'ALLIES ARE A TIRESOME LOT'
THE BRITISH ARMY IN ITALY IN THE
FIRST WORLD WAR

Wolverhampton Military Studies

www.helion.co.uk/wolverhamptonmilitarystudies

Submissions

The publishers would be pleased to receive submissions for this series. Please contact us via email (info@helion.co.uk), or in writing to Helion & Company Limited, 26 Willow Road, Solihull, West Midlands, B91 1UE.

Titles

No.1 *Stemming the Tide. Officers and Leadership in the British Expeditionary Force 1914* Edited by Spencer Jones (ISBN 978-1-909384-45-3)

No.2 *'Theirs Not To Reason Why'. Horsing the British Army 1875-1925* Graham Winton (ISBN 978-1-909384-48-4)

No.3 *A Military Transformed? Adaptation and Innovation in the British Military, 1792-1945* Edited by Michael LoCicero, Ross Mahoney and Stuart Mitchell (ISBN 978-1-909384-46-0)

No.4 *Get Tough Stay Tough. Shaping the Canadian Corps, 1914-1918* Kenneth Radley (ISBN 978-1-909982-86-4)

No.5 *A Moonlight Massacre: The Night Operation on the Passchendaele Ridge, 2 December 1917. The Forgotten Last Act of the Third Battle of Ypres* Michael LoCicero (ISBN 978-1-909982-92-5)

No.6 *Shellshocked Prophets. Former Anglican Army Chaplains in Interwar Britain* Linda Parker (ISBN 978-1-909982-25-3)

No.7 *Flight Plan Africa: Portuguese Airpower in Counterinsurgency, 1961-1974* John P. Cann (ISBN 978-1-909982-06-2)

No. 8 *Mud, Blood and Determination. The History of the 46th (North Midland) Division in the Great War* Simon Peaple (ISBN 978 1 910294 66 6)

No. 9 *Commanding Far Eastern Skies. A Critical Analysis of the Royal Air Force Superiority Campaign in India, Burma and Malaya 1941-1945* Peter Preston-Hough (ISBN 978 1 910294 44 4)

No.10 *Courage Without Glory. The British Army on the Western Front 1915* Edited by Spencer Jones (ISBN 978 1 910777 18 3)

No.11 *The Airborne Forces Experimental Establishment: The Development of British Airborne Technology 1940-1950* Tim Jenkins (ISBN 978-1-910777-06-0)

No.12 *'Allies are a Tiresome Lot' – The British Army in Italy in the First World War* John Dillon (ISBN 978 1 910777 32 9)

'Allies are a Tiresome Lot'

The British Army in Italy in the First World War

Wolverhampton Military Studies No.12

John Dillon

Helion & Company Limited

For Susi, with love

Helion & Company Limited
26 Willow Road
Solihull
West Midlands
B91 1UE
England
Tel. 0121 705 3393
Fax 0121 711 4075
Email: info@helion.co.uk
Website: www.helion.co.uk
Twitter: @helionbooks
Visit our blog http://blog.helion.co.uk/

Published by Helion & Company 2015

Designed and typeset by Bookcraft Ltd, Stroud, Gloucestershire
Cover designed by Paul Hewitt, Battlefield Design (www.battlefield-design.co.uk)
Printed by Gutenberg Press Limited, Tarxien, Malta

Text © John Dillon 2015
Images © as individually credited
Maps drawn by George Anderson© Helion & Company Limited 2015

Front cover: British and Italian officers study a map in northern Italy shortly after the arrival
of British forces from the Western Front in November 1917. British officers belong to the 26th
Battalion, Royal Fusiliers (124th Brigade, 41st Division). (Imperial War Museum Q 26509).
Rear cover: Wooden grave marker put up by Sergeant Davenport's unit, this has been
replaced by the CWGC headstone. (© Michelle Flanaghan, Sergeant Davonport's great-
granddaughter)

ISBN 978-1-910777-32-9

British Library Cataloguing-in-Publication Data.
A catalogue record for this book is available from the British Library.

For details of other military history titles published by Helion & Company Limited contact
the above address, or visit our website: http://www.helion.co.uk.

We always welcome receiving book proposals from prospective authors.

Contents

List of Illustrations

List of Maps

The Wolverhampton Military Studies Series
Series Editor's Preface

As series editor, it is my great pleasure to introduce the *Wolverhampton Military Studies Series* to you. Our intention is that in this series of books you will find military history that is new and innovative, and academically rigorous with a strong basis in fact and in analytical research, but also is the kind of military history that is for all readers, whatever their particular interests, or their level of interest in the subject. To paraphrase an old aphorism: a military history book is not less important just because it is popular, and it is not more scholarly just because it is dull. With every one of our publications we want to bring you the kind of military history that you will want to read simply because it is a good and well-written book, as well as bringing new light, new perspectives, and new factual evidence to its subject.

In devising the *Wolverhampton Military Studies Series*, we gave much thought to the series title: this is a *military* series. We take the view that history is everything except the things that have not happened yet, and even then a good book about the military aspects of the future would find its way into this series. We are not bound to any particular time period or cut-off date. Writing military history often divides quite sharply into eras, from the modern through the early modern to the mediaeval and ancient; and into regions or continents, with a division between western military history and the military history of other countries and cultures being particularly marked. Inevitably, we have had to start somewhere, and the first books of the series deal with British military topics and events of the twentieth century and later nineteenth century. But this series is open to any book that challenges received and accepted ideas about any aspect of military history, and does so in a way that encourages its readers to enjoy the discovery.

In the same way, this series is not limited to being about wars, or about grand strategy, or wider defence matters, or the sociology of armed forces as institutions, or civilian society and culture at war. None of these are specifically excluded, and in some cases they play an important part in the books that comprise our series. But there are already many books in existence, some of them of the highest scholarly standards, which cater to these particular approaches. The main theme of the *Wolverhampton Military Studies Series* is the military aspects of wars, the preparation for wars or their prevention, and their aftermath. This includes some books whose main theme is the technical details of how armed forces have worked, some books on wars and battles, and some books that re-examine the evidence about the existing stories, to show in a different light what everyone thought they already knew and understood.

As series editor, together with my fellow editorial board members, and our publisher Duncan Rogers of Helion, I have found that we have known immediately and almost by instinct the kind of books that fit within this series. They are very much the kind of well-written and challenging books that my students at the University of Wolverhampton would want to read. They are books which enhance knowledge, and offer new perspectives. Also, they are books for anyone with an interest in military history and events, from expert scholars to occasional readers. One of the great benefits of the study of military history is that it includes a large and often committed section of the wider population, who want to read the best military history that they can find; our aim for this series is to provide it.

Stephen Badsey
University of Wolverhampton

Acknowledgements

My first book; but without the help and encouragement of others it would not have seen the light of day. Following early retirement in 2005 I enrolled as a Mature Student at Reading University. History had been a favourite subject of mine while at Oakham School in the early 1960s; it was there that Major 'Bertie' Bowes demonstrated how military history could come alive if it was taught with genuine enthusiasm. At Reading Frank Tallett encouraged me through my BA and MA courses and, crucially, persuaded me to go on with a PhD. Pursuing a doctorate meant ploughing a fairly lonely furrow and without the guidance and criticism of my two supervisors, Christopher Duggan and Richard Bosworth, there would have been no thesis from which to produce a book.

Some eight or ten years before he died my wife and I started to travel with Richard Holmes on his tours of the First and Second World War battlefields of France, Belgium and Holland. Richard's passion for his subject, and his ability to pass that on to all who traveled with him, was hugely influential in my wish to make military history the focus of my degree. I like to think that Richard would have had some encouraging words to say of the result. As good a raconteur as Richard was, those trips would have been less pleasurable without the company and friendly encouragement, usually passed on over a few glasses of Belgian beer, of 'Jack' and 'Gerry' (you know who you are). Sometimes people help without being aware of it and for that I thank 'Bill' who I met on a cruise on the Nile; emails during our respective university courses, dissertations and book ideas have been a useful reality check. One of the soldiers who served in Italy was George Walton and I am very grateful to his grand-daughter, Clare Pilkington, for allowing me free use of the transcript of the postcards George sent home to his family, they help to remind us that war was not all generals and battles. But my biggest vote of thanks goes to my wife, Susi; without her support and encouragement over the last nine years there would have been no early retirement, university or book. That the project has got this far is as much down to her as to me.

When the manuscript has been written, and friends have encouraged, it still needs a publisher to see the project through to conclusion. I owe a debt of gratitude to Duncan Rogers of Helion & Company for putting enough faith in the book to take it to publication. Patrick Butcher at Helion has guided me through the process of delivering a 'book' rather than a Microsoft Word document; George Anderson who turned rough sketches into maps, while Michael LoCicero cast his editor's eye over the whole. As ever, any errors or omissions are my own.

Introduction

On 4 August 2014, in the Flemish town of Ypres, the trumpeters of the Fire Brigade played the Last Post under the arch of the memorial to the missing at the town's Menin Gate; 100 years had passed since the start of what the British call the First World War. It is almost impossible to stand quietly, with a dry eye, while the trumpets sound the last notes of the refrain that marks the end of the working day, and indicate that the soldier has gone to his final rest. For many of those who attended the ceremony, and the thousands who visit the cemeteries of the Western Front every year, the battlefields of France and Flanders – Loos, Arras, Ypres, Passchendaele, and so many more – epitomise the Great War.

The last soldier who fought in that conflict is now dead, the war has moved from memory to history. But how does that history represent an event which touched so many families directly and, arguably, led on to Hitler and the second great European war? The war poets are interpreted as having laboured on the futility of it all (although Wilfred Owen and Siegfried Sassoon were decorated for bravery), as do later writers such as Pat Barker and Sebastian Faulks; historians in the mould of Alan Clark[1] and Denis Winter[2] gave us the 'butchers and bunglers' thesis, which was taken to the level of entertainment by the stage and screen productions of *Oh! What a Lovely War* and that television favourite, *Blackadder Goes Forth*; more recent historians, such as John Terraine and Gary Sheffield, have taken a more considered view of the problems that faced Sir Douglas Haig and the General Staff and have proposed that many lessons were learnt, techniques did change and improve – and at the end, the Allies 'won'. Sadly much of the school syllabus material, through which recent generations learnt about the war, was based on the earlier 'futility and sacrifice' literature. Also, the trench conditions in France and Flanders became the paradigm for a soldier's lot in World War One; 'without mud it wouldn't be the First World War'.[3] Recent historians have come out against the way in which that material, particularly in the 1960s, distorted the public memory of the conflict and the motivation of those who fought in it. Andrew Roberts, somewhat harshly, described it as 'generational-betrayal

1   A. Clark, *The Donkeys* (London, 1961).
2   D. Winter, *Haig's Command. A Reassessment* (London, 1991).
3   D. Todman, *The Great War. Myth and Memory* (London, 2005), p.41.

literature';[4] Brian Bond suggested that as a result of the way in which the war had been portrayed since the Armistice, 'the 'real' historical war ceased to exist in November 1918', only a few historians had 'sought to preserve, order and interpret the events of the war objectively'.[5] Richard Holmes in *Tommy*, summed up the situation well; '[the war] usually enters our minds not as history, but as literature'.[6] These various issues cloud the lens through which the First World War is viewed, but there is one more, highlighted by Hew Strachan in *To Arms*.[7] In his book Strachan identifies what he saw as a major omission in the British military histories published to that date; they were Anglo-centric, with too much emphasis on the Western Front. He made the point that it was a *world war*, not a European conflict with side-shows. Unfortunately the British contribution to the war in Italy has been largely ignored by British military historians, having suffered from the limitations marked out by Strachan. This book, the result of a PhD thesis, aims to bring the Italian Expeditionary Force out of the shadow of the conflict in Flanders and throw some light on the life and experience of the soldiers who made up its ranks, not just the action in which they participated, but also their life beyond the fire-step.

In the Second World War, under Mussolini, Italy was Germany's ally, but the reverse was the case in 1914-1918. The Foreign Office files in the National Archives outline the lengths to which the Foreign Office, and particularly the Foreign Secretary (Sir Edward Grey) went to prise Italian politicians away from a position of neutrality (where they were prepared to join whichever side made them the best deal), to one of belligerent together with Britain, France and Russia. In later chapters there are frequent references to the poor opinion held by Sir William Robertson, Chief of the Imperial General Staff (CIGS), of the Italians; he considered them to be of little military worth and an inconvenience to which he had to attend and also supply troops. He was the chief military adviser to the Prime Minister and the War Cabinet, yet there is little acknowledgement that, however frustrating as an ally, they filled that role very much at the behest of Sir Edward Grey; Britain wanted the Italians as an ally, however weak their military heritage. This dichotomy is given little mention in British histories, the focus being on their 'inconvenience'. In his excellent coverage of the build-up to the war, *The Sleepwalkers*, Christopher Clark says nothing of the way Italian politicians used Clause VII of the Triple Alliance treaty to enable them to declare their neutrality. In that dark period before war was declared, when Italy could have made its position clear (and possibly influenced subsequent events), Clark clearly positions the country as the least of the Great Powers; there were 'five autonomous players of equal importance [...] six, if we add Italy'.[8] The issues around Italy's obligations

4   A. Roberts, *A History of the English-Speaking Peoples Since 1900* (London, 2006), p.105.
5   B. Bond, *The Unquiet Western Front* (Cambridge, 2002), p.26.
6   R. Holmes, *Tommy. The British Soldier on the Western Front 1914-1918* (London, 2004), p.xvii.
7   H. Strachan, *The First World War. Volume 1: To Arms* (Oxford, 2001).
8   C. Clark, *The Sleepwalkers. How Europe Went to War in 1914* (London, 2012), p.xxiv.

and 'get-outs' within the treaty obligations of the Triple Alliance, together with the struggle that the British Foreign Office had with Italian and Russian politicians to obtain the former's entry to the Entente against the Central Powers, are explored in Chapter One. Where other histories have given little coverage to this topic, but have laboured Italy's 'unreliability', they lack context without the background to Britain's efforts to get that country on-side.

The focus accorded to the Western Front in British accounts of the war is understandable, most of the country's soldiers fought there, and it is the location for most of the iconic battles that have entered the British psyche, particularly the Somme (especially the first day) and Passchendaele. However, it was not the whole war, not all battles were for little gain, and the experience of soldiers on other fronts was not necessarily the same as that in Flanders. The differences between the Italian and the Western Fronts are covered in subsequent chapters. The context in which the war is presented must move on from the legacy of the literature of the post-war decades; one of futility, bunglers and Donkeys. Michael Howard expressed the challenge to historians in his introduction to *A Part of History*:

> Only recently have historians begun to escape this obsession [the futile viewpoint and a quest for blame], to see the conflict [...] as a 'part of history': a terrible and tragic event, certainly, but one that must be understood in its context, and explained rather than condemned.[9]

It is also important that the war should be understood from the point of view of the men fighting it, and that means looking beyond the trench, the mud and the battles. The majority of a soldier's time was spent out of the line, as Chapter Five describes, and a concentration on the infrequent periods of action in which they were involved gives a distorted picture of their experience. Paul Fussell (an American and a cultural historian) in his influential book, *The Great War and Modern Memory*,[10] focused on the output of the poets for an understanding of the war, and in doing so perpetuated the futility interpretation of the Western Front. As Robin Prior and Trevor Wilson point out in their critique of Fussell,[11] there is nothing in his book to make the readers aware that far more of the soldiers' time was spent playing football, or cheering the female impersonators in the divisional concert group, than was spent in fighting. The importance of sport and entertainment may have been ignored by Fussell, but not by John Fuller. The latter has studied the vital importance of morale issues to the troops and their fighting efficiency and his points are brought out in Chapter Five; maintaining

9   M. Howard (ed.), *A Part of History. Aspects of the British Experience of the First World War* (London, 2008), p.xiv.
10   P. Fussell, *The Great War and Modern Memory* (Oxford, 1975).
11   R. Prior and T. Wilson, 'Debate. Paul Fussell at War', *War in History*, Vol. 1 (1994), pp.63-80.

the spirit of the IEF was an important function of the regimental officers, particularly on a relatively quiet front, such as Italy. The diary comment of one such officer who served in France, and then with the IEF, puts some perspective on the view that life was all death and futility; 'Could you ever have guessed how much I should enjoy the war'.[12]

In the last two or three decades military histories have moved on from the focus on a central 'big man' (Napoleon, Wellington, Haig) and the operations – 'guns and drums' – that he conducted, to try to visualise war from the stand-point of the individual soldiers, to take a cultural history perspective. To that end this book uses letters and accounts from some of the men who served in Italy to explore their everyday experience, these, together with the files at the National Archive and the Imperial War Museum also give an insight to the important issues of health, the medical services, morale and (a big issue for those in authority), discipline. In the last three years important studies have been published into the experience of the junior officers (John Lewis Stempel[13] and Christopher Moore-Bic[14]); the labour battalions (John Starling and Ivor Lee) who supported the front-line troops – and were a large part of the IEF disciplinary statistics; the importance of rations and feeding the troops (Rachel Duffett[15]). Using these various sources it is possible to draw a more rounded picture of the lives of those young men, one that does not have them tied to trenches and dugouts.

As well as looking at the war from outside the paradigm of the trenches of the Western Front this book sets out to explore the 'side-show' of the Italian Front, as seen by the British Tommy from late 1917 until after the armistice. Although this theatre of action was quiet, in comparison with Flanders, that cannot be the only reason why it gets so little coverage in British histories of the conflict. Italy was a difficult ally, right through the war. The decision to take the country into the conflict, following ten months of neutrality, was taken by the political elite, with little enthusiasm shown by the general population. Unlike the other members of the Entente, Italy entered the conflict with specific territorial gains as a war aim. As the war progressed the country was seen, especially by Britain, as intent on fighting a 'separate war' to achieve those objectives, and frequently raised the possibility of withdrawal from the war if the Allies did not accede to Italian aims, or did not reinforce its army to the extent that it felt necessary. Robertson, in his role as CIGS, was particularly irritated and frustrated by Italian attitudes and their tendency to postpone or cancel planned offensives. British annoyance, leavened with a good dose of chauvinistic superiority towards their

12   G.H. Greenwell, *An Infant in Arms. War Letters of a Company Officer 1914-1918* (London, 1935), p.251.
13   J. Lewis-Stempel, *Six Weeks: The Short and Gallant Life of the British Officer in the First World War* (London, 2011).
14   C. Moore-Bic, *Playing The Game: The British Junior Infantry Officer on the Western Front 1914-18* (Solihull, 2011).
15   R. Duffett, 'Beyond the Ration: Sharing and Scrounging on the Western Front', *Twentieth Century British History*, Vol. 22 (2011), pp.453-473.

ally, together with the perceived reluctance of the Italians to give due credit to British and French military support in the October 1918 offensive against the Austrians, all seem to have influenced British historians towards the Italian Front. Writing the official British account of the IEF, Edmonds commented on 'the Italian one-sided method of writing history', and that they had not acknowledged the 'vital assistance' given to them by their allies.[16] That said the conflicts on the rivers Isonzo and Piave have not been completely overlooked. While general histories of the war give only cursory nods to Italy, there are a few notable exceptions. Mark Thompson[17] produced an excellent narrative account of the conflict from the point of view of the Italian troops (with barely a mention of the British), while John Gooch's book, using archival sources, provides an in-depth analysis of the war fought by the Italian army. The only two accounts of the war in Italy, specifically from the British viewpoint, are those by George Cassar[18] and John and Eileen Wilks[19] (both from the 1990s), both of which give detailed accounts of the military actions fought by the IEF, but little on the life and routine of the soldiers. Two aspect of the IEF which this account explores, but are overlooked by other writers, are the post-armistice demobilisation phase, and the time spent as part of the international force holding the peace in Fiume.

It should be stated at this point that this book does not attempt to follow the military actions in which the IEF was involved in blow-by-blow detail; Edmonds, Cassar and Wilks do this admirably for the British, while Thompson and Gooch do likewise for the Italians. What it does do is use archival material to look more closely at some aspects of the IEF's experience than the other writers. Greater use is made of the courts martial records, allowing a broader view of the discipline of the British troops in Italy, how it differed from the BEF, and why the sentencing regime appeared to vary from that in France. Again, using British sources, this account raises some questions over the planning of the final assault against the Austrians, in October 1918, in which the IEF played an important part; was it planned some weeks ahead (as the official Italian report claims), or was it spatchcocked late in the day to regain territory before peace negotiations started.

The 1914-1918 war has gone beyond remembering, now that all those old soldiers have died, but Remembrance is still an important yearly ritual, especially so in these centenary years. The way in which the war should be commemorated is the subject of some current debate within the World War 1 Centenary Advisory Board; should its tone be 'modest, inclusive and reverential', as Sebastian Faulks would advocate, reminding us that it was 'an avoidable calamity' – though this view does not come

16   J.E. Edmonds and H.R. Davies, *Military Operations Italy, 1915-1919* (London, 1949), p.358.
17   M. Thompson, *The White War. Life and Death on the Italian Front 1915-1919* (Croydon, 2009).
18   G.H. Cassar, *The Forgotten Front. The British Campaign in Italy 1917-1918* (London, 1998).
19   J. and E. Wilks, *The British Army in Italy 1917-1918* (Barnsley, 1998).

through in the soldiers'[20] letters from Italy. Or should it take Hew Strachan's line that 'Germany was a militarist and imperialist regime which had to be defeated and from that point of view the victory is a serious victory'. By 1918 the men of the IEF were tired of the war, but there is little in their letters or post-war accounts to indicate that they saw it as futile, or that they believed themselves to have been duped into taking part. According to the official censor they had 'an immense and widespread longing for any reasonable and honourable settlement that will bring the war to a close – but not at Germany's price', if they did that 'Just think what an insult it would be to all the lads who have gone west'.[21] The First World War is overshadowed by the Second; it is easier to understand the need to fight Hitler and Nazism (especially when it is featured so much in school history classes), than why an obscure assassination in the Balkans should cause Britain to take up arms and lose so many men. While the public can agree on the need for the centenary events they are 'much less aware what the war was about'.[22]

This book has not set out to explain the causes of the war, Christopher Clark, Margaret MacMillan[23] and others have done that admirably, but it does explore Italy's role, why Britain was so keen to involve that country and the way in which the war on the Italian Front was experienced by British troops. These men had come from the hell of the Ypres Salient and their letters, post-war accounts and the archival records allowed a comparison to be made of many aspects of the soldiers' lives on those two fronts. By focusing on the lives of the men of the Italian Expeditionary Force it is hoped that this book will close a gap in the historiography of the British army's war in Italy in 1918, going beyond what Hew Strachan has called 'the parochial preoccupations with the mud of the Western Front'.

20   N. Hellen and R. Brooks, 'Don't mention that we won the First World War', *Sunday Times*, 13 January 2013, pp.1-2.
21   IWM: Doc. 4041, M. Hardie, *Private Papers*, report October 1917.
22   Hellen and Brooks, *Sunday Times*, comment by H Strachan, 13 January 2013, pp.1-2.
23   M. MacMillan, *The War That Ended Peace. How Europe Abandoned Peace for the First World War* (London, 2013).

1

Italy's war prior to Caporetto:
"The all-important thing is to secure Italy's signature to the alliance"

On 28 June 1914 the car carrying the Austrian Archduke Franz Ferdinand and his wife Sophie, Duchess of Hohenberg, took a wrong turning in the city of Sarajevo. This mistake gave Gavrilo Princip, a Bosnian Serb activist, the opportunity to successfully complete the planned assassination of the heir to the Austrian throne. That the spark which would light the European tinderbox should be struck in the Balkans was both a surprise, and yet unsurprising. To the man on the London omnibus, why should a killing in a city whose name he could not pronounce – even less, locate on a map – mean that his country would go to war? But to the European politicians and diplomats (who would not have to do the fighting), a European war had an inevitability about it. The Great Powers were building up their military forces; German and Italian ambitions for empire had brought about tensions over Morocco and Libya in 1911; pent-up frustrations and nationalism had caused the major European states to face off during the two Balkan wars of 1912 and 1913. Two of the myths of the war tell us that German railway timetables and the falling dominoes of international alliances caused the war that followed the assassination. Like all myths, they hold a grain of truth, but they are not the whole story. With the recent centenary of the outbreak of that conflict there have been a number of excellent books published explaining how Europe came to tear itself apart in such a horrific way. These various authors demonstrate how belligerent statements by major actors (the Kaiser and the Austrian and German Chiefs of Staff); the lack of clarity over the commitment of Britain to support France in the event of war; Russian attitudes to Pan-Slavism; the German 'blank cheque' to Austria; imprecise communications between diplomats and politicians; and a misunderstanding of each nation's motives, could lead very quickly to a continental conflagration and a World War.

The date chosen for the visit of the Austrian couple was inauspicious; it was St Vitus's Day. On that date in 1389 a Serb-led army in Kosovo had been defeated by the forces of the Ottoman Turks, and it had become a memorial day for the martyrs who died there. A visit by the archduke, heir to the Austro-Hungarian crown, was a reminder to nationalist groups that Bosnia (and the Slavs who lived there) was part of the empire of the Dual Monarchy. The 28th of June, by one of those coincidences that occur in history, was also the wedding anniversary of Franz Ferdinand and Sophie. The smoky atmosphere of Belgrade coffee-shops was a forcing ground for nationalist groups and their various plots, reminiscent of the later novels of Eric Ambler and Alan Furst, and among those activist movements was Ujedinjenje ili Smrt! ('Union or death!'), also known as the Black Hand. Joint founder of the group in 1911, and principal architect of the assassination plot, was a young officer in the Serbian army, Dragutin Dimitrijević – known to history as 'Apis'. The plan, which did not go as intended, had three principal players: Gavrilo Princip; Muhamed Mehmedbašić, a Muslim from Herzegovina who had already failed earlier that year to kill Oskar Potiorek, the Bosnian Governor; and Nedeljko Čabrinović. As the weather in Sarajevo that day was warm the royal couple were driven through the city in an open-topped car, the second of a five-car convoy. Armed with grenades and pistols the assassins were spaced out along the route, with Princip being one of the last. If all had gone to plan one of the others would have killed the Archduke and Gavrilo Princip would not have had the notoriety of setting the spark to a European war. Failing for a second time in that year, Mehmedbašić (the first of the group) did not manage to throw his bomb. All good plans should have a back-up; unfortunately Čabrinović, further along the route, threw his grenade only for it to bounce off the royal car and explode under the one following, injuring some of the officers riding in it. Bravely, Franz Ferdinand insisted on continuing with his itinerary to the Town Hall, where he and the Mayor were to deliver speeches to the assembled crowd. One can imagine how hollow the words sounded as both men spoke of their excitement and pleasure at the enthusiastic reception accorded the royal visitors; while at the same time, officers of the entourage received treatment for their wounds from Čabrinović's bomb. It was on the way back from the Town Hall that Princip was given his fateful opportunity. The drivers of the cars in the cavalcade had not been told of a change of route and as a result they turned into Franz Joseph Strasse, where Princip had taken up position. With no reverse gear the car had to be physically pushed backwards, giving Princip his chance. Unable to throw his bomb, he fired off the two shots that killed the Archduke and his wife. This shooting, which of itself presented no existential threat to Britain (which was more pre-occupied with Irish Home Rule than the killing of a Gilbert and Sullivan-type archduke), France or Russia, was the catalyst for the Great Powers of Europe going to war in August 1914. But what stance would Italy take in the aftermath of the assassination?

Since 1882 Italy had been a member of the Triple Alliance, together with Germany and Austria-Hungary,[1] an agreement which had been periodically renewed, most recently in 1912. While it may seem sensible that Italy aligned itself with Austria, after all they shared a common border on the Isonzo and in the Alps, it was not a comfortable arrangement. Italians regarded the Dual Monarchy as a traditional enemy, and

---

1   From this point on 'Austria' will frequently be used for 'Austria-Hungary'.

one which occupied land that the Italians regarded as their own – the Trentino and Trieste. It would not have escaped the notice of nationalists that, by aligning themselves with Austria, the Italians had effectively renounced their claims to these territories which were now held by an ally. But Italy's position in the Triplice was further complicated by an arrangement with France, signed in 1902. Both those countries had interests in North Africa and under the Prinetti-Barrère agreement Italy recognised French 'rights' in Morocco, in return for French liberality towards Italian schemes in Libya. Additionally, should either be the subject of direct or indirect aggression, the other would observe 'strict neutrality'. This proviso 'in effect nullified Italy's part in the Triplice';[2] it allowed French politicians to assume Italian neutrality in the event that their country became involved in hostilities with Germany. In August 1911, when asked how France took Italy into account in his planning for a possible war with Germany, General Joffre (Chief of the French General Staff) replied; 'Italy will make no move. Her interests lie on our side, not on that of Germany and Austria'.[3] But it was not just the arrangement with France which allowed Italy to put aside its obligations to its Triplice allies; Clause VII of the Triple Alliance stated conditions under which Italy could adopt a position of neutrality.

The agreement signed by Austria-Hungary and Italy stated that any 'temporary or permanent' occupation of territory in the Balkans should not take place 'without previous agreement' between the two states,[4] and any agreement would be based on 'reciprocal compensation for every advantage, territorial or otherwise'. So, in the event of Austria occupying Serbia, Italy could claim compensation, and that would be most likely to include the Trentino and Trieste – *Italia irredenta* – which Vienna would be unwilling to cede to an ally which it regarded as having avoided fulfilling its treaty obligations. In 1913, during the Second Balkan War, Austria had told the Germans and Italians of their intentions towards Serbia and been persuaded by them to back off. Now, with Franz Ferdinand assassinated, Germany promising their famous 'blank cheque' support, and national 'honour' at stake, Vienna did not want to make the same mistake again. This time Italy would not be informed of Austrian intentions. The terms of the ultimatum presented to Belgrade were to be communicated to the Italians at the last minute as a 'sop' to them to prevent them from hearing of them first 'through the press'.[5] Italy was in a bind. Because Austria did not involve the Consulta in any 'previous agreement' regarding its intentions towards Serbia, Antonio di San Giuliano (Foreign Minister) and Antonio Salandra (Prime Minister) could claim that there was no *casus foederis* under Clause VII of the Triple Alliance; Italy was not obliged to join Germany and Austria-Hungary in any consequent hostilities. At this

2   W. W. Gottlieb, *Studies in Secret Diplomacy during the First World War* (London, 1957), p.137.
3   D. Owen, *The Hidden Perspective. The Military Conversations 1906-1914* (London, 2014), p.114.
4   Gottlieb, *Secret Diplomacy*, p.162.
5   Gottlieb, *Secret Diplomacy*, p.165.

point it should be said that the Italian ministers had not wanted to be told of Vienna's intentions, they adopted the position of the deaf-mute. Had they been made officially aware (as skilled diplomats they could sense what was really happening between Vienna and Belgrade) then they would have had two choices; openly oppose an ally for a second time, as in 1913, but this time without Germany also calling for restraint; or support the Dual Monarchy in a war which was against all Italy's interests, and where Austria was unlikely to deliver *Italia irredenta* as compensation, should the Triple Alliance come out of the conflict as victors. The Italian historian Luigi Albertini was scathing in his assessment of the stance taken by Salandra and San Giuliano, they had shown a 'total absence of all sense of horror at the tragedy that was about to be enacted and did not raise a finger to avert it'.[6] Or, as a more recent historian expressed it; Italy had 'wriggled out of its alliance obligations on the grounds that the Habsburgs had provoked the conflict after Sarajevo'.[7] The Italian ministers were in a unique position; because Austria had occupied Serbia without consulting, so they felt able to repudiate their commitments as an ally under the treaty, while at the same time claiming that the Austrians were bound (by the same treaty that the Italians were walking away from) to deliver Rome's claims to compensation. The attitude adopted by the Italian negotiators in July 1914 was one of the 'outstretched empty hand',[8] and it would not be the last time in the war that the country would be accused of wanting more than its efforts had warranted.

Alexander Watson's comment on Italy having 'wriggled' out of the treaty is a view frequently expressed in English histories of the war; while Italy's stance was legal, it might have lacked a little honour, but these writers overlook Austria's role. In *August 1914* Barbara Tuchman wrote of Italy that; 'when the test came, [that country] had skipped aside on the ground that Austria's attack on Serbia was an act of aggression which released Italy from her treaty obligations'.[9] But Austria and Germany were co-signatories to the treaty, both knew the content of Clause VII, indeed the former was so aware of its implications that Austrian politicians deliberately refrained from informing the Italians beforehand, in the knowledge that (as in 1913) Italy would be most likely to adopt neutrality. In the light of Austria's manoeuvring to avoid prewarning Italy, it is difficult to agree with Günther Kronenbitter that Italian neutrality 'came as an unpleasant surprise to the military leaderships in Vienna and Berlin'.[10] Italy is invariably portrayed in English histories as having played a devious hand and wriggled out of its obligations, at the same time little disapproval is levelled at Austrian politicians for their shameless avoidance of involving Italy on the grounds that it was

---

6   Cited in Gottlieb, *Secret Diplomacy*, p.168.
7   A. Watson, *Ring of Steel. Germany and Austria-Hungary at War, 1914-1918* (London, 2014), p.49.
8   J. Joll and G. Martel, *The Origins of the First World War* (London, 2007), p.40.
9   B., Tuchman, *August 1914* (London, 1994), p.129.
10   G. Kronenbitter, 'The Austro-Hungarian Experience of Coalition Warfare, 1914-18', *RUSI Journal*, Vol. 159 (2014), p.76.

likely to result in that country invoking the very clause they were attempting to work around. This slightly pietistic stance ignores Britain's similarly legalistic position on the military talks between the War Office and the French, and whether these involved an obligation on Britain to send the British Expeditionary Force (BEF) to France immediately hostilities were declared by Germany.

To counter the threat posed by the Triple Alliance the two major states on Germany's borders, France and Russia, had their own mutual support agreement. The opportunity for this came about when, in 1890, Germany failed to re-sign its Reinsurance Treaty with Russia, so opening the door for France to jump through. Under this bilateral agreement each would come to the other's aid if attacked by a member of the Triple Alliance. Although Britain stood outside these formal European alliances, it had allowed itself to become entangled with France in an 'entente', rather than a full-blown treaty. It would become a criticism of Britain (and particularly of the Foreign Secretary, Sir Edward Grey) that, by failing to state unequivocally whether or not it would support France in a war with Germany, it did not do enough to avert the escalating crisis. Grey insisted to the last that Britain was not legally obliged by the 'entente' to join the conflict – but as with Italy's stance, it was not a comfortable one. What was the arrangement that Grey believed to be non-binding on Britain?

Since 1906 there had been talks (with the blessing of Grey) between Britain and France over their possible military cooperation, especially in the event of France being attacked by Germany, and these took on greater urgency and relevance in the years immediately preceding the outbreak of war. The progress of these discussions, and the political issues they raised within the British Cabinet, are explored in depth in David Owen's book,[11] as well as that by Margaret MacMillan[12] In 1908 Brigadier Sir Henry Wilson had taken on the role of Director of Military Operations in the War Office. A confirmed Francophile, who spoke excellent French, Wilson was an exponent of Britain sending an expeditionary force to the continent in the event of a German invasion of France. Although there was no formal military treaty Wilson worked with the French to determine the size, composition and transportation of just such a British force, should events prove it to be necessary. The successful deployment of the BEF, in August 1914, was testament to the work done by Wilson and his staff, in cooperation with the French. Alongside the planning for the use of British troops on the continent of Europe, British and French naval staffs reassigned priorities for their respective navies. Events in Morocco had demonstrated that North Africa and the Mediterranean might be a flash-point between France and Germany, consequently France needed to increase its naval strength there, but that could only be done by exposing its North Sea and Atlantic bases. Britain agreed that it would move its own ships from the eastern Mediterranean (leaving France to cover that area) to Gibraltar;

---

11   D. Owen, *Hidden Perspective.*
12   M. MacMillan, *The War That Ended Peace.*

in return Britain would provide the naval cover for France in the Channel and the North Sea.

In his book David Owen draws on his experience as a previous Foreign Secretary to draw some parallels between the Anglo-French military conversations and Tony Blair's ignoring of the Cabinet when he took Britain into the 2003 Iraq war alongside the United States. Grey did not inform the Cabinet of the on-going talks, and the way in which they were becoming a moral, if not a legal, obligation. To compound his error Grey did not inform Herbert Asquith of them when the latter took over as Prime Minister in 1908. The first occasion on which Asquith was made aware of the potential involvement of the BEF in France was in a private letter from Grey in April 1911; the Cabinet was not told until November of that year.[13] Owen makes the case that Grey broke all conventions by effectively committing Britain to involvement in a war, without prior notification of the Cabinet. Further, he makes the point that in November, when they were made aware of the content of the talks, the Cabinet could have insisted that an expeditionary force was no longer a given of British policy – they did not.[14] They could have declared that, in the event of a German war, the British navy would have enforced a close blockade of Germany, so making Berlin reconsider military action without sacrificing the core of Britain's small, professional army.

While the 'fuzzy logic of the Franco-British alliance',[15] did not represent a formal treaty between the two nations, Paul Cambon (French Ambassador to London), regarded it as a 'moral Entente'.[16] Sir Winston Churchill (First Lord of the Admiralty) summed up Britain's difficulty. What if France, whose northern coasts were defence-less 'on the advice of and by arrangement with' the British, was attacked by Germany: 'Every one must feel who knows the facts that we have the obligations of an alliance without its advantages, and above all without its precise definitions'.[17] Grey, maintaining to the end that Britain did not have to support France, was given the 'cover' to do just that by the German violation of Belgian neutrality, to which Britain was a signatory in 1839. His conundrum was well put by Barbara Tuchman:

> Britain was committed to support France by virtue of something that was not a commitment. He [Grey] must present Belgium as the cause without hiding France as the basic cause, he must appeal to Britain's honour while making it clear that Britain's interest was the deciding factor.[18]

But, to return to Italy's position. Under the terms of the Triple Alliance, Italy had been able to adopt a position of neutrality, but this presented its own problems. The

13   Owen, *Hidden Perspectives*, p.122.
14   Owen, *Hidden Perspectives*, p.133.
15   C. Clark, *Month of Madness*, Radio series, BBC 4, broadcast on 26 June 2014.
16   MacMillan, *War that ended Peace*, p.501.
17   MacMillan, *War that ended Peace*, p.500.
18   Tuchman, *August 1914*, p.119.

German Ambassador in Rome, Baron Ludwig von Flotow, had told San Giuliano 'in the plainest manner possible the extremely regrettable impression which such an attitude [neutrality] would make on us, and then called to his attention the consequences which might develop for Italy in the future as a result'.[19] If Germany and Austria were victorious then they would not forget the way they were deserted by their ally, but if they lost and Italy had taken no part, then Britain, France and Russia would be under no obligation to award the Trentino and Trieste as 'compensation'. Italy was a country with few natural resources, dependent on Germany, France and Britain for imports of steel, coal and food cereals; why should these countries continue to export, to a neutral, those materials which were needed at home for the war effort? Neutrality was not a comfortable place, maybe the answer would lie in continuing to negotiate with both sides. Could it be that 'alongside the possibility of being bribed to fight there existed the opportunity of being bribed not to fight'.[20] That would allow the country to follow Salandra's vision of *sacro egoismo* and get the best deal. Many British histories of the war (if they make any mention of Italy) imply that the Italian Front was an irritable side-show to the main event, rarely do they detail the extent to which Sir Edward Grey went to obtain Russian and French acceptance of the need for Italian participation on the side of the Entente. Italy played the jackal at the feast, determined to barter its entry into the conflict to the highest bidder, but its hand was forced by the Allied victory at the battle of the Marne; a setback to Italian diplomacy as well as to the German advance. This reversal of fortune on the Western Front took Italian politicians by surprise; if they were not careful then an Allied victory over the Central Powers could mean the end of the war with no Italian involvement. If that were to happen, then there would be no chance of recovering the Trentino and Trieste. Or, as it was put to an Italian at the Paris Embassy by George Clemenceau, 'Italian action to-day would no longer have enough value to justify the important political and territorial concessions which we [the Italians] are claiming'.[21] They had to get into the war.

It should be acknowledged at this point that the Italian declaration of neutrality had been indirectly beneficial to the Allies. In February 1914 General Albert Pollio (Chief of the Italian General Staff) had promised the Germans that, in the event of war, three Italians corps would go to Germany's assistance. This required the French to position similar troop levels on their southern border to counter that eventuality. However, when war came Italy removed itself from the conflict: 'Had not Joffre been certain that the Italians would remain neutral he would have been compelled to leave on the Franco-Italian Frontier troops *without whom the Battle of the Marne could not have been fought*'.[22] [My emphasis.] By staying out of the conflict the Italians had

19   L. Snyder, *Historic Documents of World War 1* (New York, 1958), p.92.
20   J. Gooch, 'Italy during the First World War', in A.R. Millett and W. Murray (eds.), *Military Effectiveness, Volume 1, The First World War* (London, 1988), p.157.
21   Gottlieb, *Secret Diplomacy*, p.218.
22   E. Spears, *Liaison 1914* (London, 1968), pp.431-2.

helped to reverse German numerical superiority over the French of 25 divisions to 17, to one where the Germans were facing a French force of 41 divisions. In the nine months following August 1914 Grey worked hard, in spite of Russian reservations, to persuade Italy to join the Entente, while Italian politicians talked to both sides.[23] With the Allies making their move to try to force the Dardanelles, Italian politicians became worried that there could be a dismemberment of the Ottoman Empire and no spoils for Italy. As Sir James Rennell Rodd (British Ambassador in Rome) put it; Italy had to decide whether to 'continue to be one of the Great Powers, or to remain content to be in future the first among the secondary States of Europe'.[24] Rodd was an Italophile and few of his contemporaries in the Allied embassies would have regarded Italy as ever reaching Great Power status, let alone 'continuing' to be one.

Italy was wooed by both sides, less for its military prowess than for the fact that it could tie down opposing forces on its borders and so complicate the planning of the other side; or as one historian has noted, 'Pre-1914 Italy was a Power on the make, looking for a bargain package deal which would offer the least of the Great Powers a place in the sun'.[25] In the opinion of Helmuth von Moltke (Chief of the German General Staff) what mattered was not 'that Italy should actively support us with strong forces but that the Triple Alliance as such should enter the war united';[26] while the Russian Minister for Foreign Affairs, Sergei Sazonov, 'did not place [the] fighting qualities of the Italian army very high'.[27] As the bidding war for Italian participation gathered momentum, so the Italian demands increased. In August 1914 the call had been for *Italia irredenta*, for the Trentino and Trieste. By March 1915 the Italians wanted a large number of Dalmatian islands, greater involvement in the affairs of the Balkans and territory in Asia Minor. The growing frustration with Italian demands, as the price of their joining the Entente, comes through in the telegrams passing between the Foreign Office and the embassies in Paris, St. Petersburg and Rome. Italy's appetite for gains from the war was 'not moderate', it had 'increased since August' and the Allies could not be expected to 'accept these exorbitant demands as they stand'.[28] By 1 April the Russians had reached the limit of their willingness to accede to Italian claims on the Dalmatian coast and it was time for the British to 'tell the Italians that this is the limit of territorial concession'. Sir Edward Grey instructed Rodd to inform the Italian Minister of Foreign Affairs that, in order to accommodate Italy, the Allies

23   TNA: FO 371/2507, telegram from Buchanan to FO, 30 March 1915.
24   TNA: FO 371/2375, Rodd to Grey, 6 March 1915.
25   R.J.B. Bosworth, *Italy, the least of the Great Powers: Italian foreign policy before the First World War* (Cambridge, 1979), p.viii.
26   L. Albertini, *The Origins of the War of 1914. Volume 3*, trans. I Massey, (Oxford, 1965), p.317.
27   TNA: FO 371/2507, Buchanan to Grey, 4 April 1915.
28   TNA: FO 371/2507, handwritten notes on Italian conditions for cooperation, 6 March 1915.

had allowed 'serious inroads upon the principles of nationalities'[29] – a cause for which the Entente claimed to be fighting the Central Powers. There was already a belief in the Foreign Office that they had signed up to terms 'which we really will have very great difficulty in meeting'[30] when the war ended and peace negotiations started. On 26 April 1915 Italy signed the Treaty of London, described by Max Hastings as 'a transaction that reflected discredit on both contracting parties'.[31] Under the terms of the treaty Italy was to prosecute the war 'in common with France, Great Britain and Russia *against all their enemies*'.[32] [My emphasis.] However, showing the propensity to frustrate their allies which continued through the war, the Italians claimed that they needed a further month to be ready to fight, and Germany was excluded from the declaration. There was no better way to convince the British, French and Russians that the Italians would consider the conflict on their front to be somehow 'separate', and most British histories of the conflict have treated it accordingly.

By failing to include Germany in the 24 May declaration of war Italy 'separated the Italian cause from that of the great powers of the entente'.[33] From the viewpoint of their new allies, the Italians were out of step with the aims of their partners; the destruction of Prussian militarism and the lofty ideal of national self-determination. Germany was in an alliance with Austria-Hungary and it is difficult to see what Italy hoped to gain by excluding that country from the declaration of war. Berlin was not likely to play the Italian game by treating them as neutrals, indeed they had been warned that if they attacked Austria-Hungary then they would find German troops alongside the Austrians. As Rodd reported to the Foreign Office on 23 May 1915; a 'State of War with Germany is therefore also regarded as existing'.[34] While most British histories of the war treat Italy's entry almost as a footnote – after all, they were only in it for Trieste, weren't they – Hew Strachan accords it rather more significance.

> Had Italy not intervened, the Russian defeat at Gorlice-Tarnów [April 1915] would have become a permanent turning point in the strategic balance in Europe with far-reaching consequences for the further history of the war. In the event Italy's intervention and the success against Russia cancelled each other out.[35]

This author had the privilege of taking part in a number of European battlefield tours, with Richard Holmes as guide, covering actions from both World Wars. On

---

29   TNA: FO 371/2507, Grey to Rodd, 1 April 1915.
30   TNA: FO 800/377, Nicolson to Buchanan, 3 May 1915.
31   M. Hastings, *Catastrophe. Europe Goes To War 1914* (London, 2013), p.415.
32   TNA: FO 371/ 2508, 15 April 1915.
33   R.J.B. Bosworth, *Mussolini's Italy. Life under the Dictatorship 1915-1945* (London, 2006), p.62.
34   TNA: FO 371/2375, Rodd to Grey, 23 May 1915.
35   H. Strachan, *The Oxford Illustrated History of the First World War. New edition* (Oxford, 2014), Kindle locn. 922.

these, as well as his 'War Walks' series on television, Holmes was a strong advocate of the principle that you can only really understand a battle if you have walked the ground. The modern battlefield tourist only needs to visit one or two locations on the Isonzo to appreciate the vastly different terrains of the Italian and Western Fronts. The restored Italian trenches at the Kolovrat outdoor museum, at an elevation of 1,100 metres, give a commanding view over the River Isonzo, some 1,000 metres below.

To the north of this viewpoint, beyond Kobarid, towers the vast bulk of Mount Rombon, its 2,000-metre summit still snow-covered in June. From there the defensive wall of mountains sweeps round in an arc, to the east of the Isonzo, to meet the Bainsizza and then on to the Adriatic. Close to the small town of Caporetto, modern-day Kobarid, is Napoleon's Bridge, rebuilt since it was destroyed during the retreat from the Austro-German breakthrough at Caporetto. The bridge spans a narrow, steep-sided, gorge through which flows the River Isonzo (Soca to the Slovenes); swift and deep, the colour of milky jade from the limestone rocks. To the visitor it is impossible to imagine one army attacking another in these deep defiles. And yet they did.

As different as the ground was between the Western and the Italian Fronts, there was one similarity; in each case one side held the strong defensive position leaving the other to make the expensive assaults. In Flanders the Germans normally held the higher ground, with the British and French having to make the expensive, attritional,

Figure 1.1 Italian trenches above Caporetto. (© J. Dillon)

Figure 1.2 River Isonzo near Caporetto. (© J Dillon)

frontal attacks. The situation in Italy was similar. Like the Germans, the Austrians held the strong defensive positions, but this time they were atop mountain peaks and ridge-lines, and frequently snow-covered. Even today, a century after the fighting has stopped, the Presena glacier in the Trentino retreats and reveals the bodies of dead Italian *Alpini*. These alpine heights stretch in an arc from the western end of the Dolomites eastwards through the Carnian and Julian Alps to the Carso at the head of the Adriatic and Trieste, and in so doing they dominate the Venetian plain to which the Italians had retreated after Caporetto.

In spite of the difficulties presented by the terrain, and the heavy casualties it exacted on the attacker, British commanders maintained that the Italians were not pulling their weight. While criticism can legitimately be levelled at Cadorna for the way in which he conducted the war on his front (and this will be covered in later chapters), to draw the conclusion that all the Italians were poor soldiers is unjustified.

When the conflict started Italy had only been a unified nation for a little over fifty years, and unlike Britain, France and Russia there was no long, proud, military tradition for the Italian army to draw on. To many of the Allied commanders who had to work with the Italians, their new ally was defined by stereotypes. They were a 'leisure loving race. The whole country, the whole atmosphere is made for laziness'.[36] Italy, like Ireland, was a poor country from which many had emigrated in droves, especially to the cites of the United States, Britain, Australia and Canada; in the last two they were only admitted in small numbers as they were deemed to be 'black' by the locals. Many had been agricultural workers before leaving, but in their adopted homes they gravitated towards navvy work, or roles in the food and hospitality industries; waiters, hotel workers and fresh-fruit vendors. Rather than be respected for hard work, the Italians were stereotyped as something of a joke, as ice-cream vendors and street organ-grinders. A British soldier, commenting on the Italian soldiers retreating from Caporetto, likened them to 'Sanger's Circus',[37] one of the most successful in Britain at that time. The British Ambassador in Rome, accustomed to the panache with which London could mount ceremonial events, reported to the Foreign Office on the funeral of the Italian Foreign Minister, Antonio di San Giuliano: 'The arrangements made for the funeral were more than usually characteristic of the extraordinary lack of organisation which governs most public functions in this country'.[38] But the chauvinistic comments went deeper than the circus and ice-cream. According to one historian, Americans considered Italians to be 'untrustworthy', 'morally corrupt' and 'congenital liars'.[39] To Rodd they were a 'mercurial people', but 'not so tough as that [*sic*] of the northern nations'.[40] The Australians, wishing to preserve their 'white racial purity' were particularly harsh: Italians were 'dirty dago pests', carriers of 'stilettos and disease'[41] – the stiletto was synonymous with a stab in the back. But, whatever the views of the Americans and Australians, it was the stereotype of the Italian soldier as one that 'could not fight'[42] which resonated with the British commanders. The defeat of the Italian army by the Ethiopians, at Adowa in 1896, and their less than glorious attempts to incorporate Libya into an Italian empire in 1911, left them in no position to enter a major European war – and did nothing for their reputation with the British, who conveniently overlooked their own defeats by 'non-whites' at the Dardanelles and Kut. Brigadier-General Charles Delmé-Radcliffe was head of the British Military Mission in Italy during the war, and his appreciation of the fighting characteristics of the Italians would have been echoed by many: 'It is not wise to expect the same

---

36   A. Acland, Private papers, Liddle Archive, GS 0003, p.108.
37   N. Gladden, *Across the Piave* (London, 1971), p.25.
38   TNA: FO 371/2007, Italy: General correspondence, Rodd to FO, 19 October 1914.
39   M. Ledeen, *D'Annunzio. The First Duce* (New Brunswick, 2009), p.13.
40   TNA: FO 371/2687, Rodd to FO, 22 December 1916.
41   K. Agutter, 'Captive Allies: Italian Immigrants in World War One Australia', *Australian Studies*, 1 (2009), p.3.
42   Bosworth, *Mussolini's Italy*, p.43.

fighting value from Italian troops as from British, French or German troops'.[43] No matter how many died on the Isonzo front in 1916 and 1917, they were caricatured as poor fighters, disorganised, comic and Catholic. The stereotype stuck with them through the Second World War, indeed the issues with Silvio Berlusconi, 'Bunga-Bunga' parties and their economy still make Italians the butt of jokes today.

Lord Cavan, the commander of the British troops in Italy after the departure of Sir Herbert Plumer, had a much more favourable view of the Italians, regarding them as good soldiers who were poorly led. He recognised the unique character of fighting in the mountains, and that the British were not trained for it. In August 1918, with no offensive planned on the Italian Front, he expected to have to winter in the country and resume fighting in the following spring. With no skills or training for winter survival in the mountains Cavan suggested to the War Office that the IEF should pull back to the plains: 'I do not think it is advisable that we should turn ourselves into *Alpini* with all the special equipment and training that would be required to keep men healthy and well through the winter'.[44] In many ways life was harder for the conscripted Italian peasants than it was for their British contemporaries. General Cadorna believed in harsh punishment but failed to recognise that the masses which made up a citizen army were 'swayed by other laws'.[45] Socialism was gaining traction in the industrial cities of the north, the seasons and harvest governed the lives of the agricultural workers from the south and, except for the 'nationalists', the vast majority cared little for Trieste and the war. Although the Italian military penal code did not allow for decimation, Cadorna assumed the authority for himself and urged his commanders to do likewise. Units which were considered to have failed to perform would have all the mens' names put into a knapsack, and then some would be drawn and the unlucky soldiers summarily executed; a lieutenant, three sergeants and eight men were shot from one unit which had broken during an Austrian attack in May 1916.[46] In April 1918, months after the defeat at Caporetto, while the British and French troops were in Italy, a decree was issued which stated that deserters 'shall be punished by death after degradation'.[47] But it was not only discipline, frequent attacks and the physical discomforts of life in the mountains which blighted the life of the Italian soldier; leave was infrequent and his pay and separation allowances were insufficient to maintain his family at home. One of the consequences of the deployment of British troops to Italy was that it allowed the Italian soldier to see how badly his pay and allowances compared with that of his ally. This issue was considered to have such a detrimental effect on Italian morale that it was discussed by the British War Cabinet in May 1918. The decision – 'without precedent when dealing with a

---

43   TNA: WO 106/761, British Mission Italy: Reports, Delmé-Radcliffe to WO.
44   TNA: WO 106/852, memo from Cavan to CIGS, 1 August 1918.
45   C. Sforza, 'Cadorna and Diaz', *Foreign Affairs*, 8 (1930), p.286.
46   J. Gooch, 'Morale and Discipline in the Italian Army, 1915-18', in H. Cecil and P. Liddle (eds.), *Facing Armageddon. The First World War Experienced* (London, 1996), p.440.
47   TNA: FO 371/3229, copy of an article in the Italian *Official Gazette*, 29 April 1918.

Sovereign Power'[48] – was taken to approach the Americans and make a joint offer of additional money to the Italians to improve the soldiers' allowances. However, as the Italians 'were in frequent need of financial help', it was felt that this 'free gift' would make it difficult to resist any future demands; as well as poor fighters, they were also stereotyped as constantly shaking a begging bowl. So, poorly paid, short of leave and subject to harsh discipline, how fair was it for British commanders to discount these men and their 'side-show' war?

The focal point of Italian offensive action was on the Isonzo front, where Cadorna launched one attritional assault after another – the histories document eleven, with the Austro-German breakthrough at Caporetto as the twelfth. Casualties in that unforgiving environment were high. Despite Robertson's constant carping on the Italian soldiers' ability to fight, as a percentage of the population Italy suffered as many dead (1.6%) as Britain and Ireland.

Table 1: Military deaths in Italy and Britain[49]

Country	Killed as % of those mobilised	Killed as % of males 15–49	Killed as % of population
Italy	10.3	7.4	1.6
Britain	11.8	6.3	1.6

The big difference in the casualty figures between Britain and Italy, which was commented on by Cavan and others, was the percentage of casualties who were taken prisoner; 26% for Italy against 6.6% for Britain. The high percentage of casualties who were taken prisoner reinforced the stereotype of the Italian as a reluctant fighter, never mind that the percentage of casualties who died was the same as Britain at 28%.[50] Later chapters will discuss the poor level of training of the Italian troops, the lack of heavy artillery, and the fact that Cadorna and his subordinates had not learnt and adopted the changing techniques of static warfare; all of which contributed to the heavy losses on the Isonzo front. Thousands of men were killed for very little territorial gain. In 1915 Cadorna lost 400,000 of which 66,000 were dead and in the eleventh battle (the last before Caporetto) there were 166,000 casualties of whom 40,000 were killed. Cavan was right; they were good soldiers who were poorly led. In any army troops who feel that their lives are being needlessly wasted will desert but, as with most combat statistics, the figures need to be used with caution.

Does the raw data of desertion statistics justify the charge that Britain's Latin ally was more ready to leave his place of duty than the stoic Anglo-Saxon. Mark Thompson

---

48   TNA: CAB 23/6, minutes of WC 410, 13 May 1918.
49   N. Ferguson, *The Pity of War 1914-1918* (London, 1998), p.299.
50   Ferguson, *The Pity of War*, figures extrapolated from tables on pp.295-99.

cites 101,685 Italian cases in which the soldier was found guilty, with 'around 38,000' British tried for the offence (of which a smaller number would be found guilty);[51] on this raw comparison the Italians were more likely to desert. However, Thompson does state that his is a narrative history, 'not based on methodical research into primary sources'.[52] Those sources need examination. The Italian total quoted by Thompson covers those found guilty of having deserted in Italy – that includes those caught away from the active front. To compare the incidence of British and Italian soldiers deliberately avoiding their place of duty we must include those arraigned for the offence in the UK, as well as those tried at the front. The Statistical Analysis of the war (WO 394 series in the National Archives) records courts martial trials at home in Britain, as well as 'Abroad'; it is this figure that must be used. Thompson's 38,000 is close to the 42,574[53] cases dealt with 'abroad' between the start of the war and the end of 1919, and so forms only a partial comparison with his Italian figure. There is also an important distinction to be drawn between the definition of desertion in British and Italian military law. The British authorities required that for a case of desertion to be proved then the prosecution had to convince the court that there had been 'intent' on the part of the soldier not to return to duty. This was not the case in Italian trials where absence was synonymous with desertion. With this evidential requirement in mind the correct comparison is with a British total for desertions as well as those tried for absence. In their study of British military executions Corns and Hughes-Wilson detail 126,818,[54] such cases, while John Gooch cites the Italian total (not just those found guilty as with Thompson) as 189,425.[55] Thompson's juxtaposition of Italians found guilty of a summation of (in British law) two different offences, with British soldiers tried (but not proven guilty) of only one of the Italian charges leads to a false conclusion; there were 2.68 Italians accused of leaving their post for each British soldier similarly arraigned. The more realistic comparison is drawn from comparing 189,425 Italians with 126,818 British troops; a ratio of 1.5 to 1.0, giving a very different narrative.

Lloyd George, critical of the way in which Haig and the General Staff were prosecuting the war in France, was a strong advocate for a different approach from that of his military advisers; one which he hoped would prove less costly in British lives. In January 1915, as Chancellor of the Exchequer, he put a paper before the Committee of Imperial Defence entitled 'Suggestions as to the Military Position'. It was his view that Britain was having to secure the 'continuous exertion and sacrifice'[56] of its people (in the face of heavy attritional losses), while 'hesitating neutrals' with large armies were still in doubt as to their position; a less than veiled criticism of the Italians who,

51   Thompson, *White War*, p.275.
52   Thompson, *White War*, p.440.
53   TNA: WO 394/6, table on p.642.
54   C. Corns and J. Hughes-Wilson, *Blindfold and Alone. British Military Executions in the Great War* (London, 2001), p.216.
55   Gooch, *Morale*, p.439.
56   TNA: WO 106/308, memo p.3.

at that point, were still negotiating with both sides. Why could Germany not be attacked indirectly, for example from Italy against Austria-Hungary, with the aim of 'knocking the props [from] under her'? According to Lloyd George the people of Britain were tired of the 'banal telegrams' from army headquarters which talked of 'making a little progress' and 'recovering trenches'; telegrams which exaggerated slight success in France and Flanders, while suppressing reverses. At least one historian has suggested that while Lloyd George railed against the heavy losses in the BEF his advocacy of an indirect attack on Germany was not aimed at a reduction in Allied losses, just those of British soldiers. Trevor Wilson has suggested that Lloyd George wanted British soldiers to be used against 'lesser adversaries' – Turkey or Austria-Hungary – while others took on the Germans. It was for this reason, according to Wilson, that Lloyd George (by then Prime Minister) was calling for an Italian offensive in 1917. If the Austrians were attacked then Germany would need to go to their assistance, with the Italians having to fight German troops: 'But this would be taking place at the expense of the Italians and not of our men [...] It would be the first time that the Italian resources of manpower had been properly utilized to pull their weight in the war'.[57] At the time of his comment Lloyd George had discounted Cadorna's nine assaults on the Isonzo, their defence against the Austrian attack in the Trentino in 1916 and over 400,000 men killed.

The division between Lloyd George and the General Staff over the approach to be taken to defeat Germany has been simplified as that between the 'peripheralists',[58] who advocated operations in Italy, Salonika and the defeat of Turkey, and the 'Westerners' with their concentration on defeating Germany in France and Flanders. This antipathy was evident during the decision to deploy British troops to Italy in late 1917. By his earlier comments on banal telegrams from Robertson and others, Lloyd George was demonstrating that he had little respect for the information and advice delivered to him by what he regarded as a closed military clique. On the other hand, Robertson's opinion of politicians' grasp of military matters was equally trenchant: 'Men object to being killed by amateur strategists'.[59] In Britain the military commanders prosecute a war at the behest of the politicians, it is the latter that declare war, set the war aims, determine who their troops will be allied with, and what direction the war will take. It is the role of the military leaders to utilise the forces available to the best of their ability, so as to achieve the political ends. The Prime Minister had the power and authority to overrule or remove the senior commanders, rather than constantly criticise their abilities – he chose not to do so and consequently had Robertson as an unwilling partner in the British support to Italy after that country's defeat at Caporetto.

57   T. Wilson, *The Myriad Faces of War* (Cambridge, 1986), p.440.
58   J. Gooch, 'Soldiers, Strategy and War Aims in Britain 1914-18', in B. Hunt and A. Preston (eds.), War Aims and Strategic Policy in the Great War (London, 1977), pp.21-40.
59   D.R. Woodward (ed.), *The Military Correspondence of Field-Marshal Sir William Robertson* (London, 1989), p.56.

In January 1917 the Allies held a conference in Rome to discuss strategy for the war at which Lloyd George (newly elected as British Prime Minister) tabled his views on the opening of new fronts against Germany, one of which should be in Italy. In his opinion the Italian army had the numerical strength to mount an offensive on their own front, but he acknowledged that they lacked sufficient heavy artillery to make this a success. To rectify that shortage he suggested that the Allied General Staffs should produce a plan for the concentration of the required guns in Italy, with additional batteries to be loaned by Britain and France.[60] In December 1916, prior to the Rome meeting, Robertson was aware that this solution might be proposed and (displaying his reluctance to go along with the suggestion) had written to Haig on the matter:

> I understand there is a desire to lend some of your big guns to Italy for the next few months in return for the despatch of Italian divisions to Salonika or Albania [...] I daresay that everything will come out right in the end [...] You know what my advice will be if and when I am referred to, and I shall see that I am, and I shall suggest that before anything is done you should be asked to what extent your operations etc, would be interfered with by such an arrangement. If you are asked for this opinion I hope you will not mince words. *There is a very dangerous tendency becoming apparent for the War Cabinet to direct military operations.*[61] [My italics.]

Robertson did not want the guns (or any element of the BEF) to go to Italy and resented what he saw as political interference in military affairs. In his view the Germans had to be defeated on the Western Front, and any movement of forces away from France lessened the chances of achieving that aim. The extent to which he tried to out-manoeuvre Lloyd George is illustrated in a comment in the memoir of the secretary to the War Cabinet, Sir Maurice Hankey. Ordinarily the issue of the loan of the artillery batteries (to be discussed at the Rome meeting) would have been addressed between Robertson and Cadorna, before the meeting started. However, Lloyd George asked Hankey to take on this responsibility, but the latter was not quick enough; 'he [Robertson] had made no secret of his hostility to any project of the kind. Early as I was [to see Cadorna], Robertson had been there before me'.[62] When Cadorna was asked to join the political meeting (the generals had a military conference in parallel with that of the politicians) to discuss the proposed loan of the guns, he disappointed Lloyd George by raising all sorts of objections; it would take time to send them; the loan period was inadequate; the means of fire-control were inadequate,

60   TNA: WO 106/765, *Allied co-operation in operations on Italian Front*; memo from Lloyd George.
61   Woodward, *Robertson*, pp.131-2.
62   M. Hankey, *The Supreme Command, 1914-1918 Volume Two* (London, 1961), p.606.

and then there was the use of the railways – Cadorna had certainly been 'got at'. In his memoir Lloyd George used a military metaphor to express his annoyance; 'the military chiefs were left in possession of the field'.[63] The Rome meeting closed with a requirement for Cadorna to put forward plans of his own, detailing how an offensive on the Italian Front might be carried out, and what he would require from the Allies to assist him with that.

In spite of the reluctance of Robertson and Haig, Britain's military involvement in Italy was drawing closer. Having effectively scuttled Lloyd George's suggestions at the Rome Conference, Cadorna came back with his plans for an offensive which included a request for the Allies to supply 300 heavy guns and eight divisions.[64] Just as Italy had frustrated the Entente leaders during the negotiations for the Treaty of London, so the Allied military chiefs now found themselves losing patience with Cadorna and the *Comando Supremo* over the requested assistance. In March 1917 Cadorna was convinced that the Germans, who were withdrawing along the Ancre on the Western Front, would divert divisions to join the Austrians in the Trentino, or along the Isonzo. The Italians feared that if there was an attack on their northern flank, this would cause them to withdraw from the Julian front to the Tagliamento River, or even to the Piave.[65] In conversation with Delmé-Radcliffe, Cadorna stated that any such withdrawal 'would be a severe blow to the Entente'. He went on to suggest that this might lead to 'certain influences' in this country 'bringing about a separate peace'.[66] Cadorna was eluding to socialist agitation and propaganda which was at that time finding its way into the Italian army, and which he would later blame for his military defeat at Caporetto. The threat of possible Italian withdrawal from the war, if they did not get what they wanted – and this was not the only example – reinforced the view of the Allies that they 'do not seem to feel that this is a crucial war for the independence and existence of the country. They perhaps think of it as a big Libyan campaign'.[67] Based on the force that Cadorna was convinced would be massing against him, a calculation which would be ridiculed by Robertson, the Italians increased their request for British and French support – they now wanted the guns and 20 Anglo-French divisions.[68]

In March 1917 Robertson, together with the French General Maxime Weygand, met Cadorna at his headquarters in the small town of Udine, about 20 miles behind the Isonzo front; it was here that plans were drawn up for the transport and supply of British and French divisions, should a decision be taken to deploy them to Italy. However, in the meeting Robertson and Weygand disagreed with Cadorna over the

63   D. Lloyd George, *War memoirs; 3* (London, 1934), p.1448.
64   TNA: WO 158/23, *C-in-C & CIGS correspondence and signals*; memo from CIGS to War Cabinet, 17 March 1917.
65   TNA: WO 106/1512, correspondence between Cadorna and Nivelle, 6 March 1917.
66   TNA: WO 106/1512, memo from Delmé-Radcliffe to Robertson, 14 March 1917.
67   J. Whittam, 'War and Italian Society 1914-16', *War and Society*, 1 (1975), p.153.
68   TNA: WO 158/23, minutes of War Cabinet, 16 March 1917.

number of Austrian divisions facing him as well as the suggestion that the Germans were moving troops from the Western to the Italian Front. According to British intelligence, the Italian forces were twice as strong as those opposing them.[69] Robertson, in a later comment to Sir Henry Wilson, demonstrated his opinion of the Italians: 'What a rotten lot they are'.[70] Although Cadorna's request for 20 divisions was turned down it was agreed that, if Italy were to be attacked in overwhelming force, then the Allies would send troops and equipment as provided for by the Inter-Allied Military Conference held at Chantilly, 15-16 November 1916. To prepare for this eventuality Robertson sent Brigadier-General Crowe to Italy to work with the Italian and French staffs on a 'Convention in the event of Co-operation of British Troops':[71] this spelt out in detail the logistics involved in a deployment. The work of this group ensured the successful move of British troops in October 1917.

Although Crowe's assignment was a positive outcome of the Udine conference, that did not mean that Robertson had relaxed his opposition to the need for any move of British troops. On 1 March he had told the War Cabinet that 'each Ally should be able to defend his own front'.[72] In this statement he saw no irony in the fact that the British were in France helping to defend the French. In Robertson's view, 'To move troops about from one front to another for *defensive* purposes was unsound in many ways, and was to be strongly deprecated'. [Italics in the original.] And that was especially the case if the move was based on an incorrect assessment of the opposing forces, as he believed Cadorna's was. Robertson was convinced that the Italians, by believing their own inflated assessments of the number of Austro-German troops, and their ability to quickly move from the Western to the Italian Front, were becoming in awe of their enemy and allowing him to establish a moral superiority over themselves: 'There is no reason why the Italians should already have curled up, as they have, on the defensive and be contemplating the defeat of their country'.[73] Cadorna may have made requests which Robertson considered were unreasonable, but that was not the same as 'contemplating defeat'. Continuing in the same vein he criticised the contribution of Italy as being less than Britain 'had a right to expect', and that agreements made under the Treaty of London should be reconsidered by the Cabinet. In his view, unless Italy was prepared to put up a 'better fight' than it currently seemed capable of, then it 'also ought to be prepared to accept something less than her full demands'. As Chief of the Imperial General Staff (CIGS), and military adviser to the Prime Minister and the

69   TNA: WO 106/765, summary of the Udine meeting, 23 March 1917.
70   Imperial War Museum (hereafter 'IWM'): DS/MISC/80, Diary of Sir Henry Wilson.
71   TNA: CAB 45/83, *Official Report of the Convention in the event of Co-operation of British Troops in Italy.*
72   TNA: CAB 23/2, *Cabinet minutes and papers; nos. 83-153*, minutes of War Cabinet 83, 1 March 1917.
73   TNA: WO 106/1512, addendum to note to the War Cabinet of 12 February 1917, written 29 March 1917.

War Cabinet, Robertson was influential and he made plain that he was not impressed with Cadorna's military assessments, or Italy's contribution to the Allied effort:

> [The] Italian want of energy and courage are placing upon our shoulders a greatly increased burden, and from a military standpoint I am very doubtful whether we can sustain this burden sufficiently long to ensure a victory as will compel the enemy to cede the territories specified in the existing Agreements.[74]

Robertson was an 'old soldier' from the mould that produced the stiff-backed defenders of Empire. During the retreat from the Marne, in which some at British headquarters had demonstrated 'incompetence'[75] – resulting in the troops being short of food – Robertson (then Quartermaster-General) 'hit upon the ingenious solution of dumping supplies at crossroads on the most likely lines of retreat'.[76] This may have been wasteful, but it worked. It was this positive approach to problems that caused him to constantly criticise the Italians for what he perceived (often unfairly) to be their tendency to fold in the face of adversity. In 1917 Robertson was taking a pessimistic view of the situation facing the Allies of the Entente; he considered the French government to be 'unstable' and there were 'signs of war weariness [...] and a desire for peace' in that country, 'to say nothing of pacifist and other intrigues'. He was concerned that Britain and America might, in the end, 'be the only stable and determined members of the Entente'.[77] Robertson had a chauvinistic appreciation of the contribution his country was making towards the defeat of Germany, whilst belittling Italian efforts. However, this skewed perspective ignored the fact that, in late August 1914, French commanders had cause to 'grind their teeth in exasperation at an attitude [of the British] which seemed to take no account of realities';[78] Sir John French had proposed pulling the BEF out of the line for ten days to refit. Max Hastings' summation of that first month of the war reminds us that Britain's contribution was not always as positive as Robertson wished to portray it when criticising the Italians:

> In August 1914, however, the BEF conducted only a long retirement interrupted by two holding actions. German miscalculation and bungling, together with French mass and courage, did much more than British pluck to deny the Kaiser his victory parade down the Champs-Elysées. But this does not diminish the fascination with which posterity views the BEF's first actions.[79]

74   TNA: WO 106/1512, p.3 of note written 29 March 1917.
75   Hastings, *Catastrophe*, p.214.
76   Spears, *Liaison*, p.215.
77   TNA: WO 106/796, *Situation in Italy; November 1917*, Robertson's report, 14 November 1917, p.3.
78   Spears, *Liaison*, p.288.
79   Hastings, *Catastrophe*, p.201.

Although Robertson was critical of the Italian effort, the response from Britain to Cadorna's request for assistance was more positive, if not as fulsome as the Italians had hoped: no infantry divisions would be deployed, but ten batteries of field guns and howitzers were sent to strengthen the Italian artillery. Soon after their arrival the troops' letters home were reflecting two themes that would recur in the messages sent to families by those who arrived later in the year; the problems with Italian food and their greater feeling of safety in Italy. First impressions were that the Italians were 'good soldiers and nice chaps', but the rations left something to be desired. Unlike the later deployment of the IEF, who were supplied by the Royal Army Service Corps (RASC), this first draft of gunners was victualed by the Italians. This arrangement resulted in an 'Anglo-Italian' menu; less meat, bacon, cheese and tea than the British soldier was used to, but supplemented by macaroni, rice, coffee, wine and lemons. The wine may have been welcome, but letters home grumbled about 'the monotony of macaroni and rice and stew'.[80] We will see in a later chapter that *Tommy* was not happy unless griping about something and what he had to eat was right up there on the list of moans. Quick to complain, he also recognised that life in Italy was more comfortable than that in the trenches of the Western Front, a point well caught by one young officer: 'What worlds away is this country with its wonderful cloudless sunshine from the dismal flat lands of the Western Front!'[81] Whatever their views on pasta, the gunners were received with enthusiasm by their Italian colleagues; gun positions had been prepared for them and adorned with 'messages of welcome.[82] Acceptance by the Italian infantrymen would not come so readily. The foot-soldiers considered artillerymen, be they British or Italian, as '*imboscati*'; a derogatory term for those who spent their time in the safety of the rear areas of the battle zone. Because the Italians had not developed the counter-battery techniques needed to bombard Austrian artillery, the enemy – in turn – rarely shelled Italian guns. As a result there was an undeclared 'live and let live' mindset amongst the gunners; one which Tony Ashworth suggests could also be detected in some areas of France and Flanders.[83] As a consequence of this tendency not to shell each other's guns, the Italian infantry believed that the artillery had an easy life. This sentiment had also existed among the infantry of the BEF, until counter-battery fire was adopted by the British and the Germans. As the guns became primary targets for both sides, so the life of the gunners became less enviable. By the end of the war the artillerymen of the BEF made up 7.6% of the British casualties in France, while in Italy they accounted for 9.7% of those in the IEF.[84] The lower intensity of the artillery exchanges in Italy also resulted in less destruction in the area

80   H. Dalton, *With British Guns in Italy: A Tribute to Italian Achievement* (Teddington, 2007), p.44.
81   Dalton, *British Guns in Italy*, p.24.
82   TNA: WO 106/773, *Impressions of the Italian Army during the autumn retreat 1917*, Jan 1918.
83   T. Ashworth, *Trench Warfare 1914-1918. The Live and Let Live System* (London, 1980).
84   TNA: WO 394/12, Statistical Abstract, report 28, p.148.

immediately behind the front than was the case in France; 'battles were still separate and distinct in Italy, with perceptible periods of lull, less apt than in France to become one blurred series of gigantic actions'.[85]

The first batteries to go to Italy had left Britain in April, with a follow-up reinforcement in July.[86] Among them was a young battery commander, Hugh Dalton, who became a Labour Chancellor of the Exchequer in 1945 – perhaps best remembered for inadvertently giving away budget details before he delivered his speech to Parliament, and being sacked for doing so. Dalton commanded his battery during the eleventh and twelfth battles of the Isonzo, alongside the Italians, and was one of those who wrote well of the Italian soldiers.

> Only those who went out to the Italian Front before Caporetto, and saw with their own eyes what the Italian Army had accomplished on the Carso and among the Julian Alps, can fully realise the greatness of the Italian effort.[87]

In 1919 he published an account of his time in Italy, the sub-title of which – *Tribute to Italian Achievement* – betrays his love of the country and its people. The language Dalton used to describe his experiences demonstrates the background and educational differences between himself (and many of the young officers who had joined the colours since the outbreak of war) and Sir William Robertson. While Dalton received a classical education at Eton (followed by King's College Cambridge and the London School of Economics), Robertson, the son of a village tailor and postmaster, attended the village Anglican school and went into domestic service at the age of 13. In 1877, by then he was 18, Robertson joined the army as an ordinary soldier and served in India and the Boer War. He has the distinction of being the only soldier to rise from 'ranker' to Field Marshal, which would have given him a unique perspective of the army and the men who served in it. Having no truck with the romantic views of Italy, as exemplified by many like Dalton, he regarded the country as a 'side-show' on which British troops were wasted.

In July 1917 Cadorna made yet another request for artillery assistance. He was developing his plans for a further assault on the Isonzo and wanted the British and French to supply him with 100 guns to assure success. July was not a good time to ask. At the end of that month the British began a major offensive in Flanders; officially designated as Third Ypres, it is more commonly known as Passchendaele, and is synonymous with mud, slow progress and great loss of life. General Ferdinand Foch, Chief of the French General Staff, was in favour of sending the guns, writing that Cadorna 'must not be given a reason whether real or otherwise not to attack at the

85   Dalton, *British Guns in Italy*, p.23.
86   Edmonds, *Italy*, p.31.
87   Dalton, *British Guns in Italy*, p.11.

right moment'.[88] This time it was the French who were suggesting that the Italians needed little excuse to avoid fighting. But Foch was not proposing to reduce his own artillery strength; he suggested that the batteries should come from the French First Army, at that time part of Haig's command. Haig and Robertson were adamant that these could not be released without having a detrimental effect on the planned offensive in Flanders, and an argument in writing developed between the British generals and Foch. During August Delmé-Radcliffe wrote that it would be wrong to miss the opportunity presented by the Italian offensive to gain a 'signal military victory' against the Austrians. Picking up this point Lloyd George argued the case for sending the guns, stating that the War Cabinet had a responsibility 'not to allow the most promising opening which events have thrown our way in any western theatre to come to nought for want of opportune support'.[89] The Prime Minister's enthusiastic statement speaks more of his wish to see an attack on Germany's 'props' than a real assessment of the success of Cadorna's previous Isonzo offensives. The disagreement over the artillery batteries was settled after a meeting between Haig, Foch and General Philippe Pétain, and by September the guns were on their way to Italy. But Cadorna was to try his allies' patience one more time – in September, after Haig's guns had arrived in Italy, he called off his plans for an attack.[90] Robertson telegraphed Delmé-Radcliffe, urging him to speak to Cadorna and tell him that the Anglo-French front had been 'deprived of a hundred guns' to assist Italy. Uncharacteristically Robertson also wanted the Italian C-in-C told that 'I beg General Cadorna to consider the grave effect on the Allied cause if he should remain inactive at this juncture'[91] – begging was not something which came naturally to the British CIGS. On 24 September Robertson reminded Cadorna that the artillery batteries had been sent to Italy on the basis that they would be used 'for offensive purposes' but, as the Italians had now adopted a 'defensive attitude', the guns should be withdrawn immediately from Italy as the British required 'to send them to another theatre'. Once again the Italians had disappointed their allies by an apparent lack of total commitment to the war. A telegram from Robertson to Haig in late September shows just how little enthusiasm he had for British involvement on the Italian Front:

> You will be pleased to hear that as Cadorna has said he must go on the defensive the Cabinet are awfully sick with him, and I think also with themselves! I do not

88   TNA: CAB 21/89, *Development of military plans of the Allies during 1917; Support to Italy*, letter from Colonel Spiers to CIGS, 16 July 1917.
89   House of Lords, Parliamentary Archives (hereafter 'PA'): LG/F/44/3/19, Lloyd George papers, letter to CIGS, 26 August 1917.
90   TNA: WO 158/24, *Communication between C-in-C BEF and CIGS*, telegram from CIGS to Haig, 21 September 1917.
91   TNA: WO 106/770, Telegrams; March-October, telegram from CIGS to Delmé-Radcliffe, 22 September 1917.

anticipate that we shall ever hear any more about your sending divisions to the Italian Front.[92]

Robertson was wrong. Exactly one month later the Austro-German forces inflicted a crushing defeat on the Italian army at Caporetto, resulting in the urgent deployment of British and French divisions to Italy.

1917 and the defeat at Caporetto

On 24 October 1917 the Italian army suffered a military defeat, known to history after a small town on the River Isonzo – Caporetto (now Kobarid in Slovenia). The Austro-Hungarian army, spearheaded by German divisions and storm-troops, achieved a significant breakthrough on ground held by the Italian Second Army. For the army and the country, Caporetto was a humiliation. All dreams of becoming a Great Power, of establishing an Italian empire, dissolved before the reality of this military disaster; 'Italy lurched to the edge of utter defeat'.[93] Where Benedetto Croce had spoken enthusiastically (only a month before the battle) of the army helping Italians to achieve 'national and political cohesion',[94] those illusions were shattered by Caporetto. As with the preceding eleven battles on the Isonzo this book is not the place for a detailed account of the events of the Twelfth, they are well covered elsewhere, with Mark Thompson's *White War,* and Gooch's *Italian Army,* deserving special mention. However, given that it was the pre-cursor to the deployment of British troops to the country, a brief overview of those events in October helps to set the scene.

The collapse of the Italian Front was dramatic and rapid, causing Cadorna to fall back some seventy miles to the River Piave where he was able to stabilise and hold a new defensive line. Any further retreat from this position threatened Venice, the Po valley and the ability of Italy to remain in the war. Whatever Robertson's earlier comments on the inadvisability of sending troops from one front to another for defensive purposes, the Italians had to be kept in the war. During the Austro-German advance the Italian Third Army (under the Duke of Aosta) fought well but the collapse of Second Army on their left exposed Aosta's flank, forcing him to make an orderly withdrawal, first to the River Tagliamento and then to the Piave. Caporetto was undeniably a *military* defeat for the Italians. Cadorna had been at pains to deflect criticism of his own command failings by issuing a statement that blamed the spread of socialist propaganda among the troops, and a consequent weakening of their morale; he missed the point that morale issues were a reflection of leadership, and his army had been beaten militarily. Two days after the start of the Austrian attack he told

92   Woodward, *Robertson*, pp.226-7.
93   R.J.B. Bosworth, *Mussolini* (London, 2010), p.100.
94   C. Duggan, *The force of destiny: a history of Italy since 1796* (London, 2008), p.398.

Figure 1.3 Mountains East of Caporetto which would have been held by the Austrians.
(© J. Dillon)

Delmé-Radcliffe that 'some of the troops did not fight well'[95] and that if 'peace propaganda' was allowed to continue in the country 'he will not be responsible for the Army which has undoubtedly been affected and is not so reliable as it should be in the case of some units'.[96] The Italian soldiers were poorly led by Cadorna who tried to expunge his culpability for the defeat by blaming his men; there had been 'treason on the part of his troops, who had made no effort to oppose the attack'.[97] The comment was seized on by Robertson as reinforcing his already low opinion of the Italian army; 'the situation ought never to have arisen having regard to relative numbers and terrain', the Italian troops were 'so unreliable'.[98] Credence must be given to some of Cadorna's criticism of the spread of 'pacifist propaganda', but it should not be allowed to detract from the

95   PA: LG/F/44/3/27, memo 495 from Delmé-Radcliffe to CIGS, 26 October 1917.
96   PA: LG/F/44/3/27, memo 497 from Delmé-Radcliffe to CIGS, 26 October 1917.
97   TNA: CAB 23/4, *Cabinet minutes and papers; nos. 227-308*, minutes of War Cabinet 262, 1 November 1917.
98   PA: LG/F/44/3/30, Robertson to Haig, 28 October 1917.

command failings of himself and some of his subordinates, especially Second Army's commander, General Luigi Capello. Prior to the battle Cadorna ordered Capello to make his dispositions for defence, but he was ignored and Cadorna failed to ensure that his orders were acted on by his subordinate. In a note to the government Cadorna stated that within the army, 'the spirit has been lacking and is still lacking; and when the spirit and will to fight is lacking in a soldier, everything else is lacking also'.[99] This shameful attempt to blame his soldiers for his own failings was summarised by Thompson who makes a reference to Cadorna's father, General Raffaele Cadorna, who had led the invasion of the Papal States in 1870 and then captured Rome for the new Italian state in September of that year:

> [Capello] did not commit himself to Cadorna's defensive design until late afternoon on 23 October: less than 12 hours before the start of the Twelfth Battle [Caporetto]. Incredibly, Cadorna failed to see that the practical unity of his command had been compromised, perhaps beyond repair. There was no clenched fist in charge of the army, as his father had insisted there must be. His worst nightmare had come true, and he could not see it.[100]

In spite of the Commander-in-Chief's attempts to blame the result of the battle on the unwillingness of his men to fight, those same troops stopped, turned and halted the Austrian advance on the River Piave, and so demonstrated a level of morale which proved to be 'much stronger than Cadorna had feared'.[101]

Regardless of his commander's orders, Capello was determined to put in place his own design for a counter offensive strategy. Poor communication between him and Cadorna, together with the Second Army commander being confined to bed with kidney trouble in those last crucial days of October, resulted in the two men working against each other. It was not until Capello returned from sick-leave that he fell in line with Cadorna's defensive plans – only a day before the Austro-German assault hit them. In the days prior to the attack the Italian command had obtained information from various sources indicating that it would take place in late October and that it would be against Cadorna's Isonzo front, between Tolmino and Mount Rombon. The Italian commander felt sufficiently confident of his preparations against just such an assault to inform the War Minister and the King that the steps he had taken allowed him to 'await the enemy's blow with serene confidence of being able to repel it victoriously'.[102] Unfortunately the British criticism that Italian commanders and Staff Officers did not visit the front frequently enough, and relied on subordinates carrying out written orders – which the originators made little attempt to ensure had been

---

99   R. Seth, *Caporetto. The Scapegoat Battle* (London, 1961), pp.176-8.
100 Thompson, *The White War*, p.300.
101 Gooch, *Morale and Discipline*, p.443.
102 J. Gooch, *The Italian Army and the First World War* (Cambridge, 2014), p.232.

actioned – was borne out at Caporetto. Apart from poor leadership and staff work the Italians were defeated by superior German tactics: the use of gas in the preliminary bombardment incapacitated many of the Italians in the forward trenches; the Italian artillery was very poor at counter-battery shelling; and the Germans had developed the technique of indirect fire with little or no pre-registration of their targets. On top of these factors was the German use of storm-troop tactics. Instead of attacking with large formations, these units were split up into small autonomous groups led by NCOs. Advancing individually they went round strong-points and machine-gun pits which would then be taken by the second line of the advance; this method of advance avoided the attackers being cut down in attritional attacks on fortified positions, so stalling the attack at the first line of defences. Employing these tactics the Italians quickly found that the Germans were behind as well as in front of them. With their 'disregard for any semblance of a linear advance'[103] units moved forward rapidly, rather than allowing themselves to be over-sensitive to exposed flanks and so be held up by individual fire positions. One man who came to prominence in the attack that day was the German Lieutenant, Erwin Rommel; in one account[104] of the attack on Mt. Matajur, he and his men are reported to have taken the surrender of some 9,000 Italian officers and men for the loss of only six dead and 30 wounded. Rommel's advance across that difficult terrain is recreated today by some of the guides from Kobarid museum who lead groups of US Marines on the same arduous climbs.

In the days following Caporetto the Italian army, including the artillery batteries on loan from Britain, retreated some 70 miles until, on 10 November, it stopped and formed a defensive line on the River Piave. By the time that Cadorna's army reached the river it had lost 10,000 dead, 30,000 wounded, 265,000 as prisoners and 350,000 had been separated from their units as they fled before the Austrian advance. Retreats are most often characterised by confusion and chaos and this had been no exception, as newly arrived British officers were quick to point out. Lord Cavan, who would be the first commander of the British force in Italy, remarked that he had seen thousands of men withdrawing with 'scarcely a rifle among them and very few officers'.[105] Robertson, who travelled to Rome immediately after the Italian defeat, was typically scathing in a note to Haig; 'a more disgraceful sight than the returning Italians, without arms & [sic] equipment, was never seen. *They are not for it*'.[106] [My italics.] Lloyd George, stereotype at the ready, declared that while the Italian soldier was brave, he did not have the resolution of his northern neighbour: 'The dangers of retreat are not so great amongst the stolid races of the north as in the armies of a quick,

103 B. I. Gudmundsson, *Stormtroop Tactics. Innovation in the German Army, 1914-1918*, (Westport, 1989), p.133.
104 J. and E. Wilks, *Rommel and Caporetto* (Barnsley, 2001), p.112.
105 TNA: WO 79/70, *Earl of Cavan; Campaign in Italy, 1917-1918, draft account*, handwritten notes p.3.
106 Woodward, *Robertson*, p.251.

imaginative, susceptible people such as the Italians'.[107] The Prime Minister's chauvinistic statement would be tested the following spring when the Germans burst through the front of Gough's Fifth Army and 21,000 British soldiers (including the author's grandfather) were taken prisoner on the first day of that offensive.

The Italians stopped, turned and then held the Austrians, but a myth grew up that this was not done until the Allies (British and French) arrived. A deal of the responsibility for this 'legend' is due to Marshal Ferdinand Foch. He accepted responsibility for the French point of view, expressed in the *Revue des Deux Mondes* that the defence on the Piave 'was due to the intervention of Marshal Foch'. Cadorna then disputed the claim with articles in *Rassegna Italiana* and the British *Army Quarterly*.[108] The Italian C-in-C is justly criticised for his preparations for the defence at Caporetto, but it is incorrect to say that the Italians did not take up the Piave line on their own. To his credit, Cavan disputed the *Revue's* report and praised the Duke of Aosta's Third Army for holding up the Austrians which, '[gave] time for the French and British not only to complete detrainment, but also to march the ninety miles to the Montello unmolested by the enemy'.[109] Cavan wanted the record put straight:

> The Italians unaided stopped the rout and held the enemy on the Piave. It should never be forgotten that the French and British reinforcements did not arrive in the fighting section of the Italian Front until the pursuit of the enemy was definitely checked.[110]

In spite of Cavan's declaration, the myth that the Italians could only stop and hold the Austrians with Allied assistance has persisted into later histories. In a recent book on the rise of western military power Professor James France, an historian who specialises in the crusades, asserts that the Piave line was held and stabilised 'only with British and French assistance'.[111] Myths die slowly.

Caporetto was a stinging defeat for the Italians but the Italophile historian George Trevelyan, never averse to a little hyperbole, divined (in flowery prose) a positive side to the disaster:

> Now followed, as if from a blue sky, that tremendous cataclysm which almost ruined Italy and bade fair to ruin the cause of her Allies, but ended in giving to her a new national purpose and discipline, and to the Allies a closer unity.[112]

---

107 D. Lloyd George *War Memoirs; 4* (London, 1934), p.2311.
108 L. Cadorna, 'The End of a Legend', *Army Quarterly*, 7 (1924), pp.235-44.
109 Lord Cavan, 'Some Tactical and Strategic Considerations of the Italian Campaign in 1917-1918', *Army Quarterly*, 1 (1920), pp.11-18.
110 TNA: WO 79/70, handwritten note, p.8.
111 J. France, *Perilous Glory: The Rise of Western Military Power* (London, 2011), p.292.
112 G.M. Trevelyan, *Scenes from Italy's War* (London, 1919), p.163.

With the success of the Austro-German attack, the Italians could reasonably expect the British to deploy divisions to the country under the arrangements previously agreed by the Crowe reconnaissance of early 1917. Nevertheless, with the BEF still mired in its offensive at Passchendaele, Robertson was reluctant to remove troops from the Western Front to support Italians whom he did not believe were pulling their weight: they needed to get a grip; they should display 'more courage and less panic'; they should remember 'what we did at Ypres and the French at Verdun'.[113] Robertson was once again displaying his complete disdain for Britain's ally but, to be fair to him and Haig, they were under great pressure from Lloyd George over their slow progress against the Germans in Flanders (not to mention the heavy losses), and he did not need this Italian distraction.

The British were taken aback by the rapidity with which the Italian defences on the Isonzo were over-run. In the period immediately prior to the attack, and the first few days of the collapsing defence, the intelligence sent to the War Office from the British attaché in Rome had presented an overly sanguine appreciation of the situation. Three days before Caporetto Delmé-Radcliffe had reported that the Italians were expecting an attack, but the 'morale of Italian Army [sic] is excellent and officers and men are all confident of frustrating enemy's offensive',[114] i.e., there was no cause for concern. On 26 October Robertson responded, in some frustration, with a summary of the optimistic telegrams he had received from Delmé-Radcliffe, pointing out that they did not in any way prepare London for what happened:

> after making every allowance for the unexpected I cannot reconcile above [list of optimistic telegrams] with your 492 [telegram of 21 October] in which Cadorna suspects morale and loyalty of his troops, orders a withdrawal from the Bainsizza and prepares to withdraw whole of his armies to the Tagliamento.[115]

Again, believing that the Italians were persistently inflating the number of enemy divisions, Robertson and his staff could not understand how Cadorna considered himself to be numerically inferior to the opposing force, 'he should be superior even if nine or ten German divisions have arrived'. Two days into the Austro-German offensive Delmé-Radcliffe had declared that the Italian losses were 650 guns and 40,000 prisoners, but that Cadorna was facing the situation with resolution and 'has no intention of allowing himself to be overcome by it'[116] – and yet only days later the front collapsed. With such poor intelligence from the military attaché in Rome to London, there is no wonder that the War Office was confused as to the true situation. Robertson was convinced that the Italians were in a funk; Cadorna 'should have no

113 TNA: WO 106/770, memo CIGS to Delmé-Radcliffe, 26 October 1917.
114 TNA: WO 106/770, Delmé-Radcliffe to CIGS, 21 October 1917.
115 TNA: WO 106/770, CIGS to Delmé-Radcliffe, 26 October 1917.
116 PA: LG/F/44/3/27, Delmé-Radcliffe to CIGS, 26 October 1917.

difficulty stopping the advance' because of his numerical superiority and the terrain the enemy would have to cross. He compared the situation with that which had faced the Romanians and, in his opinion, if that nation had succeeded 'surely the Italians could do the same if the troops but fight moderately well'.[117] As far as Robertson was concerned a panic prevailed, and this had spread to Delmé-Radcliffe and his staff and the embassy; 'I do not understand why you should be burning your archives'. Nevertheless, putting his reservations to one side, Robertson now recognised the inevitable and Britain would have to deploy troops to Italy: 'Cadorna ought not to require help but we may have to help in order to prevent the total collapse of Italy which would be a serious matter'.[118]

Although Robertson had now concluded that British military support to Italy was a necessity, it was still a political decision. That this was the case is demonstrated in his instruction to Haig not to discuss the issue with the French or Italian authorities; 'that would place us in an awkward position *if the Cabinet decide against assistance*' [my italics].[119] In his advice to Lloyd George, 27 October, Robertson was still equivocal. He told the Prime Minister that Italy still had 'stacks of men' and there was 'no military necessity to send troops to her provided the Italian troops fight reasonably well'. As CIGS it was Robertson's job to advise the politicians on the military options and then to implement their decision, however, he was in favour of 'waiting until Cadorna asks for them [troops], unless you think that for political reason we ought not to be outdone by the French. We must not get rattled over this business, but of course we must stop the rot if we can'.[120] The reference to being 'outdone' by the French is an interesting comment on an internal dynamic of the alliance; it appears to have also been competitive. Robertson was still strongly of the view that sending units to Italy was the wrong thing to do; it weakened the army where it should be strongest (beating the Germans on the Western Front), and the Italian situation was one of their own making – they just needed to 'man up' to their opponents. Lloyd George responded the same day (from his golf club) that Britain should assist Italy, but his letter contained the hint of a rebuke for the way in which the generals were dealing with their ally:

> If we mean to exercise a dominant influence in directing the course of the War we must do so in the way the Germans have secured control i.e. by helping to extricate Allies in trouble. We cannot do so merely by lecturing them at Conferences. We must help them, then we will have earned the right to dictate to them.[121]

---

117 TNA: WO 106/770, CIGS to Delmé-Radcliffe, 26 October 1917.
118 PA: LG/F/44/3/27, CIGS to Haig, 27 October 1917.
119 PA: LG/F/44/3/27, CIGS to Haig, 27 October 1917.
120 PA: LG/F/44/3/27, CIGS to Lloyd George, 27 October 1917.
121 PA: LG/F/44/3/28, Lloyd George to CIGS, 27 October 1917.

Lloyd George's choice of verb – dictate – implies a chauvinistic superiority by Britain over its ally, but there are also other subtle meanings that might be read into it. Is it a mild rebuke of Robertson for his hectoring against Italian methods – first help, then criticise. Or is it a hint at the stance to be taken by Britain at a future peace conference where, when the spoils came to be divided, assistance rendered to them would put Italy in a weaker position? This author tends to the first interpretation. The War Office response was sent that day to the Prime Minister; two divisions had been given notice that they would be dispatched as soon as possible.[122]

Whatever misgivings Robertson may have had at the need to send troops to Italy, the decision was taken that they should go and the military had to get on with it. In spite of the limited transport facilities available between the Western Front and northern Italy, and an on-going major offensive at Passchendaele, those responsible did an excellent job. In the early weeks after Caporetto five British divisions, with artillery and equipment, as well as five squadrons from the Royal Flying Corps, were moved to Italy. It was now time for the British soldiers and their commanders, whatever their views of Italian fighting abilities, to familiarise themselves with a war theatre very different from Flanders, and to work closely with an ally who had recently suffered a humiliating defeat.

122 Woodward, *Robertson*, p.241.

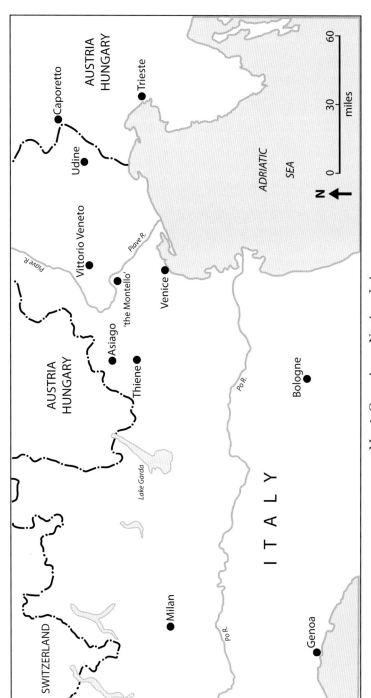

Map 1 General area, Northern Italy.

2

The dispatch of British divisions: "It was like entering another world"

Reluctant as Robertson was to send troops from the Western Front to Italy, he now had his instructions from the Prime Minister. The plans (drawn up by Crowe) to dispatch two divisions from Haig's armies were set in motion. However, none of this stopped Robertson's carping: 'I do not question this decision – indeed, I fully agree with it *for the time being*'.[1] [My italics] Robertson held the view that if the war was going to be won, then it was Britain who would have to do the winning. He had serious reservations about the Italians; it would be idle to rely on any prospect of them launching an offensive in the coming winter, and it was by no means certain – in his view – that the Allies could 'keep Italy in the war', as he considered it not unlikely that the Italian army would 'again collapse'. In his role as CIGS, and military adviser to the government, Robertson was asking the War Cabinet whether or not 'we shall be justified in continuing to throw good money after bad', he was concerned that Britain might end up shouldering the brunt of the struggle against Germany. After three years of war, heavy casualties, and with British troops stretched from Flanders to Mesopotamia, Britain needed strong partners to see the conflict through. However, reflecting on the mutinies in the French army in 1917, Robertson declared that there were 'many signs of war weariness in France and of a desire for peace'. Also, he was afraid that Britain and America could end up as 'the only stable and determined members of the Entente' and diluting the army's strength by taking on more commitments abroad would not, in his view, help the war. In spite of his criticism of meddling politicians, and his dislike of Lloyd George – at one point he described him as 'an under-bred swine'[2] – Robertson's job was to implement the government's strategy, and that meant supporting Italy. To that end he instructed Haig to send two 'good' divisions to Italy, under the command of a 'good man'. Haig chose the 23rd and 41st Divisions from XIV Corps, commanded by Lieutenant General the Earl of Cavan. These were New Army units (raised after Lord Kitchener's call for volunteers) which had seen recent

1   TNA: WO 106/796, Robertson's report, 14 November 1917.
2   Woodward, *Robertson*, letter to Kiggell, 9 August 1917, p.213.

action and would be going to Italy as experienced and hardened troops. It was quickly decided that two divisions would not be sufficient so the 5th, 7th and 48th, as well as the staff of XI Corps under Lieutenant General Sir Richard Haking, were added to the deployment to make up the British Italian Expeditionary Force (IEF). With the increase to five divisions the command of the IEF was moved from Cavan to General Sir Herbert Plumer (commander of Second Army in France), on 16 November 1917.

The decision to send the IEF was necessarily taken in a hurry, as illustrated by Cavan's account of his in-depth briefing before moving to take on the role. According to Cavan, Robertson met him in Flanders and told him to:

> Get into the car and tell your chauffeur to follow. We can talk in the car and I am in a hurry to get to Haig's headquarters. You've got to go to Italy, and your job is to put new heart into the Italians.[3]

Cavan naturally asked what he was to command, when he should start and where he should go; he was told to 'discuss it with Haig's staff as soon as you can'. With that, Cavan got out of the car and returned to his headquarters to take up his new position – Italy may have been something of a rushed assignment, but we can assume his briefing was a little more comprehensive than Cavan's notes would have us believe. The 23rd Division were similarly taken by surprise, on 28 October, when they received their warning order to move, the opening paragraph of which stated that 'The Division complete will be in readiness to move by rail forthwith; destination unknown'.[4] The divisional history goes on to state that on 31 October the officers were briefed by Sir Douglas Haig that they would be going to Italy and while many officers had guessed the destination, 'to the rank and file the announcement came as an inspiring revelation'. Knowing that they were going to Italy would indeed have been a revelation to the men; Norman Gladden (a Private in 23 Division) later wrote that on 7 November they entrained for 'oonoesware' [sic] and it was only on the 10 November, as they reached Toulon, that 'we knew that Italy was our destination'.[5] Similarly Bombardier Ronald Skirth (293 Field Battery) had no idea they were bound for Italy until they arrived at Savona.[6] While something of a surprise, the move was popular with the men after their recent experience of the fighting in Flanders. The reports of the official censor are in the archive at the Imperial War Museum, and are drawn from Captain Hardie's reading of the letters the soldiers sent home: 'On the whole, Tommy is not displeased with the change of scene'. In their view Italy 'was much better than Ypres', it was 'Child's play here compared with Belgium'. The mood was summed up by one man from the 2nd King's Own Scottish Borderers: 'It's a real holiday out here, the best

---

3   TNA: WO 79/70.
4   H.R. Sandilands, *The 23rd Division 1914-1919* (London, 1925), p.209.
5   Gladden, *Piave*, p.5.
6   D. Barrett (ed.), *The Reluctant Tommy. Ronald Skirth* (London, 2010), p.116.

war I have been in. Our billets are good, the wine is fair, the weather grand and the people treat us A1. What could be better'?[7]

Robertson had told Lloyd George that sending the troops to Italy would be 'really *very* hard on our men after what they have recently gone through'[8] [italics in original]; that was certainly not the view of the men, for whom the war would be considerably different from that they had experienced to date. In their last eleven days in the line in Flanders 23 Division suffered 1,229 casualties of which 13 officers and 262 other ranks were killed.[9] This compared with a total of 6,925 casualties for the whole of the year in which the IEF was deployed to Italy.[10] A young Lieutenant with the Duke of Cornwall's Light Infantry described the difference for his parents; 'after the experience one had in France, speaking comparatively, there was no war in Italy. It was more of a picnic usually, but noisy at times'.[11]

The troops may have been cheerful at the prospect of leaving Flanders, but the journey to Italy would be long, slow and uncomfortable – but most considered it a price worth paying. The route lay along 700 miles of railway track from France to the disembarkation points in Italy. Although it receives little attention in British histories of the war, this rail-route, and its onward extension to the port of Taranto on Italy's southern coast, was vital to the Allies. Situated at the north of the 'heel' of Italy, and with a magnificent harbour, Taranto was the main supply base for troops and supplies being transported to and from the war theatres of Salonika and Egypt. The port had facilities for a transit population of 15,000 white and native troops as well as 500 hospital beds for the sick and wounded from those two fronts. In later chapters the point will be made that the medical and disciplinary statistics of this rear-echelon depot base 'skewed' the data for the IEF. Historians and researchers have drawn conclusions from the data for 'Italy' and applied these to the fighting units, care must be taken to separate the statistics for front-line troops from those based outside the active war zones. But, to return to those troops who were arriving in Italy from the BEF. Because the railway from the Channel ports, all the way to Taranto, was in regular army use, and had established *haltes-repas* (resting points) along its length, the deployment of the IEF was able to proceed smoothly. Heavily utilised as the network was – as well as troops it was the main supply route for the food and raw materials of which Italy was desperately short – in the two months of November and December it carried an additional 715 trains,[12] many full of men leaving 'that accursed Ypres Salient which none of them ever wanted to revisit'.[13]

---

7   Hardie, Private Papers, report October 1917.
8   Woodward, *Robertson*, p.240.
9   Sandilands, *23rd Division*, p.209.
10   TNA: WO 394/12, *Statistical Abstract of Information regarding the Armies at Home and Abroad*.
11   Acland, Private Papers, p.100.
12   A.M. Henniker, *Transportation on the Western Front 1914-1918* (London, 1937), p.302.
13   C.T. Atkinson, *The Seventh Division 1914-1918* (London, 1927), p.437.

In today's world of high-speed trains a 700 mile journey might well be over within half a day, but for the soldiers en-route to Italy there was a cold and draughty five days ahead of them. In his study of Officer-men relations in the British Army, Gary Sheffield stresses the attitude of paternalism that was drilled into young regimental officers: 'By 1917, it was no longer valid, if indeed it ever had been, to think of officers and men as belonging to two distinct, watertight groups, possessing no knowledge of each other's conditions'.[14] However, paternalism did not stretch to sharing the conditions of the men, if it could be avoided. The soldiers of the IEF found themselves – in November – 30 or more to a cattle truck, on which was stencilled the notice that each could hold 'Hommes 40, Chevaux 8'. Officers, like Dalton, travelled in an altogether different style; on one occasion he recorded a meal on the train at which 'ice was served with the wine'.[15] Another young subaltern, in charge of a draft of men on their way to Italy in September 1917, noted that when the train stopped for the night the gunners' coach was detached 'so that they slept in a siding – we [the officers] after meal at station [*sic*], slept in the station hotel'.[16] The disparity between their travelling conditions did prick the conscience of some young officers: 'It must be pretty trying for the men, herded together, 40 to a plain truck, for all the world like luggage in a guards-van'.[17]

On their way south the *haltes-repas* facilities would have been welcome opportunities for toilet-breaks and some food, but the provision was not always adequate to the need; after all, thirty men spending hours in a cattle truck could lead to all wanting 'natural relief' at the same time. Major Owen Morshead described one such halt on a hot day at Marseilles:

[T]he many hundreds of men were of course not allowed to leave the immediate vicinity of their respective trains – and there were no sanitary facilities. By the time we left conditions were already almost unbearable – and what it will be like after some thousands more troops have been held up there I shudder to think.[18]

As we will see in later chapters the British were often quick to criticise the Italians, army and civilians, for the poor state of their sanitation, but Morshead's example demonstrates that the IEF was not above reproach. The wagons in which the men travelled obviously had little in the way of catering facilities so the men were dependent on being fed at the en-route stops. The food (like all army fare) was basic, leading to much griping and grousing (for which the men were famous); soup kitchens served

14   G. Sheffield, *Officer-Man Relations, Morale and Discipline in the British Army, 1902-22*, PhD, (King's College, London, 1994), p.261.
15   Dalton, *British Guns in Italy*, p.13.
16   A. Wade, 'Youthful memories of war (2)', *Journal of the Western Front Association*, 27 (1989), p.29.
17   IWM: Doc. 05/50/01, O. Morshead, *Private Papers*, diary 19 November 1917.
18   IWM: Doc 05/50/01, Morshead, diary 20 November 1917.

Figure 2.1 British troops of the 14th Corps aboard a leave train.
(© Imperial War Museum Q 26117)

up an unvarying menu of 'bully stew, pork and beans followed by hard rice grains in tepid water … Hell! When shall we taste real food again?' There was, however, one redeeming characteristic of a steam engine – it produced masses of hot water, essential for the soldiers' all-important brew of tea. It did not take them long to discover that the driver could press 'a magic knob and boiling water hisses out from near the wheels into the dixies of tea-leaves'.[19] When it came to tea, the soldier would always find a way.

While the 'coaches' were insalubrious, and the food lacking in variety, the troops recognised that they were escaping from the hell they had come to know in France and Flanders. They found themselves travelling through a completely different land-scape, most of them never having been so far from home before. The impression that this made on the men comes through in the their post-war accounts, like that of Norman Gladden who was carried away by 'glimpses of the peaks of the Maritime Alps towering beyond, and vineyards and orchards filled with vines and fig and palm and many subtropical plants, which were new to me'.[20] Such sights, after the mud they had come to know, allowed the men to believe they could survive the war.

19   Barrett (ed.), *Reluctant Tommy,* p.111.
20   Gladden, *Piave,* p.6.

The first two divisions of the IEF arrived in Italy in November. The 23rd started detraining in the Mantua area on the 11th of the month, with the 41st doing the same on the 16th; the Official History recorded it as a 'nightmare' with the Italian railway organisation having completely broken down.[21] However, 'goodwill prevailed' and the British troops were well received. All the way through Italy the soldiers had been waved to by the Italians; they had been showered with flowers, and the town of Savona had posters printed in Italian and English wishing the British 'best wishes and heartfelt greetings ... Let Victory be with us'.[22] While most of the men wrote home that they had been met with flowers and smiles, not all reflected the sentiments of the Savona proclamation. Acland noted that in Turin, a city singled out by Cadorna as a hot-bed of socialist propaganda, their arrival was resented by some; the locals thought that the British were there 'for no other reason than to keep them [the Italians] at it [the war]'.[23]

When the divisions embarked for Italy they did so with no decision having been taken as to where they would join the line; the situation was too fluid. However, after arriving in the country and taking stock of the strategic situation, Cavan and Cadorna agreed that the British would occupy the defensive line on the Montello, high ground near the River Piave, which they would take over from Italian troops. To reach the line from their disembarkation points the men would have to march on the local roads, with full packs and equipment, for three or four days. But, as with sport, even a route-march could involve an element of competition. Battalions were required to report the number of 'stragglers' at the end of each day, and each unit would take pride in having as few men as possible 'fall out'; the 7 Division history records that the troops stood up well and that 'stragglers were few and far between'.[24] However, five days traveling in cattle trucks was no real preparation for a sixty-four mile march in three days, and the war diary of the medical officer in 23 Division gives a more accurate picture; first day 178 stragglers, second day 71 and a further 360 on the third day. Those who fell by the wayside were collected by a Red Cross unit bringing up the rear. The British soldiers were proud of their discipline and turnout and judged the Italians lacking when compared against their own high standards. Civilians were described as 'drably-garbed', while they were shocked at the 'slackness' of the Italian military guards they encountered en-route and the way that Italian soldiers 'often [used] their rifles as supports' when standing around.[25] But the Italians were recovering from a military defeat while the British were pleased to be away from Flanders – this was bound to be reflected in the outward demeanour of both. Also, British soldiers frequently sang while on the march, sometimes bawdy ballads, sometimes

21   Edmonds, *Italy*, p.91.
22   TNA: WO 95/4240, *War Diary 23 Division*, the diary has a copy of the poster.
23   Acland, *Private Papers*, p.104.
24   Atkinson, *7th Division*, p.438.
25   Gladden, *Piave*, pp.9-28.

sentimental reminders of home. Italian peasants were recorded as being 'wide-eyed' and stopping their field-work as they heard the troops of the IEF march by singing *Keep the Home Fires Burning* and *Take me back to Dear old Blighty*. For men like Private George Walton, fresh from the Western Front, this was all so different:

> Sharp touch of frost yesterday but got out a lovely warm day. Went on a route march and saw the mountains in the distance covered with snow. Been all round the village, chestnuts and apples chiefly on sale. Starting upon the native bread ration. Love to both. Geo.[26]

Walton had been in the country for less than a week when his post-card finished with a comment on one of the soldiers' favourite subjects; food. The local bread that he referred to was not the white loaf that the British soldier normally received in his rations. While they complained at the monotony of the army diet, the troops did not take well to changes they were unfamiliar with, and dark bread was certainly not something they took to. Some of the men, like Harry Lamin, wrote home asking their family to send them the bread they were missing; 'I have had no white bread lately we have been on Italian rashing [rations] would be glad if you could send a parcel I have not had any for weeks'.[27] [Syntax of the letter as in original.] The same issue was taken up by Gladden at the beginning of December; 'we were cheered by the issue of a small ration of white bread from the army Bakehouse, our first since leaving France'.[28] Three things could seriously affect a soldier's morale; mail, leave and food – and it remains so in today's modern army. In France the men had become used to being able to buy bread in the local village as a supplement to their army ration, but that option was closed to them in Italy by a General Routine Order which stated clearly that 'The purchase of bread by the troops from local shops and bakeries is forbidden'.[29] But this directive was not a case of the army being heavy-handed. Italy was so short of food that cereals had to be sent from Britain and America to ward off the results of bad harvests. As a consequence the local communities did not have the resources to supply the soldiers with additional bread over and above their daily ration; 700 grams of bread per day, 350 of meat and a further 200 grams of potatoes. When it came to food, *Tommy* liked what he liked, and that did not include anything 'foreign'. One of the few things Private Frank Hancock noted of a trip he made to Rome was that in one restaurant he had been able to get 'good soup, roast beef and two veg'.[30] But what-ever their views on the local food, the men knew that they had moved to a relatively

26   G. Walton, Private Papers, held by his granddaughter, Clare Pilkington.
27   B. Lamin, *Letters from the Trenches. A Soldier of the Great War* (London, 2009), p.102.
28   Gladden, *Piave*, p.27.
29   TNA: WO 95/4197, *Adjutant and Quarter-Master General*, GRO, 23 November 1917.
30   F. Hancock, Private papers, Liddle Archive, GS 0701, January 1919.

quiet part of the war, and their chances of going home at the end of it had improved. Approaching the Montello, Vere Cotton wrote to put his mother at ease:

> I don't fancy it is a particularly fierce front when one gets there. [...] Reports from the line describe it as a haven of rest where one shell per diem per square mile is about the average to be expected. The first airplane I have seen this month has just gone overhead.[31]

While many in the IEF regarded Italy as a 'peace front'[32] some also harboured the nagging feeling that they were missing the real war, especially after the German assault on the Western Front in March 1918. When news of that offensive filtered through to them Gladden and his mates felt that they were 'cut off in Italy from the rest of the world'.[33] It was almost a 'survivor's guilt'; while they had an easy time, those in Flanders were doing the real fighting against the Germans. This was summed up in the letter of one anonymous soldier, though not all would have agreed with him: 'We feel hopelessly out of it with such big things going on in France, but really I would give worlds to be there and help the lads to stop the Bosche'.[34] Apart from the distance from the 'real' war, the feeling of isolation in Italy would be reinforced in the coming year with the shortage of home leave and then the belief that they were neglected when demobilisation started at the end of the war. But the men of the IEF had made real the chorus of one of their songs from Flanders:

> 'Far, far from Ypre-es I long to be,
> Where German snipers can't get at me'.[35]

Now it was time for *Tommy* to adapt himself to Italy and the Italians.

---

31 IWM: Doc. 93/25/1, V.E. Cotton, *Private Papers*, diary pp.144-5.
32 Trevelyan, *Italy's War*, p.199.
33 Gladden, *Piave*, p.97.
34 Hardie, report February – July 1918.
35 M. Arthur, *When This Bloody War is Over. Soldiers' Songs of the First World War* (London, 2001), p.70.

3

Working with the Italians: "Allies are a tiresome lot"

There will have been many occasions during World War Two, and more recently in Bosnia, Iraq and Afghanistan, where senior military commanders agreed with Sir William Robertson's statement to Haig that, 'Allies are a tiresome lot'.[1] Although this comment was made of the French and Russians, his letters to Haig leave no doubt that it applied equally well to Italy in 1917 and the early months of 1918. Italy was irksome not only because of the need to send military support – diverting it from the Western Front – but because the country was not self-sufficient in food and raw materials. Without shipments of cereals and coal from Britain and France there were serious doubts over Italy's ability to continue in the war. Hew Strachan in *The First World War* stated that 'Italy had enough food to feed itself'[2] following Caporetto. However, Arthur Balfour (Secretary of State for Foreign Affairs) informed the War Cabinet in October 1917 that, while the military situation in Italy was grave (this was only days after the Italian defeat), 'the position of that country in respect of food was no less serious'.[3] The meeting went on to record that the dispatch of the IEF might be 'rendered abortive' if Italy were 'compelled to withdraw from the war owing to the inability of her Allies to help her feed her population'. Food shortages were so serious that in November 1918, in Milan, the civilian meat allowance was reduced to just 300 grammes per person, per month,[4] while at the same time the British soldier expected to get 350 grammes every day. This need to deliver food and raw materials to Italy placed a severe strain on the limited rail links to the country and came on top of the needs of the IEF; each one of the five divisions required 25 trains to deliver 30 days of provisions. Would it not have been possible to lessen the strain on the rail network by the use of shipping – unfortunately not. Where the train journey took five days, it required 38 days between allocating a cargo to a ship in Britain and its arrival at the

---

1   Woodward, *Robertson*, p.99.
2   H. Strachan, *The First World War* (London, 2006), p.252.
3   TNA: CAB 23/4, War Cabinet 260, 30 October 1917.
4   TNA: FO 371/3229, telegram from Rodd, 6 November 1918.

base depot in Arquata.[5] As if the long journey time were not enough, the ships were also vulnerable to sinking by German submarines. To mitigate this risk, when it was necessary to use sea-transport, the ships were escorted through the Mediterranean. However, this highlighted another area of friction between the Italians and their allies. From the perspective of the British and the French the Italians were not pulling their weight with the escort duties 'to convoy the supplies which we were sending to them [the Italians]'.[6] The Allies were critical of the Italian reluctance to risk their navy at sea, as a result their capital ships stayed in harbour, they had resorted to the concept of the 'fleet in being'.[7] The reluctance of the Italians to fully commit their naval assets infuriated the Allies, who were expected to risk their own vessels to escort vital supplies to Italy, and was a major reason for Britain and France to refuse to allow their ships to operate in the Adriatic under Italian command.

While Britain and France assisted Italy with the supply of coal and food, there was one way in which Italy could return the favour – labour. The building and mainte-nance of the defence works on the Western Front was very labour intensive and much of the 'rest' time of soldiers was taken up by the need to provide 'fatigue' and 'working parties'. The requirement for manual labour at the front is one of the neglected topics of the war (or as Richard Holmes would say 'scarcely the stuff for aspiring regi-mental historians'), but admirably covered in a recent book, *No Labour, No Battle*.[8] In November 1917 Lloyd George was asked to raise with the Italians the suggestion that they should send up to 100,000 labourers to France, as they were 'first class workers if not fighters'.[9] Once again the stereotype of the non-fighting Italian is employed in the argument. The issue was subsequently taken up by the War Cabinet in January 1918. In that meeting it was suggested that Italian labour could serve as a *'quid pro quo'* for the 'troops, guns, ships, coal and wheat supplied to Italy by this country'.[10] After all, Foch had already secured an agreement for the Italians to supply a similar number to France, so why shouldn't Britain get its share? The minutes of the War Cabinet for 20 February demonstrate an underlying veneer of racism towards the Italians, who were considered to be not quite 'white'. It was recorded that the deployment of Italian labour, as well as alleviating a problem on the Western Front, would have the additional benefit of being able to stop the shipment of Chinese 'coolies' from the USA; and 'each coolie saved would give us an American soldier'.[11] The implication was that Italian soldiers and Chinese 'coolies' were on a par when it came to military

5   TNA: WO 394/5, Statistical Abstract, pp.268-9.
6   TNA: CAB 23/6, War Cabinet 431, 17 June 1918.
7   R. Sicurezza, 'Italy and the War in the Adriatic', in H. Cecil and P. Liddle (eds.), *Facing Armageddon* (London, 1996), p.182.
8   J. Starling and I. Lee, *No Labour, No Battle. Military Labour during the First World War* (Stroud, 2009).
9   PA: LG /F/14/4/78, letter, 24 November 1917.
10   TNA: CAB 23/5, *Cabinet Minutes and papers; 309-378*, War Cabinet 322, 15 January 1918.
11   TNA: CAB 23/5, War Cabinet 350, 20 February 1918.

effectiveness. Sadly, although Italy did supply men, and over 12,000 were deployed to the British sector, the British and French did not treat them well; their accommodation and food was poor and they were sent home after the German offensive in March 1918. In the event Italian labour was used on the British sector 'for less than two months and it was not a great success'.[12]

After the defeat at Caporetto, and the subsequent decisions to send British and French divisions to support the Italians along their new front on the River Piave, the question was raised of who should be Commander-in-Chief of all forces in Italy. In the days immediately following the Italian retreat senior British (Cavan) and French (General Émile Fayolle) commanders submitted their assessments of why they believed that Cadorna had failed to prepare the Italian army to withstand an expected assault. Their reports, based on their experience in Flanders, reflected the Allied view that Italians had not kept abreast of developments in modern warfare: Cadorna's artillery was ineffective at counter-battery fire; he put too many of his men in the forward trenches (no defence in depth); his Staff Groups lacked the competence to plan and command operations; he failed to 'rotate' men through the front-line trenches so that they became tired and worn-out; he assumed that if he issued an order it would be acted upon, no steps were taken to ensure that they were carried out by his subordinates. If British and French troops were to fight alongside Italians, under an Italian commander, then they had to have confidence in that man's ability – Cadorna did not meet that test. The need for change was summarised by the British War Cabinet, 13 November 1917.

> The chief contributory cause to the present disaster was the inefficiency which had been revealed of the Italian Higher Command and General Staff, and we had accordingly made *the first condition of our assistance the replacement of General Cadorna and his staff.* The Headquarters Staff had been quite unable to grip hold of the situation and to keep in touch with and control the movements of the Italian forces. The dispositions were bad, the Staffs generally inefficient, and no communications had been maintained. Both our own and the French Military Advisers had represented that General Cadorna was quite unfitted to retain the supreme command of the Italian forces.[13] [My italics.]

To ease the replacement of Cadorna, and smooth ruffled feathers, he was nominated as the Italian representative to the newly formed Supreme War Council at Versailles. On 9 November General Armando Diaz (a Neapolitan) succeeded Cadorna (a Piedmontese in the Savoyard tradition of the army) as Commander in Chief. Prior to this appointment the largest formation that Diaz had commanded had been a Corps within the Italian Third Army, he now had to step up to the role of providing

---

12   Starling, *No Labour, No Battle*, p.315.
13   TNA: CAB 23/4, War Cabinet 272, 13 November 1917.

leadership to a multi-national army. But the British were also making command changes within the IEF. At the outset we saw that Robertson (in the back of a car) made Cavan commander of an IEF of only two divisions, but Cavan – like Diaz – was a Corps commander. With the increase of the IEF to five divisions a full General was deemed necessary to lead it, and Lloyd George decided that Plumer, after his success at Messines,[14] was the man for the job. With Third Ypres (Passchendaele) still the focus of the British, this was a bad time for Haig to lose Plumer from Second Army, as he noted in his diary on 7 November: 'Was ever the Commander and his Staff sent off to another theatre of war in the middle of a battle?'[15] Plumer was no less reluctant to leave, as he wrote to his wife the same day, 'I am very sick about it and do not want to go in the least'.[16] Although Plumer had preferred to stay in France, his success over the Germans at Messines Ridge gave him great credibility with Diaz. The respect accorded to the new British commander allowed him to convince the Italians to accept some of the help and suggestions that the British believed were essential for them to fight a modern war, suggestions which might have been considered patronising from someone with a lesser reputation. However, Plumer was recalled to the Western Front in February 1918 because of the worsening situation there, immediately prior to the Germans' March offensive. The transfer of Plumer back to France was felt by the British Ambassador to be regrettable, the commander's 'unfailing tact' had allowed him to make recommendations to the Italians 'which were not only not resented but actually welcomed'.[17]

Cadorna's replacement allowed the British and French to persuade the Italians that they needed to introduce more training for their Staff Officers and troops, and to update their tactics, but this would require sensitivity and tact:

> Their [the Italians] susceptibilities are very much on the alert, and even in General Diaz' entourage there is a strong feeling of resentment against any interference whatever on our part. It therefore behoves us to proceed as warily as possible with a view of [sic] accomplishing our purpose, if possible, in time without offending our Allies' susceptibilities.[18]

The stereotypical Italian was seen as 'susceptible' to taking offence, 'lachrymally emotional'[19] was one writer's description, and would react badly to advice, which would be regarded as criticism. The drive for change started as soon as the British

---

14   Plumer masterminded the blowing of the huge mines which resulted in the British taking Messines Ridge in June 1917.
15   G. Sheffield and J. Bourne, *Douglas Haig. War Diaries and Letters 1914-1918* (London, 2005), p.339.
16   G. Powell, *Plumer. The Soldiers' General* (Barnsley, 2004), p.235.
17   J.R. Rodd, *Social and Diplomatic Memories 1902-1919* (London, 1925), p.350.
18   TNA: WO 106/805, *Italy*, General Fayolle's report, December 1917, p.21.
19   F.M. Ford, *Parade's End* (London, 1982), p.178.

took over the defensive positions on the Montello from the Italians. Built to comply with the Italian practice of putting most of the men in the forward line, there were no reserve trenches and no attempt at defence in depth; 'the troops are massed on the first line in whole Battalions, sometimes Regiments, the men are elbow to elbow, but generally with no reserves in the rear'.[20] Plumer had his men set about building strong-points and bunkers, as well as re-siting machine guns, thus providing depth to their position above the Piave. Similar suggestions for change had been made to the Italian units on the British flanks, but they had been ignored. Demonstrating the tact for which Rodd had applauded him, Plumer arranged for an inspection of his lines by Diaz, on the grounds that a visit by the Allied Commander in Chief would please the British troops. Flattered, Diaz obliged. In the following days Plumer noticed that the Italians on his flanks had set about improving their defences in line with the British example.[21]

General Sir Charles Harington was Plumer's Chief of Staff and represented him at the War Cabinet in February 1918. In that meeting Harington gave it as his opinion that the best assistance that could be given to the Italians was to 'instruct them, so that they might learn from the lessons we had learned during the war'.[22] Although Harington's viewpoint might be seen as patronising (there is no acknowledgement that the war in the mountains was very different from that in Flanders), the British and French were convinced that they had learnt some hard lessons in Flanders and that they had changed their tactics accordingly, unlike the Italians who were still fighting the war in the same way as in 1915. But the British were wrong to assume that their ally ignored technological change. The first bombs dropped on enemy positions from aircraft were Italian; they were used in Libya in 1911. Also, in April 1913, 'Signor J.B. Araldo of Spezia' had offered the design for his 'bomb dropping apparatus' to the British.[23] Araldo's invention allowed the release of the weapon by a lever operated by the pilot, rather than requiring a passenger to 'throw the bombs' over the side – the War Office decided not to adopt the device and continued to man-handle bombs over the side of the cockpit until 1915.[24] Betraying some of the arrogance that the Italians always believed the French displayed towards them, Fayolle's report demonstrated that he had totally discounted the value of the Italians as a military force after Caporetto; 'even in the most favourable circumstances, it would not be possible to leave the Italian army to its own devices within any measurable distance of time'.[25] While Harington put forward the case for the Allies to provide training for the Italians, Haig's Head Quarters (GHQ) was less keen. Fayolle had suggested that British and French officers might temporarily swap places with some of their Italian

20   TNA: WO 106/805, General Fayolle's report, p.11.
21   Edmonds, *Italy*, p.107.
22   TNA: CAB 23/5, War Cabinet 345, 13 February 1918.
23   TNA: FO 371/1660, Italy, 1913. Letter, 19 April 1913.
24   R. Barker, *The Royal Flying Corps in World War 1* (London: 1995), p.72.
25   TNA: WO 106/805, General Fayolle's report, p.24.

colleagues to facilitate the cross-pollination of ideas, but that proposal would be shot down. GHQ had no objections to a 'limited number' of Italian officers being attached to units in France, but, in their view, seconding junior British officers to Italy would not increase their knowledge for campaigning in Flanders. They had missed the point that if only one side (the Italians) was considered as needing to learn from the other, then it would be regarded as humiliating, and would be rejected. Then, to show that GHQ really had little interest in the proposal, they suggested that sending British officers to Italy would be unfair as it 'would probably deprive them of their chance for leave'.[26]

The concern expressed by Plumer at Italian staff work was not mere pedantry. As a junior partner (in terms of troops on the ground) in the military alliance in Italy, the IEF would have to rely on the thoroughness of Italian planning in any future offensive. In the short time that he had been in the country Plumer had been assessing the Italian Staff and making his own value judgements. In his opinion Italian officers did not visit the font line enough, as a result they assumed that all orders issued had been carried out, and there was no attempt to see them through to completion; their staff work was 'so theoretical that they do not understand the practical difficulties of their orders'.[27] Was Plumer merely displaying British arrogance in front of an ally who had recently suffered a devastating defeat? This author does not believe so. Plumer was making his assessment based on his success on the Western Front, where he had commanded the British Second Army; at that point he had the experience that Diaz lacked. There was nothing to be gained by Plumer in denigrating his Italian ally, he now had an independent command and it was in his interest to have a successful working relationship with the Italians. When he gave it as his opinion that senior Italian officers did not inspire confidence in subordinate commanders, it was based on what he observed at *Comando Supremo*. In his criticism of the Italians Plumer was at least objective, and had the aim of encouraging them to make what he felt were necessary improvements. Not unnaturally, when he did see changes for the better, he credited some of that to the Italian staff groups having been 'much impressed by the frequent visits of British Commanders and Staffs'. However, their progress could be likened to the curate's egg:

> There has certainly been some noticeable improvement in their Staff work lately, but they are generally speaking much below the standard necessary for the conduct of operations on any large scale.[28]

---

26 TNA: WO 106/762, *Brig. Gen Delmé-Radcliffe British Mission Italy: Reports*, memo from GHQ, 22 September 1918.
27 TNA: WO 106/810, *Report by General Plumer on the condition of the Italian Army; 20 January 1918*, p.3.
28 TNA: WO 106/810, Plumer's report, p.3.

Plumer's assessment would be tested in the final offensive of Vittorio Veneto, which resulted in the capitulation of the Austrians and an armistice with that country a week before the Germans signed theirs.

Whatever opinions the senior British commanders held of their Italian allies, those of the British soldiers of the IEF were on a more mundane level. British troops were, by and large, proud of their own discipline and turnout and believed these were a measure of a unit's efficiency, and it was against these standards that they judged the Italian soldiery when they arrived in the country. The initial impressions of many were not good. Arthur Lambert saw them as 'unshaven and shabby' with dirty boots, rusty bayonets and seemingly unfriendly. But this was an army which had suffered a major defeat and a withdrawal of some seventy miles: 'Caporetto was very recent and the memory hurt!'[29] One junior officer, 2nd Lieutenant J. Faviall, was distinctly unimpressed by what he saw of the retreat:

> We were not so taken with our first sight of the Italian army retreating after the disaster at Caporetto. First a fleet of cars carrying officers; some hours after [came] the bedraggled units of the Italian army; their horses thin their harness horrible, their men dejected.[30]

The War Office was keen to know how the Italian soldiers were perceived by their British colleagues and to that end the official censor was required to make an assessment in his reports, based on the comments in the soldiers' letters home. However, these vignettes gave only brief glimpses, with little context to put them into perspective. 'The Italians are no-bon' wrote one of them in December 1917, using the anglicised French from the trenches in Flanders,[31] while another remarked that the Italian soldiers were referred to by the British as 'Orange-Suckers'. But, as Hardie noted, the British Tommy had a 'whimsical contempt for all that is not British'. According to the censor the soldiers had begun their time in Italy by despising the 'ice-cream vendors', but their fear of being let down by the Italians had given way to a new trust in them as soldiers.[32] It should be remembered though that, when Hardie made these comments, action on the Italian Front had been very limited with no opportunity for the British soldier to assess his Italian ally in combat. Two conflicting opinions in the censor's report demonstrate the problem inherent in putting too much emphasis on the content of a small number of soldiers' letters: in one man's view 'I don't think there will be any more running away by the Italian troops', while another considered that 'the Italian soldiers here do not want to fight'. These two opinions are wildly conflicting – though written only a month apart – but they are both valid. Private soldiers had a very

29   A. Lambert, *Over The Top. A "P.B.I." in the H.A.C.* (London, 1930), p.95.
30   J.V. Faviall, Private Papers, Liddle Archive, GS 0543, p.9.
31   Hardie, report for October 1917.
32   Hardie, report for February-July 1918.

limited view of the war around them and could only comment on their own experience. However, as a method of assessing the morale of the Italian army, it had many flaws – it is to be hoped that not too much reliance was placed on Hardie's analysis.

Unlike most of the men, who had only incidental contact with Italian troops, Ronald Skirth struck up a genuine friendship which he recounts in his reminiscences.[33] Skirth spent time in France and Italy as a member of an artillery battery, but his account has to be treated with caution: the IWM notes that it is a 'very interesting but anecdotal and disjointed ms [sic] memoir'. A conscientious objector, who still took a part in the war, Skirth found ways to reconcile his moral objections to killing with his position as an NCO on the gun line based on the Asiago plateau. Having done art at school, he was a competent sketcher and was allowed to spend a lot of his time alone in observation posts, making drawings of the terrain on the Austrian side of the front for use by the battery commanders. Frequently, when he should have been working on his mountain survey, he was truanting at an Italian First Aid post where his friend Giulio worked as an ambulance driver.[34] Skirth recounts trips they made together to local villages and to an Italian Service Men's Club, where he was the only British soldier. As he could play the piano he was eagerly accepted, especially as the Italians loved to sing:

> How different were the sing-songs there from the ones at the French *estaminet*!
> No 'Mademoiselle from Armentières' or 'I want to go home', but folk songs such
> as 'Santa Lucia' and 'Sorrento' and operatic arias and choruses.[35]

If Skirth really did make these excursions then it is amazing how he got away with it, had an officer or NCO visited his observation post and found it vacant, Skirth would no doubt have been court martialled for absence. In the main the British soldiers had very little contact with their Italian military counterparts, but they did look for opportunities to meet local civilians (often referred to as 'natives' in letters home), when off-duty time would permit, which usually meant in the rear-areas behind the front. It is often overlooked, but British soldiers spent most of their time away from the front-line. Roughly speaking, one third would have been in the line, one third further back in support areas and then one third in the rest and training areas. It was the time spent in the rest areas which would have given the most opportunity to mix with the local civilians. Typically each battalion would have had three or four rotations through the rest areas, each of about four weeks. Walton, who sent home over a hundred postcards, kept his family regularly informed of his periods out of the line, yet he had been in Italy for almost five months before letting them know that he had 'spent a day in my 1st [sic] town but was too busy to see

33   IWM: Doc. 9023, R. Skirth, *Private Papers*.
34   Barrett (ed.), *Reluctant Tommy*, p.163.
35   Barrett (ed.), *Reluctant Tommy*, p.164.

much till late'.[36] Ernest Crosse, padre for the 7th Division, referred to the time spent out of contact with local people as 'exile from civilisation'.[37] The point was similarly made by an old soldier who was interviewed in 1978; asked to recall instances of contact with Italian civilians (other than when on a leave pass) he replied, 'Well, not many because there were very few. I don't think I can recall any particular case'.[38] Many of the letters and memoirs from France tell of the visits to a local estaminet for eggs, chips and wine (the motive for meeting locals was often to buy food to supplement a monotonous army diet) but, as Sergeant W. Bradley wrote, these opportunities were rarer in Italy than in Flanders: 'In Italy there were few if any of these places [estaminets] to go to when off duty as all the natives lived in with the cattle during the winter months'.[39]

It was from these restricted opportunities for contact that the British troops formed their opinions of the Italians; 'Driving on the right's a bloody nuisance';[40] the children 'stole anything and everything they could get their hands on'.[41] Frequently their remarks displayed a hint of British superiority, as Lambert showed when he wrote of soldiers going window shopping; 'Italians looked at the Englishmen with curiosity and a little envy, and the compliment was returned, very much minus envy and a great deal of suppressed mirth'.[42] A scan of the letters and memoirs of these men, miles from home, often for the first time, reveals that the topics given the most 'column inches' were the lack of home leave, their billets and the food. Graham Greenwell had joined the army from school only three months after the war started, had served in France, and in November 1917 was in Italy with the IEF. Greenwell's narrative is a positive one (too much so for a mention in Fussell), delighted with his new accommodation (which he regarded as much better than that in France), he wrote that the people he was billeted with were extraordinarily kind, providing three kinds of wine for lunch but 'giving the troops some awfully strong black stuff which knocks them absolutely silly'.[43] While Greenwell does not say so, could this have been the soldiers' introduction to that acquired taste, *Fernet Branca*? But, like the soldiers, he was not averse to making general comments based on single incidents; Italian soldiers were 'the most appalling thieves', a condemnation that seems to have been based on the theft of some cooks' clothing. Edward Brittain (brother of Vera) wrote less endearingly than Greenwell; the small Italian farms in which they were billeted were 'very dirty' with '6 to 10 small, screaming children in each'. Also, while living with these families personal items kept disappearing causing him to write of the Italians, 'this is

36   Walton, postcard, Easter Sunday 1918.
37   E.C. Crosse, *The Defeat of Austria As Seen By The 7th Division* (London, 1919), p.3.
38   J. Todd, transcript of interview with Peter Liddle, March 1978, Liddle Archive, GS 1607.
39   W.J. Bradley, Private Papers, Liddle Archive, GS 0389, p.21.
40   Barrett (ed.), *Reluctant Tommy*, p.127.
41   Bradley, Private Papers, p.21.
42   Lambert, *Over the Top*, p.98.
43   Greenwell, *An Infant in Arms*, p.202.

a wonderful nation for scrounging'.[44] Others saw a generous side to those they met; Faviall recalled their landlord giving them 'a bottle of his own best vintage. Delicious white Chianti. So new to us after the grim and mercenary Belgians'.[45] George Walton (in his postcards home) recalled his landlady, on a cold day in December, putting 'a bowl upon the table containing hot wood ash so I may warm my fingers'. He then followed this with the comment that 'I think this crowd we have got among are the biggest cadgers I have met'. To be fair to the soldiers, they could only draw conclusions from the limited exposure they had to the Italian civilians – some saw good, some bad. On this topic the final word goes to an anonymous soldier who seemed to have found a second mother: 'The good [land]lady at my present billet insists on washing my underclothes for me and I have to exercise great tact in getting her to take any payment for the labour thus entailed'.[46]

Whatever interesting word pictures the soldiers may have drawn of their Italian landladies and their families, food (and their hankering after the meals they had at home) was still the main topic. First in the firing-line of food they did not like was that north Italian staple made from maize – polenta; described by one of their trench journals (tongue-in-cheek) as 'an a-maizing mixture'.[47] It was described by Gladden as 'doughy' and 'poor stuff' but was fine when mixed with jam (a fixed point in the British army menu) 'or added in lumps to thicken the eternal bully beef stew'.[48] However, many of his mates would not even make this concession, which Gladden saw as surprising 'considering the poor stuff many of them must have put up with at home'. Gladden spoke as a middle-class civil servant who had worked for the Post Office in Reading before the army called, but many of those in his unit would have come from the poor working-class districts of the industrial cities – Yorkshire Pudding would have been the staple of many of their Sunday lunches. But even Skirth, pro-Italian in most things, saw polenta as a poor second to its Yorkshire equivalent; 'in texture and flavour it resembled a batter pudding as much as chalk resembles cheese'.[49] Something of the yearning of these men for the meals of home was summed up by Gladden: 'what would we not have given for a real steak and mashed potatoes'.[50] George Walton was an educated man – a teacher, married with a family and called up at the age of 39 – and after a year in Italy, he was still unprepared to try 'new' food: 'I do not think I will ever learn to eat Italian food', and when offered a pumpkin '[I] could not persuade myself to tackle [it]'.[51] While pasta and polenta were not to the palate of most of

44   A. Bishop and M. Bostridge (eds.), *Letters from a Lost Generation. First World War Letters of Vera Brittain and Four Friends* (London, 1999), pp.392-5.
45   Faviall, Private Papers, p.9.
46   Hardie, report for February-July 1918.
47   IWM: *The Fifth Glo'ster Gazette* (The Trenches, 1915-1919), p.254.
48   Gladden, *Piave*, p.33.
49   Skirth, Private Papers, Vol.3, p.250.
50   Gladden, *Piave*, p.14.
51   Walton, postcard, 5 October 1918.

the men, there were compensations to being in a Mediterranean climate; 'we can get plenty of fruit out here oranges and apples etc'.[52] One young Captain told his family that, 'we are feeding right royally these days on Italian fruit'.[53] In July 2010 this author visited the trenches above Caporetto and was surprised to find the ground covered in wild strawberries, Walton picked them on the high ground of the Asiago plateau in 1918 and thought they would have been complete with 'Gloucester cream'. It is easy to see how different the scene was from the front they had left in Flanders. However, the troops' preoccupation with food did not blind them to the situation at home, they were aware that food was in short supply as a result of the German submarine success against shipping from America. Some of them acknowledged this in their letters, while still asking those at home to send out items that they were missing at the front; 'it must be bad for you in England being so short of food', and though hoping for those little extras from the family, they did acknowledge that 'we are not so bad off for food out hear [sic] and cannot grumble, not in war time'.[54] Although the troops continued to grumble about the food, usually the monotony of it, they did not go short, but were always on the look-out for anything that would supplement army rations.

Contact between the British soldiers and Italian civilians (apart from the landlord of their billets) would have been limited to their off-duty time in the rear areas, some miles from the front, and frequently that fraternisation involved bars and drink. The courts martial records in the National Archives give us an insight into the behaviour of the troops during the war – there are limitations on the data which are discussed in a later chapter – and it should be no surprise that alcohol played a significant part in many of the offences. With little to spend their money on, no familiarity with the language, and a wish for a break from army routine, it was not unnatural for men to go out to the bars with their mates. Unfortunately, being used to drinking beer at home, the local wine was often their downfall. In this regard the men of the IEF were no different from those in France. In an attempt to limit excessive drinking (a forlorn hope) and the bad impression this left with the local Italians, the army authorities sought to limit the hours within which the men could visit the towns and bars. Quite soon after his arrival in Italy General Plumer issued an order which restricted the men's access to cafés, bars, restaurants and inns to the hours between 12 noon and 2pm, and from 6pm to 8pm, with all the soldiers expected back in their billets by 9 in the evening. The disciplinary records show that good intentions do not always have the expected outcome – soldiers would find ways to get the drink they wanted. As well as attempting to limit the hours when they could drink, the troops were forbidden to attend meetings or entertainments 'other than those organised by British units'.[55] Given that the great majority of the

52   Lamin, *Letters*, pp.124-5.
53   IWM: Doc. 7033, V.E. Eberle, *Private Papers*, letter 21 August 1918.
54   Lamin, *Letters*, pp.124-5.
55   TNA: WO 95/4197, GRO, 15 December 1917.

men could not understand Italian, it is difficult to see the point of the last restriction. Working-class men, many from the industrial cities, were brought up on beer, they had not learnt to drink wine, and certainly not slowly or in small quantities. For many, this was their undoing. A trench journal carried a 'spoof' letter from a soldier to his wife, the sentiment would have been familiar to the troops reading it: 'Well, dear, the people here all drinks vino which is the Italian for wine but much cheaper. I tells yar ole dear [sic] it is good stuff for you can get blind for a liro, but I never does'.[56] The Labour Party in 2002 famously tried to introduce a 'continental café culture' to English drinking by introducing 24 hour opening hours, the project has arguably failed. Many of the British drinkers in Manchester or Marbella today no more understand the continental way of drinking than did the soldiers in Italy. One of those who did was Ronald Skirth (at least he did when he wrote his memoir, some decades after the war). On a trip to a local village with his Italian friend he had a 'demi-litre of *vino rosso* at a pavement caffé' [sic]. For Skirth the great advantage of the Italian pavement café was that 'you can sit and chat almost indefinitely without being harassed into buying more than you want'.[57] With 33% of the courts martial cases in Italy in 1918 involving drink, it can be assumed that Skirth's comrades had a less controlled approach to their imbibing.

While the body craved food and drink – not always to the extent that it was taken – the army deemed that the spirit also required nourishing, particularly on Sundays. Opening his chapter on religion and the British Tommy, Richard Holmes asked 'what hope and faith moved this vast assemblage of the proud and profane, the cynical and the contemptuous, that constituted the British army in France?'[58] With his long experience of the British soldier Holmes knew that, while they were not 'religious', they might have admitted – though not to their mates – to some greater being that they hoped would watch out for them. The majority of soldiers in France and the IEF would have claimed membership of the Church of England (C of E) on their attestation papers, a statement which covered many shades of belief and 'facilitated [their] sorting out for church parade'.[59] In 1915 the Chaplain-General claimed that 70-75 per cent of the soldiers in most infantry brigades were Anglican; but that should not be read as 'practicing' Anglicans. Knowing that they would have to attend some form of church parade on Sundays, and not wishing to be seen as not conforming, most Protestants would have declared themselves to be C of E so that they could attend with their mates. Once again Skirth summed up the attitude that would have been held by many; when asked whether he was a 'religious sort of chap' (and he did attend church at home), he answered 'sort of, but not sanctimonious, I hope'.[60] The padres

56   *The Fifth Glo'ster Gazette*, p.260
57   Barrett (ed.), *Reluctant Tommy*, p.248.
58   Holmes, *Tommy*, p.503.
59   N. Gladden, *Ypres 1917. A Personal Account* (Guildford, 1967), p.10.
60   Barrett (ed.), *Reluctant Tommy*, p.259.

and chaplains who held the Sunday services recognised that the soldiers were more detached from the church than those who ministered to their troops' spiritual needs. Julian Bickersteth, while a chaplain in France, put it succinctly; for the men 'religion is simply a name and has never touched either his heart or mind',[61] or, in the words of officialdom; 'The soldier has got religion, I am not sure that he has got Christianity'.[62] Perhaps reinforcing that view was the soldiers' penchant for putting the words of their marching songs to the tunes of well-known hymns. One of their favourites was *Fred Karno's Army*; the troops likened the 'imbecility and absurd incompetence' of the Vaudeville act to their own life in the infantry, and all to the tune of the well-known hymn, *The Church's one Foundation*:

> We are Fred Karno's Army,
> What bloody use are we?
> We cannot fight, we cannot shoot,
> So we joined the infantry,
> But when we get to Berlin,
> The Kaiser he will say,
> 'Hoch! Hoch!! Mein Gott,
> What a jolly fine lot
> Are the ragtime infantry!'[63]

Many who considered themselves to be Protestant (including those who were non-practicing, or from the Baptist or Methodist church) declared themselves to be C of E as it was easier to go with the majority. Roman Catholics on the other hand, although in the minority, tended to declare themselves as Catholic even though it would mark them out on Sundays as 'different' – they would parade separately. In Lambert's company of 200-250 men he states that he was the only 'surviving Roman Catholic'.[64] Similarly, Bickersteth stated that in his battalion (800 – 1,000 men) the RCs 'number no more than twelve or fourteen as far as I can make out at present'.[65] In spite of these small numbers, the Catholics were 'over-represented' in Italy by the number of chaplains of that denomination. The Chaplaincy branch for the whole army, in 1918, had 1,941 for the C of E, with 643 for the Roman Catholics; a ratio of 3:1. In the IEF there were 52 C of E and 29 RC, a ratio of 2:1.[66] The Roman Catholic representation in Italy was particularly high as the normal allowance was one RC chaplain per division, of which there were only three in the IEF in October 1918 when the count was made.

---

61   J. Bickersteth (ed.), *The Bickersteth Diaries* (London, 1995), p.78.
62   M. Burleigh, 'Religion and the Great War', inM. Howard (ed.), *A Part of History. Aspects of the British experience of the First World War* (London, 2008), p.80.
63   M. Arthur, *When This Bloody War is Over.* pp.60-1.
64   Lambert, *Over the Top*, p.137.
65   Bickersteth (ed.), *Diaries*, p.72.
66   TNA: WO 394/11, *Statistical Abstract*.

Although padres and chaplains were non-combatants, many were killed in the war as they saw their place as being with their men. Interestingly Robert Graves in his well know account of the war, *Goodbye to All That*, is damning of what he felt was a lack of courage shown by some Anglican chaplains compared to that shown by their Roman Catholic colleagues. The latter were often to be found in the danger area 'to give extreme unction to the dying'.[67] However, in Italy, the Reverend Crosse recorded that in the assault across the River Piave in October 1918, all the padres in his 7th Division stayed with their units during the attack.[68] Those who shared the dangers of the troops were far more likely to gain their respect, and have a willing flock on Sundays.

Those who have served in the forces, especially in the training schools where their every hour is planned for them, will know how precious free-time is to the young serviceman – this author had three years as an RAF Apprentice, followed by three years Officer training at the RAF College, Cranwell. The majority of the soldiers in France and Italy regarded the ritual of church parade as an intrusion on what would otherwise have been free-time on a Sunday morning. Private Frank Richards was a regular soldier before the war, used to army discipline, and in his view 95 percent of his battalion 'thoroughly detested'[69] being ordered to attend the Sunday church parade. The army did not force soldiers to go into the church for the service, but it could compel them to attend parades, this fine point was summed up in Richard Aldington's book, *Death of a Hero*; 'there was, of course, no religious compulsion in the Army; that was why Church Parade was a parade'.[70] The war diary of the 8th York and Lancaster records that on the 19 January 1918 attendance at religious service was voluntary, only 'about 50 men were present'[71] out of the unit strength of 800-1,000 men. It was against this background of loose attachment to the Church of England by the individual soldiers, and the compulsory nature of church parades, that the men viewed the frequent church attendance of the Italian population – though letters from France make little comment on the church going routines of that country's Catholic population. In a letter home from Italy Lamin told his brother that: 'They go to church at all times here. I have seen them going at five in the morning and bells ringing at three. Every body [*sic*] here seems to go to church regular'.[72] For men used to very infrequent attendance at protestant churches and Methodist chapels, with their lack of pomp and ceremony, Catholic rituals were something to refer to in letters home. Private Frank Hancock had a leave pass to Rome after the armistice and visited the religious site of Scala Sancta, afterwards he recorded his impressions for his family, '[I] couldn't help but laugh

67   R. Graves, *Goodbye to All That* (London, 1929), p.158.
68   Crosse, *Defeat of Austria*, p.31.
69   F. Richards, *Old Soldiers Never Die* (Eastbourne, 1933), p.84.
70   R. Aldington, *Death of a Hero* (London, 1919), pp.273-4.
71   TNA: WO 95/4240, war diary 8 York & Lancs, 19 January 1918.
72   Lamin, *Letters*, p.141.

when I saw the people crawling up on their hands and knees'[73] – Catholic rituals would have looked very foreign to those brought up with a Protestant background. But for those soldiers who had a deeper religious faith, and required more than the official denominational parades, they could visit the local village Catholic churches, even though these buildings may have felt strange to them. One such was Ronald Skirth, but he had to overcome his 'boyhood prejudices against RC superstitions and 'popery' [which] came into [his] mind'; he admits that he had gone into a Catholic place of worship 'ready to sneer'.[74] Such comments might seem strange to a modern reader, but as a schoolboy of the late 1950s this author recalls that the 'RC' boy in the class was singled out for comment by the rest of us, and for no other reason than that he was Catholic. Skirth made use of the Catholic church in San Martino on a number of occasions and his memoir records him struggling with his upbringing when he went into these buildings:

> There was I, a born, baptised and confirmed Protestant, worshipping in a foreign Roman Catholic church, bowing down before "graven images", talking to the effigies of a saint I knew nothing about and (almost) asking a blessing of the mother of Jesus whom I had been indoctrinated to believe had no divine powers whatsoever.[75]

But Skirth, able to put aside his 'childhood prejudices', is only able to give his own impression; the conflicting view (possibly held by many) was put forward by a young officer in a letter to his mother after a visit to Rome:

> As far as the spirit of Rome goes, it's all to my mind most hideously pagan, and I came away almost a Kensitite in the fervour of my zeal against Roman Catholicism. Everything is erected to the glory of individual Popes with God a bad second. […] all you see is Christianity run to seed.[76]

Whatever the impressions formed of Catholicism by a few members of the IEF, the majority of British soldiers just regarded it as 'foreign' and moved on – as they did with the language. The Briton abroad, whether on today's package holiday, or as a soldier in France or Italy, has tended to believe that it was for the foreigner to learn English, rather than that he should learn their language. Gladden was one of the very few whose papers reveal any small knowledge of Italian,[77] while Walton wrote home – some ten months after arriving in the country – that he had 'started

73   Hancock, Private Papers, January 1919.
74   Barrett (ed.), *Reluctant Tommy*, pp.192-32.
75   Skirth, Private Papers, Vol.2, p.240.
76   Cotton, Private Papers, Part 3, pp.181-2.
77   Gladden, *Piave*, p.134.

to do a little Italian'.[78] The inability to speak the local language would have been more pronounced in Italy that among those soldiers in France, if only because of their much shorter stay on the Italian Front. The problem would not have been made easier by their being billeted in farming communities, where the families would have had little education, and the only local civilians who spoke English would have been those who had returned at the start of the war from working, often as waiters, in Britain or America. According to Lambert, after a year in Italy, thousands of men did not get further with the language than "bread", "wine", "to eat", and then greeted everyone with *"Buona Sera"* at any time of day or night. But, true to form, a lack of linguistic skills did not stand in Tommy's way; as Greenwell explained, 'they just put an *'o'* onto the end of each word and they think they are speaking Italian'.[79] And of course the Trench Journals (produced by the men, the most famous being the *Wipers Times*), could give advice to the men on how to get by in the local 'lingo'; for ordering white wine, instead of the 'Vin Blong' they were told to order in France, they should now go for 'Chianti' which was to be pronounced 'Key-Auntie'. For those who dined at the better restaurants the *Glo'ster Gazette* informed them that at the end of the meal the correct way to ask the waiter to remove the Stilton was 'Alley tootsweeto il stiltonoh'[80] – we don't know if any took the advice. But while the *Gazette* lampooned the soldiers' attempts to learn Italian, some individuals did take it seriously. The Liddle Collection in Leeds holds the diary of Frank Hancock and in this he had written a lexicon of some thirty phrases which he felt would be useful to him; along with the months of the year and the seasons he noted that 'minestro = soup' and 'bac-a-lac = fish dinner'.[81] It may not have been a wide vocabulary, but given the limited contact the men had with the local civilians, it was probably sufficient, and it showed that some did try to learn the language – as many would have done in France.

In his report for October 1917 the official censor commented that the British Tommy 'gives the same glad eye to Carlotta as to Jeanne Marie';[82] although at least one of the soldiers seemed to prefer the former; 'the girls beat the Frenchies all ends up and Oh Gee the style on Sunday'. Unsurprisingly, away from the horrors of Flanders and on the quieter Italian Front, the men soon noticed the girls. Charles Carrington, who served as an officer in France and Italy, commented that as nobody had told him that Vicenza was one of the most beautiful cities in the world 'I chiefly noticed the beautiful women'.[83] One young officer, with a fiancé at home, might have wanted to allay her fears when he wrote that 'we have no, or very few, dark-eyed

78   Walton, postcard, 10 August 1918.
79   Greenwell, *Infant in Arms*, p.202.
80   *The Fifth Glo'ster Gazette*, p.254.
81   Hancock, Private Papers.
82   Hardie, Private Papers, report October 1917.
83   C. Carrington, *Soldier From The Wars Returning* (Barnsley, 2006 edn.), p.200.

Italian beauties here'.[84] But while the men did mention the girls in their letters, the knowledge that they would be read by wives, mothers or girlfriends, often caused them to write in chaste and naïve terms; they obviously did not want to be thought of as 'fooling around'. Norman Gladden was one such; apparently unattached when he left for France, and later Italy, he records some of his observations in his memoir. To this young man (he left school in 1913) 'the beauty of the Italian girls was no myth' and those who handed out fruit and cigarettes to the troops as they arrived in the country were, to him, 'olive-complexioned goddesses'.[85] The photo archive in the Imperial War Museum has a number of photographs of the Italian women and girls who worked for the IEF, often at ammunition and supply depots, and from some of them it is easy to see the effect that their soft smile and dark eyes would have had on a young soldier.

But good looks might not survive the hard life of the Italian farm girl:

[H]er destiny as an Italian peasant woman could not have been enviable, for in the sunny south the women, so blooming in their early youth, soon become old and worn through work and the elements, as well as the small reason they have for keeping themselves attractive.[86]

For many the attractive young women were an opportunity, while others – like Gladden – found it hard to overcome a tight Edwardian upbringing. He and others did not have the ease and confidence of that 'forward minority to whom the opposite sex is always an irresistible magnet'. In his own words Gladden (and others) formed 'the less demonstrative majority [who] drew back shyly but with feelings of no less delight'.[87] Little wonder that with so little 'life experience' many of the soldiers would contract Venereal Disease when they did give in to their delight. For young men who had lived through the brutality of the war in Flanders, even platonic relationships were important and became 'an idyllically happy memory when so much else has been forgotten'.[88] For many of the men the need was for something more than platonic.

Since time immemorial, where soldiers have gone a sex trade has followed; brothels, prostitutes and venereal disease[89] were to be found in Italy as they were in France, and indeed in all other theatres of the war. Civilians at home were much exercised by the idea of young soldiers visiting brothels, especially where the army was supervising the establishments and so – as those at home believed – lowering the morals of the troops. The banner on this was raised by the Bishop of London and the Executive

84   Eberle, Private Papers, letter, 19 December 1917.
85   Gladden, Piave, p.7.
86   Gladden, Piave, p.76.
87   Gladden, Piave, p.7.
88   Gladden, Piave, p.76.
89   The topic of VD is covered in more detail in the chapter on medical issues.

Committee of the Mothers' Union against the *Maisons de Tolerance* in Le Havre.[90] For these campaigning groups there was a fear that the war would be seen not as a sacred cause, but as a 'vehicle for vice and demoralisation'. But Haig, often portrayed as a general with no feeling for his men, expressed concern that closing the brothels would simply cause the women to move to uncontrolled areas; they would become *en carte* on the streets, infection would rise and the hospitalisation of the men would have an adverse effect on the fighting efficiency of the army. Italy was no different to France in that it also had its brothels, '*Casa del' Amore*', which were frequently put out of bounds, but were sufficiently distant not to register on the radar of the Mothers' Union. In July 1918 the men were banned from two houses in Thiene and four in Vicenza, leading to the closure of Vicenza to all ranks below Major because of the high incidence of venereal cases contracted there;[91] presumably Majors and above were deemed capable of controlling their urges. Attempts by the army authorities to curb the use of brothels in Italy certainly came in for criticism by the troops, as one young soldier commented strongly in a letter:

> I have not had leave for 12 months and now I can't even get down to Rome or Florence for a few days for a "Blow Through". If they want to stop all the Venereal [*sic*] they will have to give us leave every 4 months like the French have. It is the silly old fools who can't do anything who think we can do without a bit of "French" every now and then.[92]

The censor does not indicate who the addressee was, but it was probably not the wife, sweetheart or mother of the soldier.

It may have seemed to Cavan and his advisors that closing the brothels in Thiene and Vincenza would restrict access to women, and so reduce the incidence of VD among the troops of the IEF: they were wrong. The admissions to hospital for VD, per 1,000 men, were higher in Italy in 1918 (41.8 : 1,000) than for the same period in France (32.4).[93] Once the known brothels were closed, others sprang up to take their place, and they did not need to be in towns. A farmhouse close to Gladden's billet ran a thriving 'red lamp' trade where 'the women no doubt found this a much more lucrative business than toiling in the fields or breaking stones on the roads for the government'.[94] Many of the young men in the war zones, officers as well as soldiers, were virgins in their relationships with women. Young Charles Carrington described how it felt for a young middle-class 'greenhorn' who, like others of his generation, 'had received no instruction of any kind from parents or teachers upon what are called the

---

90   TNA: WO 32/5597, *Medical: Diseases; Prevention of Venereal Disease.*
91   Gladden, *Piave*, pp.78-9.
92   Hardie, Private Papers, report for February-July 1918.
93   T.J. Mitchell and G.M. Smith, *History of the Great War based on official documents: Medical Services. Casualties and Medical Statistics of the Great War* (London, 1931), pp.174-83.
94   Gladden, *Piave*, p.144.

facts of life',[95] but now found himself exposed to brothels and temptation. The wrong place for young soldiers to learn about sex was the combination of barrack room banter and brothel, but for many that was their schooling. One young medical officer, whose mother was obviously concerned that he should avoid any sexual disease, berates her for not having been concerned enough to discuss it with him when he was younger:

> Do you not think it is rather late in the day to expect me to run straight?
>
> I know your anxieties are natural, but if you think a little, mother mine, you will realise that I have seen and heard authentically more about the ravages of venereal disease than what you have. I have dressed civilians, old men, with huge sores caused by syphilis. I have seen many a young lad reporting sick with a 'dose', poor chaps. They have not known which way to look. What I want to get at really is this – if you had, or my father had warned me not only of the loss of manhood, but the actual physical danger, incurred by associating with women of easy virtue, when I left school, it would have been more to the point.
>
> All the knowledge I possess, I have gained in devious ways, mainly through my own efforts, actuated by one of our greatest blessings, curiosity.
>
> I think I am what we call decent inherently. But, if in addition to my birth-right I had known more, you would have been saved many an anxious thought (which I assure your dear heart are needless) whilst I have been away from you.[96]

For this young man, like many others, the Edwardian pre-war world of his parents was gone, as was his innocence.

The soldiers of the IEF adapted well to Italy, and those who left personal recol-lections indicate that relationships between the troops and the local Italians were, on the whole, good. Plumer and Cavan adopted ways of working with the senior Italian commanders which were much more likely to produce results than Robertson's persistent criticism of their ally's army. However, they did consider it necessary to try to make their Italian colleagues adopt British and French methodologies for fighting; rightly or wrongly, they believed that the Italians had not kept up with the ways of waging modern war – as proven by the Italian performance at Caporetto. For the ordinary soldiers, the majority of whom were only in the country for between twelve and fifteen months, most of which was spent either on the Montello or the Asiago plateau, their opportunity to mix with the local population was limited. Unlike the troops on the Western Front, memoirs and other personal accounts from the IEF are relatively few. Also, possibly because there were no iconic battles on a par with the Somme or Passchendaele, the IEF did not spawn poets or novelists like Wilfred Owen or Edmund Blunden. The Italian Front gave us Hemingway's *A Farewell to Arms*, but that was fiction based on Caporetto, a battle which took place before its

---

95   Carrington, *Soldier from the wars returning*, p.162.
96   Hardie, Private Papers, letter, 30 June 1918 in report for February-July 1918.

author had arrived in Italy. The main opportunities for the men to fraternise with the local Italians were with the families with whom they were billeted, the owners of the local shops and bars, and the local girls. On the whole the few British memoirs of Italy were positive, it was after all much better than being in Flanders; the friendliness of the people, the splendour of the mountains, and the Mediterranean climate left an abiding impression on many. After the war Norman Gladden was to return frequently to 'that lovely land',[97] while Ronald Skirth and his wife made a holiday on the lakes of Lugarno and Como in 1961, 'intoxicated with the beauty [they] saw in every direction'.[98]

97   Gladden, *Piave*, p.218.
98   Barrett (ed.), *Reluctant Tommy*, p.170.

4

The Medical Services in the IEF: "I am in good health at present"

When armies march to war it is with the expectation that there will be casualties; some will suffer horrific wounds, others will be killed, and many will fall sick. All of these men (and in the IEF they were predominantly men) would require treatment by the army's medical services; an organisation of doctors, nurses (male and female), hospitals, medical aid posts, stretcher bearers, ambulances and hospital trains. Much of the medical infrastructure put in place by the British in Italy was based on their previous experience in France and Flanders, but there were differences to make allowances for the differing circumstances between the Western and Italian Fronts. The point has been made in previous chapters (and will be repeated in later ones) that the level of conflict which the IEF experienced in Italy was much lower than those units had been exposed to in Flanders, with the result that the medical services in Italy dealt primarily with sickness and disease, rather than battle casualties. This difference between the two fronts is starkly emphasised by one statistic: in 1918 in France the medical services treated 1.8 men for non-battle related causes for every battle injury; in the IEF the same number was 10.8, or six times as many.[1]

At this point in the narrative we should consider some of the problems which faced those responsible for the collection of the data used in this chapter, as well as the pitfalls for researchers using statistics gathered from war zones – especially when those records were paper-based.

At the end of the war the Director-General of the Army Medical Services, Sir William Leishman, recognised that their statistics for disease and battle casualties was a body of knowledge that was in danger of being lost. Few medical officers had experience of the differing medical conditions experienced in more than one theatre of war and there was a risk that the knowledge gained by the RAMC might 'fade into oblivion'. The multi-volume history of the Great War Medical Services was intended to be one way of overcoming that problem. Two volumes have been particularly helpful in the writing of this book; Mitchell and Smith's *Casualties and Medical*

---

1   Mitchell, *Medical Services*, Table 3, p.14.

Statistics[2] and William Macpherson's *Medical Service, Volume 3*.[3] One big problem for those compiling the histories lay in the conditions in which an army operated. While overworked regimental subalterns tried to stay on top of the required reports of the numbers reporting sick in their units during quiet periods, that task would have been almost impossible during periods of combat. The problem was compounded by men moving between battalions, divisions transferring between larger army formations and, in the case of the IEF, between countries. This frequent reassignment of men and their units meant that the data in the medical records was unlikely to be correctly reconciled to give accurate statistical information – the priority was to fight the war, not the correct compilation of paper-based forms. In the introduction to his book Mitchell outlined some of the challenges inherent in the army's processes, and it is important to keep these in mind when the researcher attempts to draw conclusions from the compiled data. Mitchell states that the maintenance of medical records 'fell to men neither familiar with such work nor conscious of its importance'. The exigencies of the Western Front 'demanded that patients should be rapidly transferred from one medical unit to another, and it became rare for the treatment of any given case to be completed under one medical officer'.[4] In attempting to compile his history Mitchell's team was 'inundated with records of every conceivable sort, packed in any order, and sent from units both at home and overseas'. In his view 'France was the only one to keep up trustworthy records' and as a result it was only possible to draw up tables 'giving the *approximate* casualties in the different theatres of war'.[5] [My italics.] However, in spite of Mitchell's warning on the accuracy of the information, it is still possible to draw comparisons between the incidence and treatment of battle and non-battle casualties on the French and Italian Fronts in 1918.

Before continuing with any analysis of the casualties suffered by the IEF there is one more important comment to make on the statistics used in this chapter. Recognising that incomplete statistical reports by different theatres would create anomalies in any comparison of the raw data, the Army Council called for a sampling of the completed records. For this exercise a total of 1,043, 653 admission files were compiled from all theatres, for the period from 1916 to 1920 (this date span allowed for the inclusion of those whose injuries continued into the early post-war years). The sample from each theatre was based on its ration strength; for Italy there were 11,857 records, for France 463,588. The researcher should also be aware that the data can vary with time, and the following table serves as an example. In this sample, while the total killed varies only by six, there is a large variation in the split between Officers and Other Ranks. It is not

2   Mitchell, *Medical Services*.
3   W. Macpherson, *History of the Great War based on official documents: Medical Services, Vol.3* (London, 1923).
4   Mitchell, *Medical Services*, p.x.
5   Mitchell, *Medical Services*, p.xv.

unusual to read battle histories which record differing casualty numbers depending on the source used, and the date on which that list was compiled.

Table 2: Those killed in Italy using data from 1919 and 1930

Data source	Killed, Officer	Killed, Other Ranks	Total
WO 394/12, 1919	136	1,088	1,224
Mitchell, 1931	90	1,140	1,230

Note: sources are Mitchell, 1931[6] and the Statistical Abstract report for 1919[7] in Kew.

Having delivered a 'health warning' on World War One casualty statistics it is now time to review how the medical services operated within the IEF, and how and why Italy differed from France in battle and non-battle casualties.

In all theatres the first port-of-call for a soldier who wanted to report himself sick (as opposed to a battle casualty) was the Regimental Medical Officer (RMO) in each battalion. Analogous to today's GP (although there was no National Health Service in 1918) the RMO held a daily sick-parade to which soldiers who felt sick or incapacitated could present themselves for a diagnosis and treatment. However, like our GP, the RMO had 'targets' to meet, with the battalion commander wanting the 'sick' list to be as small as possible as it was considered to 'provide a surrogate measure of morale'.[8] But, as David Englander correctly states, when reviewing sickness and disciplinary reports 'more was read into the figures than that which was classified as either criminal or sick' and the autonomy of the RMO to treat his patients could be 'curtailed by forceful commanding officers whose priorities were fixed by the gaze of their superiors'.[9] The implication is that the figures may be lower than they should be but, if all RMOs came under similar pressure, they are still valid for comparison purposes – or at least until future research shows that some were 'leant on' more than others. Men who were hospitalised, or assigned 'light duties', were often deemed by battalion NCOs to be 'skiving', and the RMO was 'soft' for letting them get away with it. The army had a monthly target of no more than 0.3% sickness, higher than that and a unit was deemed to be below operational effectiveness; bad for the reputation of its commander. By this measure the IEF's medical services did a good job. For the whole of the time it was in Italy it achieved a low 0.19%, which compared

---

6   Mitchell, *Medical Services*, Table 4, p.177.
7   TNA: WO 394/12.
8   D. Englander, 'Discipline and morale in the British army, 1917-1918', in J. Horne (ed.), *State, Society, and Mobilization in Europe during the First World War* (New York, 1997), p.135.
9   Englander, *Discipline and morale in the British army*, p.136.

favourably with the 0.16% of the BEF in 1918.[10] The slightly higher number in the IEF is not surprising given that illness and disease was a proportionately much higher problem in Italy than in France.

While the lot of ministering to the daily parade of cuts, bruises, and upset stomachs fell to the battalion RMO, he was supported by an organisation set up to deal with increasingly serious medical problems – particularly battle casualties. Today, with modern television reporting from conflict regions, we are used to seeing the rapid evacuation of severely wounded men, often by helicopter, to get the soldiers to a surgical team within the 'golden hour' and so vastly increasing their chances of survival. Such technologies were not available in the Great War, but the army medical services had developed a layered organisation which was capable of delivering increasing levels of surgical and medical skills, to battle and non-battle casualties, at different points behind the front. At the very point of this medical spear was the Regimental Aid Post (RAP), usually either built into the trench system, or very close behind it. A map in Macpherson[11] shows that on the Asiago front the IEF had eight RAPs spread through the two divisions in the forward lines. Here the casualty would receive an initial wound dressing and assessment by the Medical Officer (MO), from where he would be sent 'down the line' for further treatment. The RAP was small and had to be capable of movement as the battle front changed, as it did during the October 1918 assault across the Piave. Typically it would consist of an MO's room, racks of stretchers for about 20 patients, and a room for applying dressings. Moving further back from the line were the Advanced Dressing Stations (ADS) and the Main Dressing Stations (MDS), with casualties coming in either as 'walking wounded', on stretchers, or by ambulance. These dressing stations, being further back, could be more permanent structures, such as the ADS at Boscon, known as "Swiss Cottage" – so called because the wooden and sandbagged structure looked like a Swiss ski chalet.[12] Only a kilometre or so back from the front, on a reverse slope, this was one of four ADS and four MDS posts on the Asiago plateau. Sadly many of the men who made it to the dressing stations, whether in France or Italy, died there of their wounds and a field cemetery became a frequent adjunct to the medical post. Modern visitors to the old British front-line on the Asiago will find that the Commonwealth War Grave Commission (CWGC) cemeteries, so beautifully maintained, are named after the dressing station with which they were associated; Granezza, Boscon, Barental and Magnaboschi.

For those men who survived the treatment at the dressing stations, but whose wounds precluded their return to the front, the next stage was a move to a Casualty Clearing Station (CCS). These were much larger and more permanent facilities (able to take 200-400 patients) and were frequently sited close to a railway to allow access to the army's hospital trains. For most of its time in Italy the IEF had three CCS units,

---

10   Mitchell, *Medical Services*, Table 3, p.59.
11   Macpherson, *Medical Services Vol. 3*, map facing p.343.
12   There is a photo in the IWM archive; IWM Q 26981.

Figure 4.1 "Swiss Cottage" Advanced Dressing Station on the Asiago plateau.
(© Imperial War Museum Q 26981)

located between 10 and 20 miles behind the front. Their position changed throughout the deployment to take account of the British moved from the Montello, then to the Asiago, and finally back to the River Piave. While each CCS was large it was not designed for long-stay patients. Those casualties who required extended periods of hospitalisation were relocated, either to army hospitals in Italy, or back to England – a 'Blighty ticket'. While the IEF needed its own hospitals, it had the advantage that the army already had some in the country to minister to the troops transiting through Taranto to Egypt and Salonika. The IEF was exceptionally well served with sites at Cremona, Bordighera and Genoa in Italy, as well as Marseilles on the rail route home to England. When the planning had been done for the deployment to Italy the hospital requirements were based on the BEF experience in France. However, although they did not know it at the time, the fighting would be much less intense, leading to fewer battle casualties. As a result the IEF had the capacity to handle 6,823 patients, with the ability to utilise a further 3,000 at Marseilles. This provided the soldiers in Italy with 9.93 sick-beds for every 1,000 men, while those in France had only 4.74 – just half the proportion. Although the British in Italy did not come anywhere near to needing all the beds for battle casualties, they were almost all taken up during the severe influenza outbreak in 1918 when 'as many as thirty per cent of the strength of a division might be out of action'.[13]

The main challenges for the medical services of the IEF were disease and illness and this chapter will demonstrate that with both of these, as well as battle injuries, there were considerable differences between the experience of the troops on the Western and Italian Fronts. In the van of the battle against infection were the unsung heroes of the medical branch; the Sanitary Officer and his teams. It was their job to promote cleanliness in all aspects of a soldier's life, from the obvious toilet facilities (we met them earlier on the train to Marseilles) to the provision of clean drinking water and the working of the camp kitchens. The majority of the men who made up these teams would have had no previous public health experience – they were conscript soldiers drafted into the role – and relied on training provided by the divisional schools of sanitation. A one-week course in Italy provided instruction in such exciting topics as; 'food and food storage', 'practical demonstration on the construction of Urinals and Latrines' and, to close the syllabus, 'Infectious and Contagious Disease'.[14] 60 'volunteers' attended in December 1917. The work of the teams involved a constant regime of inspections. The war diary of the hospital at Voghera, where cold storage for food in the hot Italian climate was at a premium, gives an example of their necessity; the tinned meat (not a favourite of the troops at the best of times) 'was quite liquid'.[14] The effect of their contents on the stomachs of those soldiers with diarrhoea is best left to the imagination. Hygiene and disease prevention required a holistic approach if they were to be tackled properly, and that meant working with the Italian authorities. The army, especially when out of the front-line, lived and worked within the Italian civilian population whose hygiene standards it could not directly control. British troops frequently mentioned Italian cleanliness in their letters home, and they were normally in the negative; Lamin considered the locals to be 'not so clean as [the] English'.[15] When Gladden's unit took over a trench system from the Italians they were pretty disgusted:

> [It] contrasted pointedly with our own British methods of achieving good sanitary standards. There, clear for all the world to see, were their abandoned latrines: no order, no privacy, literally a field of filth.[16]

It was necessary for the British to work with the Italian authorities because waterborne diseases (as well as other infections) could exist in the local areas, but caused few problems for the Italians who had built up immunities. However, these could seriously affect the troops of the IEF. Because the impact on the Italians was low, they did

---

13   Edmonds, *Italy*, p.181.
14   TNA: WO 95/4259, *Detention hospital (Voghera)*.
15   Lamin, *Letters*, 8 July 1918, p.152.
16   Gladden, *Piave*, pp.25-6.

not display too much enthusiasm for making changes at the behest of the British. In February 1918 the Director of Medical Services (DMS) informed Plumer that there was a steady rise in enteric and para-typhoid cases which he believed was not helped by 'the difficulty experienced in inducing the Italian Authorities to co-operate in combating this condition'.[17] In the opinion of the DMS the British efforts to improve conditions were impeded by a lack of Italian assistance 'owing to the number of Italian civilians and soldiers in the zone of our Forces [*sic*] and the great want of sanitation displayed by them'. British concerns did not start with the arrival of the IEF. The commandant at Taranto, in September 1917, recorded that the Italian Sanitary Commission had visited his base; 'they [came] to pick our brains I imagine, judging by sanitary conditions in Southern Italy. It is to be hoped they will apply what they learn here, to the betterment of sanitary conditions in Taranto'.[18] However, while the British took a rather arrogant view of Italian sanitary standards – even today 'foreigners' are frequently considered by 'Brits' to be less fastidious over hygiene – they could not throw stones. In April 1918 an inspection of the reserve camp at Granezza criticised the conditions left by 23 Division as:

> Very unsatisfactory. Large accumulations of rubbish found under the floors of the huts (a hole having been cut in the floors through which the rubbish had been thrown). Likewise a marked deficiency of proper latrine and urinal arrangements. Also large amounts of rubbish littered around the ground.[19]

The IEF, like the army in France, put a lot of effort into the setting and maintaining of hygiene standards, not an easy task with 100,000 men living under field-combat conditions. Among the challenges was the provision of bathing facilities, essential for morale and for controlling the spread of disease.

In today's Britain access to hot water, showers and baths is taken pretty much for granted, but that was not the case a century ago in the industrial cities in which the majority of those in the IEF grew up. Few of the men would have had a bathroom at home; most would have used a zinc bath in front of the kitchen fire. This author remembers the bath hanging on a hook outside the back-door of his grandmother's house in Sheffield into the 1960s. So, we should not be surprised if letters and memoirs do not refer to frequent 'bath-nights'. While they may not have been regular the army did provide mobile bath units, most of which could process a few hundred men a day. Unfortunately the frequency of their visits could vary. The last British survivor who had fought in the war was Harry Patch – he died in 2009 – and he told his biographer that between June and September 1917, while in France, 'I never got

---

17   TNA: WO 95/4198, *Director Medical Sevices.*
18   TNA: WO 95/4255, *Taranto Base: Commandant.*
19   TNA: WO 95/4245, *48 Division: Adjutant and Quarter-Master General.*

the chance to bathe [...] I never had a bath, and I never had any clean clothes'.[20] This recollection may be the failing memory of an old soldier rather than reality. The war diaries of units in France and Italy have many references to the men being taken to the mobile bath and fumigation units where, as well as a good soak, their clothes were changed for ones that had been deloused. Many battalions record the opportunity being available on a fortnightly basis, although there could frequently be an interval of a month; not ideal, but better than the four months of Patch's memory. An example of how the interval between baths could vary is illustrated by the diary of the 8th Devonshire battalion (part of the IEF). In this instance baths were available on 24 January 1918, then a gap of six weeks to 6 March, another six week wait until 18 and 19 April, and then in May they were available on four days. Today it can be difficult to imagine going six weeks without a bath, especially in an environment where that would encourage lice, but some of our troops on remote Fire Bases in Afghanistan may well have had to do that. The situation would have been particularly awkward for units in the forward areas, especially in the front-line trenches, where bathing would simply not have been possible. Also, even for those troops in the rear areas, operational priorities often meant that they could not use the facilities even though they were available to them. In June 1918 a medical officer in the 23rd Division reported that while the baths at Fara (in the rest area) could process 900 men daily, 'only 300 to 400 on average, are actually being sent there'.[21] There is a high probability that those absent were being employed on the innumerable working parties that filled up the time the troops spent in the 'rest' areas. In the spirit of hope over experience the same officer pointed out that as it was summer, 'a bath at least once a week will be particularly necessary during the next few months'; necessary, maybe, but the war diaries demonstrate that it was unlikely to happen. However infrequent they may have been, the need for troops in a combat environment to keep themselves clean, as a guard against the spread of disease and infection, was recognised by regimental officers. In the case of one battalion where some men had not been able to attend on the first day that baths were available, they were paraded on a second day and 'certificates rendered by the O.C. Companies to the effect that all NCOs and men in their companies had had a bath'.[22] But what were these mobile bath units like? Gladden gives us an insight to one such in France, though those in Italy would have been very similar. After removing their outer clothing for delousing the men approached the baths:

> Dressed thus in our underclothing amidst the inhabited buildings of that little place we felt very much at a disadvantage, pulling our coats around us and watching fearfully lest some of the natives should stroll over to see what was

20   R. Van Emden, *The Last Fighting Tommy* (London, 2007), p.277.
21   TNA: WO 95/4231, *Assistant Director Medical Services*, 8 June 1918.
22   TNA: WO 95/4240, 8 York & Lancs, 16 January 1918.

going on. The unavoidable intimacies of army life had apparently not killed the natural modesty in which most of us had been brought up.[23]

Edwardian middle-class values died hard.

Bang the drum as he might, the Sanitary Officer had one opponent he could not defeat; *Pediculus Vestimenti* – body lice, 'one of the minor horrors of the present war'.[24] These parasites were the scourge of the soldier's life and were an inevitable consequence of dirty living conditions, insufficient opportunities for washing and infrequent changes of clothing, especially underwear. It was acknowledged by the medical officers that the soldier 'host' was part of the problem – 'one verminous man in a room is sufficient to infect others, who usually blame the room'. But that statement did not address the issue of how to provide clean clothing, make baths available more frequently than every two or three weeks, and that unless these problems were fixed the lice would win. As the *vestimenti* in their Latin name indicates, this genus of the species lived in the men's clothing with the female laying her eggs in the seams of the soldiers' clothing, particularly in areas close to warm parts of the body; under the arms and around the groin. It is hard for us to imagine how irritating (and demeaning) it must have been to play host to these parasites, but they had other side-effects which could be more debilitating. The lice fed by sucking blood from their host which allowed them to transfer disease as they moved from soldier to soldier in the close confines of the trenches and billets. While bathing helped, it did not overcome the problem if the eggs and lice were not removed from the men's clothing. The army did try to get changes of clothes to the troops, and to fumigate those they took away, but in-between these (infrequent) changes, the men had to devise their own remedies. The seams of clothing were a favourite breeding ground so they were subjected to heat from candle flames, they were squeezed to kill the eggs, and when they were in the rest areas hot pressing-irons were used to kill them. Soldiers had their own name for most things, and lice were 'Chats'. The men would sit around together killing the little horrors by whatever was their favourite technique. This pass-time was known as 'chatting', from which we now have the verb 'to chat', or talk in a group. The army never did defeat the lice, but commercial companies saw an opportunity to make a profit from them. Boots the Chemist offered 'Vermin Powder' for 9d (nine old pence) a box which family members could send to their boys at the front to combat 'the plague of parasites to which our soldiers are liable'.[25] No doubt the families at home believed they were helping their menfolk, but the opinion of the medical officers was that 'most powders and ointments now sold for killing lice are of little value'.[26] By the time the men of the

23 Gladden, *Ypres*, p.82.
24 TNA: WO 95/4231, 23 Division memo, 15 November 1917.
25 *War Budget Illustrated*, 1 July 1918.
26 TNA: WO 95/4231, 23 Division ADMS, memo, 8 June 1918.

IEF had arrived in Italy they had learnt from their experience in France how to live with the problem, however reluctantly.

Although the IEF fought a losing battle against lice, there was more that they could do for themselves to combat two serious diseases; typhoid and dysentery. The first of these required cooperation between the British and Italian authorities to ensure that clean drinking water was available to the British troops. In December 1917 six cases of typhoid fever were diagnosed among the local population of Trevignano (an area where troops were based) which was attributed by the British to contaminated water.[27] In rear areas like this, where the soldiers had more opportunity to mix with the Italians, there was an increased potential for the spread of the disease. In the view of the British medical services the problem was compounded by the lack of quarantine and inoculation programs operated by the Italians for their local population, they did not seem to subscribe to the dictum that 'prevention was better than cure'. As modern-day tourists we are used to strictures about eating salads and fruit in exotic places, such as Egypt and the Far East – gin and tonics should be taken without ice made from local water. The locals can take it, we can't. The British needed the Italians to understand that while the local conditions might do no harm to a population 'inured to these conditions by generations', they could well cause 'the outbreak of a serious epidemic among strangers to whom such conditions are strange'.[28] To help ward against these 'foreign' diseases the IEF embarked on an aggressive program of inoculation of the troops, especially against typhoid. By this means the number of men needing a 'jab' was reduced from almost 6,000 a month in July 1918 to 2,000 in September – it stayed at this figure for the rest of the year as the October offensive kicked in and the medical services had to prioritise battle casualties over sickness.

If typhoid was to be beaten, then its prevalence in the civil population and the Italian army'[29] had to be addressed. To that end a conference was held in Padua in January 1918, at the instigation of the British ADMS, attended by the British, French and Italian military and civilian medical authorities. Later, in the autumn of 1918, the incidence of typhoid in the Italian civil population fell to half that of the same period in 1917, which the British attributed to their ally adopting the measures agreed at Padua. Effective as the inoculation program was among the troops of the IEF, the incidence of typhoid in the British forward areas in Italy was eight times higher than for similar units in France. Among the IEF the figure was 0.41 per 1,000 men (32 admissions), while for the same period the BEF experienced 0.05 per 1,000 (98 patients).[30] This high infection rate, even though it affected relatively few troops, confirmed the medical authorities in their view that they had to be worried about the prevalence of typhoid on the Italian peninsular. But the disease was managed and

27   TNA: WO 95/4231, 12 December 1917.
28   TNA: WO 95/4198, 1 January 1918.
29   Macpherson, *Medical Services Vol. 3*, p.361.
30   Mitchell, *Medical Services*, Tables on pages 174 & 184.

controlled. During its time in Italy the IEF's average monthly ration strength was just short of 95,000 men and of those only 32 were admitted for typhoid, but no deaths were recorded. The situation with dysentery however was much more concerning. Typhoid could be controlled by getting each of the men to the needle for just one jab, while dysentery required all troops to exercise constant vigilance. The disease could spread quickly among troops living at close quarters, but it was 'avoidable with care'. The cases analysed by Mitchell reveal the sad fact that although the British had had some three years' experience of controlling the disease in combat areas before moving to Italy, the admissions for dysentery in the IEF made a poor comparison with that of the units in France. The rate of hospitalisation in Italy (among British and Dominion troops)[31] was 10.95 per 1,000 men, while the corresponding figure in France was 6.58.[32] Not only was the relative scale of the problem worse in the IEF than in the BEF, but it was greater in Italy than in any year of the war in France. Even more disconcerting is the fact that those admitted with the disease in Italy had a much higher chance of dying from it; 0.18 per 1,000, or nine times higher than the rate in France of 0.02.

In his book Mitchell merely records the statistics, he makes no attempt to draw conclusions as to causes for the differences between operational theatres, but we can make some assumptions. Higher summer temperatures in Italy, compared with Flanders, would have exacerbated any lapses in sanitation standards, and the difference in the terrain between the two fronts would have presented real problems. Digging latrines in the limestone of the Asiago plateau, where rock-drills were needed rather than shovels, would have been much more difficult than a similar exercise in the soft farmland of Flanders. While unit war diaries make no mention of where and how many were dug, it is highly likely that there were fewer in Italy because of the problem of digging them. While the availability and maintenance of latrines does not figure highly in histories of the conflict, they were essential for controlling dysentery and enteric diseases by limiting the spread of 'flies and filth'. Toilet facilities, particularly those in the front-line trenches, were very basic, typically consisting of a pit with a wooden plank above it on which to sit and defecate. Away from the trench lines, in the support and rest areas, petrol would have been used to set fire to the full latrines, which would have killed off any fly colonies that had established themselves. This option would not have been available in the forward areas where fires provided aiming points for enemy artillery. The open latrine pits, even though lime and soil was regularly used to cover the contents, were veritable fly-traps, especially in summer. The toilets, animal manure dumps, summer heat and a lack of cold storage for meat would all have worked against the army's efforts to control flies. These basic conditions, together with the limited opportunities for the men to wash, as well as

31 Mitchell separates British & Dominion troops from 'foreign' units such as the British West Indies Regiment and native labour units.
32 Mitchell, *Medical Services*, Table 16, p.183 & Table 17, p.174.

rudimentary food-handling and cooking facilities, would have made it difficult for a soldier with dysentery not to infect his mates. Using an apposite metaphor Greenwell described his own experience of the effects of bowel disease as a 'bombardment in the nether regions'.[33] The effect among a platoon of men in a trench environment can be imagined. As an example, 48 Division, in July 1918, had 579 admissions for diarrhoea in just that one month.[34]

A recurring theme in this book is the difference in the intensity of the combat on the Italian and Western Fronts, a fact reflected in the casualty statistics. The non-battle casualties among the British (non-labour) troops of the IEF ran at a rate of 542.2 per 1,000 men, not a lot lower than the 595 recorded for the British and Dominion troops of the BEF – so sickness rates were similar in the two theatres. However, because the IEF was involved in less fighting, the sickness admissions were a much higher percentage of the casualties in Italy (89%) than in France (57.5%).[35] But another interesting comparison can also be drawn; that between front-line, fighting troops and the non-combatant labour units. In the latter group the rate at which men were admitted as 'sick' was three times as high as for the fighting men, 1,639 per 1,000.[36] Again, while Mitchell gives no reason for this large difference, we can make assumptions. There would not have been the same motivation to 'support your mate' in a labour unit (where it is more difficult to engender *esprit de corps*), and so a greater tendency to report sick than a man in the line who might have put up with minor illness to stay with his group. Also, many of these rear echelon troops were older and held a lower medical grade, so were more likely to succumb to illness. It is important to stress again that, when comparing medical and disciplinary statistics, the data for combat and non-combat units should be separated as the conditions under which the two groups operated were very different, leading the researcher to an 'apples and pears' analysis.

By far the biggest impact of disease on the fighting troops in Italy was that delivered by the outbreak of influenza, a contagion 'which no medical service could control',[37] and the timing of which could not have been worse, coming just as the Austrians launched their June offensive against the Piave and the Asiago plateau. The epidemic took the medical services by surprise and initially they could not identify it as influenza. They were not helped by being unsure of its origin – some thought it came from sand-flies, while others believed silk-worms in farmers' cottages were to blame. The rate at which the disease spread through troops in all theatres led to incomplete record keeping, especially in France. However, the data for the IEF is more complete and demonstrates to what extent the British in Italy were affected. The influenza admissions (17,088), including labour units, were almost 30% of the total non-combat

33   Greenwell, *Infant in Arms*, p.234.
34   TNA: WO 95/4245.
35   Mitchell, *Medical Services*, pp.168 & 177.
36   Mitchell, *Medical Services*, Table 11, p.181.
37   Mitchell, *Medical Services*, p.167.

casualties (58,382). On top of that the disease accounted for 63% of all non-combat related deaths in the IEF and 24% of all the British dead in Italy, from all causes. Unfortunately direct comparisons cannot be made with the BEF as Mitchell's data is incomplete for France. However, in that country, across the ration strength (which may include labour units) the rate per 1,000 men was 157.8, which is close to the IEF figure of 147 (excluding labour units). For the large majority of men who survived the outbreak, the illness affected them for up to two weeks, though some were unlucky enough to still be hospitalised months later. Lamin described it as causing the men to lose the use of their legs, to suffer from 'sore throat and cough' and as a result they were 'isolated for a fortnight'.[38]

The IEF were in the throes of dealing with the flu outbreak when the Austrians attacked on 15 June. Of the 48th Divisional staff only two officers were fit for duty that day; Major-General Fanshawe (Divisional Commander) and his Intelligence Officer.[39] The fighting strength of battalions in the division was nominally 800-1,000 men, but influenza reduced this to an average of only 491. Greenwell, a young captain, recorded the impact on his battalion:

> the Second-in-Command and the Adjutant went off in hospital today. Both my other officers have it [flu] and nearly all the men, and everyone is looking absolutely miserable and eating nothing.[40]

The consequences for the British reaction to the Austrian attack are dealt with in a later chapter but the unfolding of the challenge for the medical services can be appreciated through some of the entries in the war diary of the ADMS.[41]

1 June: A considerable number of cases of fever are still being admitted to Medical Units and the condition does not appear to be on the decline.

4 June: 39 CCS to be devoted to treating this disease.

5 June: A large number of patients still reporting sick with the epidemic fever. […] A considerable number of men in the hills [on the Asiago] are now being attacked [by flu]. The epidemic appears to have spread up from the plains.

6 June: At 8pm this evening 601 cases of the infectious fever remain at No. 39 CCS. The personnel of this CCS has already been attacked [by flu] and has had to be supplemented by Field Ambulance personnel.

7 June: [39 CCS] practically full of cases of the epidemic pyrexia, we have arranged for No. 9 CCS to take them also.

---

38   Lamin, *Letters,* p.153.
39   Greenwell, *Infant in Arms,* p.262.
40   Greenwell, *Infant in Arms,* pp.227-8.
41   TNA: WO 95/4198.

8 June: Arrangements were being put in place for a convalescent camp under canvas to take 800 men.

11 June: 1,840 cases in CCSs, 311 in convalescent camp.

12 June: 2,145 in CCSs and 193 in convalescent camp.

The medical services were struggling to cope with the influenza cases, on top of which they also had to take the battle casualties from the 15 June Austrian attack – but cope they did. Severe as the epidemic was, it was not isolated to the middle months of the year. In September the senior medical officer reported that 'Influenza has again appeared amongst the troops and is assuming epidemic form', it was similar to that seen earlier in the year, but 'slightly more severe […] those attacked in the spring are practically immune'. Once again, the timing of the new outbreak was inopportune; the Italians, along with their French and British allies, were to attack the Austrians in late October for the final offensive of the war in Italy, but many of the men were struck down by flu. In November there were 1,650 cases among the combat troops, including 89 deaths; that was more than the 1,461 British battle casualties the medical services reported as a result of the offensive. But the epidemic was on the decline within the IEF, although it went on to take millions of lives worldwide. The ADMS, in his report for December 1918 recorded that there were only 537 cases with 49 deaths, compared with the figures mentioned above for November. With strict adherence to sanitary standards the troops could control and limit their susceptibility to dysentery and diarrhoea, but the influenza epidemic tore through them, until the medical services could isolate and quarantine the infected men.

Through good medical practice, allowing for the problems of operating in a combat zone, precautions were put in place to combat malaria, typhoid, dysentery and influenza, but there was one disease which was completely in the control of the individual men, if only they could 'just say no'; Venereal Disease (VD). The prevention seems simple and obvious, but as with all armies through the ages, VD was widespread. The letters and memoirs from France and Italy (where the writer was bold enough to mention the subject) demonstrate that men away from home had sexual needs, and there were women prepared to help them. These testaments also show us that not all the soldiers approached the issue from the same start point; married men were familiar with sex and the potential problems of sexually transmitted diseases; young men who had 'done it' were aware of how to get sex and regarded it as something of a sport; but many had no experience, and were held back by the Edwardian mores of their upbringing – women were not sex objects and brothels were to be abhorred. Men like Gladden and Skirth wrote of being disgusted (how prim they sound to today's audience) by the way many of their colleagues went searching for sex wherever they could get it but, like many who wrote years after the war, it was always 'the others' who went looking, never the writer. However, abstention among men a long way from home was easier to call for than to deliver. In 1914 Kitchener appealed to the BEF to be constantly on their guard against excesses, especially wine and women: 'You must entirely resist both temptations and while treating women with perfect courtesy, you should avoid any intimacy'.[42] The statistics for the disease would indicate that, for many, the Field Marshal's words fell on deaf ears.

Because the prevention lay with every individual the medical services could not be held responsible for the high level of disease among the troops; 'the causes are well known and officers and men, knowing how infection is contracted, individually take the risk'.[43] While the RMOs could not prevent VD, they did provide educational programs to try to limit its impact, but as the disease was the second highest cause of hospitalisation in the IEF, after influenza,[44] it was obvious that the message was not getting through. For the army the issue was less a moral one than one of efficiency as men in hospital were not available for duty. Hospitalisation times were not insignificant. The average period for gonorrhoea was 28.6 days, while that for syphilis was longer at 37.6 days. This obviously had a serious impact when 416,891 cases were admitted among British and Dominion troops for the whole war.

How did the infection rate of the disease affect the IEF? For 1918 there were 1,888 admissions from the combat troops in the Forward Area, a rate of 24.06 per 1,000, considerably lower than for France which stood at 32.36 per 1,000 for the same period. Here again the distinction must be made between combat and non-combat (labour) troops, for to include them produces a significant 'skew' in the figure for the IEF.[45] When the units based at Taranto are included then the admissions for the IEF jump to 3,956, giving a rate per 1,000 men of 41.8. This figure is well above that of the British and Dominion troops in France (32.36) where, unlike Italy, only 2.76 per 1,000 of the Indian and 3.86 of the labour troops were hospitalised with the disease. The increased incidence of VD among the troops at Taranto reinforced the low esteem in which rear-area units were held by those in the front line; not only were those men a long way from the fighting, they had more chances with the women. High as the rate was for all British troops based in Italy, considerably above that in France, it fell well below the 50.44 per 1,000 men in the British and Dominion units in Egypt and Palestine in the same period.

If exhortations to 'refrain' fell on deaf ears, what could the military do? Disciplinary action was one option, but as with medical treatment, this came after the horse had bolted. Because of the way in which the man became infected, VD was regarded by many to be a 'self-inflicted wound', and received little sympathy. Under King's Regulations (KR462), a soldier suffering from VD had to report himself sick without delay, and that order was to be read to the troops every three months to ensure that they were aware. If they complied then there was a reasonable chance that they would just be treated as a sickness casualty, albeit one who would lose all leave for the next

42   M. Harrison, 'The British Army and the Problem of Venereal Disease in France and
      Egypt during the First World War', *Medical History*, Vol. 19 (1995), p.138.
43   Mitchell, *Medical Services,* p.72.
44   Mitchell, *Medical Services,* Table 15, p.183.
45   Mitchell, *Medical Services,* pp.174 & 183.

twelve months – not a great incentive to speak up. If the man failed to declare himself infected, and was later discovered so to be, then he could face a court martial under Section 11 of the Army Act; the offender 'neglects to obey any general or garrison or other order [KR462]'. Within the IEF there are no courts martial records stating that the offender had VD but, taking January 1918 as an example, there were at least 17 cases tried under Section 11. In their fight to limit the impact of the disease on the troops the authorities also attempted to limit the access of the soldier to temptation and, a cause of much resentment, punish all for the offences of the few by periodically stopping leave within the country:

> All leave to Italy has now been stopped because young officers won't take precautions. In several places I have seen notices printed in Italian telling you what to do after. Why don't they have these notices printed in English, or else unofficially to all a few words on how to prevent getting a dose![46]

Leave restrictions were bound to be contentious with the men, especially as home leave was so difficult to get, and to lose it because someone else could not control his urges must have been doubly frustrating, as the young officer above intimates. This use of leave as a deterrent was taken up by the Director of Medical Services in one of his reports:

> On account of the number of cases of Venereal Disease contracted outside the area under our control, all leave in this country for Officers under field rank, N.C.Os and men has been stopped [...] Commanding Officers and Medical Officers have been advised to explain to the men the dangers they run in connection with Venereal Disease and to use every means at their disposal to prevent it.[47]

Attempting to control the disease by closing brothels was a policy which not all senior officers agreed with. Haig had argued against the closing of them in Le Havre on the basis that if they were 'controlled' then it was possible to monitor the health of the prostitutes who worked there, so limiting the spread of disease. It was better than driving it onto the streets. Meanwhile, the brothels in Thiene and Vincenza were constantly being closed to the men of the IEF. But control of the disease through limiting the soldiers' access to women was always going to be difficult, a fact demonstrated by a table of data[48] in Mitchell's *Medical Services*. An analysis of 91,231 admissions for sexual diseases among men of the BEF, between January 1915 and May 1918, found that while 44.7% of them were detected in France, 42.2% had picked up

46 Hardie, July 1918 report.
47 TNA: WO 95/4198, memo, 31 July 1918.
48 Mitchell, *Medical Services*, Table 14, p.74.

the infection in the United Kingdom – a fact to worry the Mother's Union who were so concerned that the army was lowering the morals of their boys. If home leave was such a virulent source of infection for the BEF, there is no reason to suppose that would not also have been the case for those serving in Italy.

With sex being such a preoccupation for many of the men away from home it would be no surprise to find that many of them 'caught a dose' more than once – there were recidivists. In the language of Mitchell's statistics the second-timers were covered by the 'relapse rate'. In Italy this ran at 11%, while in France (for the same period) it was considerably higher at 17%. What this meant was that more of the men in the IEF were catching the disease for the first time; maybe those who had held off in the wet and damp of Flanders gave in to the sultry heat of Italy and the 'olive-skinned beauties' they had noticed on their train journey south. One more thing should be said about VD, it was no respecter of rank. It would be wrong to think that infection was limited to those below officer status – young subalterns could be as easily turned by a pretty girl's smile as any young soldier. One source for the failure of young officers to resist temptation is the 'manifest' of the hospital trains. These list how many patients were carried, the number of them who were 'sitting' or 'lying', and how many were 'venereal'. The train from Cremona to Bordighera on 17 July 1918 had 24 VD patients, four of them were officers.[49] In the strictly stratified society of early twentieth-century England, a sexual disease was particularly 'bad form'. Captain Lawrence Gameson was a medical officer in France and in his unpublished manuscript he describes an incident involving a fellow officer who came to him, infected with gonorrhoea; '[the] circumstances of his getting the disease were foolish, but the potential social consequences at home were disastrous'.[50] Gameson noted that not only was the other officer guilty of a military crime (concealing his infection) but Gameson himself was guilty for treating him and not reporting it. While the treatment was successful, and the secret maintained, under military law there were two criminals.

One of the unfortunate consequences of always portraying the First World War through photographs and archive film from the Western Front is that the public is led to believe that these were representative of all theatres. However, as this book sets out to demonstrate, that is not correct. One of the many differences between Italy and Flanders is to be found in the battle and non-battle casualties. For every 1.4 men who reported sick in France in 1918 there was one more who was admitted as a battle casualty, in the IEF there were eight sick men for each one wounded or killed.[51] But it was not only the ratio of battle to non-battle casualties that made the difference. The data collection undertaken by Mitchell's team reveals significant variations between the types of wounds on the two fronts, as well as quantitative differences in some of those medical conditions which have become iconic symbols of trench warfare – trench foot

49   TNA: WO 95/4261, war diary, 43 Ambulance Train.
50   IWM: Doc. 612, L. Gameson, *Private Papers, Vol. 2*, p.366.
51   Mitchell, *Medical Services*, pp.169 & 179.

and 'shell-shock'. In their analysis the causes of battle wounds are divided into three categories; accidental or undefined, self-inflicted, or 'instruments of war' – bullets, shrapnel, bomb or bayonet.

The limestone terrain on which the IEF spent most of their time in Italy created problems for the men who had to dig trenches, but it also caused exploding shells to produce showers of high velocity rock splinters. The impact would not have been dissimilar to that on board a man-of-war in Nelson's navy where, below decks, the majority of the sailors would have been killed or injured by large, flying, splinters of wood, rather than by the cannon balls. But while rock splinters are not a defined cause of battle injury in Mitchell's analysis this author suggests that they are covered by his category of 'accidental or undefined'. In France, where the majority of shells from German artillery exploded on trenches dug in farmland, 'accidental' covered only 16.6% of battle casualties, in Italy that number was 46%,[52] the same as that for Macedonia which has a similar terrain of rock and mountains to that of the Asiago plateau. Although Mitchell makes no reference to rock splinters as a possible source of the 'accidental' battle injuries, the Italian experience of fighting in the Carso and Isonzo regions (prior to Caporetto) gives credence to the assumption. Filippo de Filippi, in his article on the geography of the Italian Front, describes the defences on the Carso as entirely different from the trenches dug in the earth of the Western Front. The effect of the enemy shells exploding on the limestone 'was extremely deadly, on account of the innumerable rock splinters, which greatly multiplied the effects of the projectiles'.[53] John Gooch, who has written much on the Italian Army, backs up Filippi's assertion; 'the increase in fragmentation caused by exploding shells [on limestone] produced 70 per cent more casualties there than on other fronts'.[54] Bad as it was to be hit by the rock splinters, the wounds may not have been as life-threatening as those produced by high velocity bullets and artillery shells, and this may again be inferred from some of the data in Mitchell's analysis. Of those who were hospitalised with battle wounds in France, 7.6% died in care; a rate six times higher than that in the IEF at 1.2%. Also, where 29% of the combat casualties in France were later returned to their unit as fit, the similar figure for Italy was much higher at 41%.[55] In summary, the limestone of the Asiago, on which the IEF spent the majority of their time in Italy, caused injuries quite different from those on the Western Front, the soldiers who were wounded had a better chance of surviving and were more likely to be returned to their unit after hospitalisation.

The unusually wet winter of 2013-14 in Britain brought home the meaning of the term 'flood-plain'; generally a low-lying area with a high water table, and tending to

---

52   Mitchell, *Medical Services*, Table 15, p.281.
53   F. de Filippi, 'The Geography of the Italian Front', *Geographical Journal*, Vol. 51 (1917), p.73.
54   Gooch, *Morale*, p.437.
55   Mitchell, *Medical Services*, Table 5, p.18.

flood easily. The description fitted Flanders in the First World War, but there the problem was exacerbated by the destruction of the drainage system under very heavy German artillery fire. In his memoir Greenwell described it as being 'waist-deep in liquid mud'.[56] Little wonder then that one soldier, enthusiastic at the move from Flanders to Italy, told his family that, 'we had come from the mud & lice of Flanders, we found ourselves in the sun & freshness of Italy'.[57] While they now had to cope with the cold, rain and snow during their winter on the mountainous Asiago plateau, they were at least free of mud on the scale that they had experienced in Flanders. One consequence of the troops' constant immersion of their feet, due to the wet conditions on the Western Front, was 'trench foot'; incredibly six men died of this in France in 1915. However, precautions could be taken to keep their feet dry, rubbing with whale oil helped, as did having boots that fitted properly. For the men of the IEF, the drier conditions helped enormously with reducing the incidence of the debilitating condition. By enforcing the precautions that could be taken the BEF (from 1915 to 1917) had reduced the infection rate from 38.4 per 1,000 men, to 11.3. This impressive reduction continued in France with the incidence dropping to only 3.8 cases per 1,000 men,[58] However, in that same year the IEF took their trench foot sickness figure to only 10 per cent of the BEF; an impressive 0.3 per 1,000 men. This was a dramatic improvement in a medical condition that was not inconsequential. Mitchell records that approximately 55% of those hospitalised for the infection were there for between one and three months.[59] The prevalence of trench foot on the Western Front was at a level where it has become synonymous with 'The War', but if that conflict is to be seen in the round, then it has to be acknowledged that not all theatres suffered from the condition to the same extent.

Apart from mud, another recurring image from the Great War is that of soldiers in hospital suffering from 'shell shock'. The ex-soldier, missing a limb, drew recognisable sympathy but the 'shell-shocked victim, unable to gain employment after the war, became one of the period's most enduring icons'.[60] The effect of long exposure to artillery bombardments, tiredness and fatigue could lead to men becoming battle-stressed; they might become deaf or mute, or lose their memory.[61] The condition, while little understood by the medical services, could be treated with rest, and time away from the front. Unfortunately the ignorance surrounding the condition could also lead to the man's officers and NCOs believing that he was simply trying to avoid his duty; he was deemed to be 'swinging the lead' or 'lacking in moral fibre'. But not all saw it that way. Young Captain Greenwell was one who had some empathy for those affected:

56   Greenwell, *Infant in Arms*, p.146.
57   Faviall, Private Papers, p.9.
58   Mitchell, *Medical Services*, Table 23, p.88.
59   Mitchell, *Medical Services*, p.302.
60   Holmes, *Tommy*, p.485.
61   M. Roper, *The Secret Battle. Emotional survival in the Great War* (Manchester, 2009), p.246.

I have got a poor chap who has suddenly gone groggy with shell-shock. He can't keep his hands still and waggles them the whole time. I have brought him down here and he is buried somewhere in the depths of the dug-out.[62]

Although there were no doubt cases where men had feigned shell shock as a means to get themselves removed from the active areas of the front, it would come to be recognised as a genuine medical condition – but one beyond the scope of this book. It could also be used as a cloak to cover failures of leadership in an officer, and so remedy a situation where he was not considered to be 'up to scratch'; in these cases shell shock became 'neurasthenia'. The term had the benefit of sounding 'medical' without the 'can't take it' connotation that went with being shell shocked. When Siegfried Sassoon wrote his critique of the war, rather than arraign him before a court martial, he was sent to the Craiglockhart Hospital for treatment, ostensibly for neurasthenia. A medical officer, James Dunn, commented pithily; 'Sassoon's quixotic outburst has been quenched in a "shell-shock" retreat'.[63] In other words this was officialdom deciding that the poet's outburst should be covered by that cloak of mental stress. It was better to have him deemed to be suffering from a mental disorder than that his views on the war should be taken as the writing of a sane man.

In his study of the British soldier, Holmes states that shell shock was 'less common than we might think',[64] and he is borne out by the figures. Although popular myths of the war portray shell shock as all pervasive among those who survived the bombardments, the medical records show only 3 per cent of the hospital admissions in France attributable to the condition. Once again the experience of those in Italy shows how different the war was away from the Western Front. Among the troops of the IEF shell shock was five times lower than that in France, at only 0.6 per cent of admissions. This reduction is directly attributable to the much lower frequency and intensity of the Austrian artillery bombardments, compared with those of the Germans. The IEF suffered no shelling on the scale of Loos, the Somme or that of the German Spring offensive in March 1918. Arthur Acland wrote dismissively of the Austrian gunners, claiming that they fired a few rounds 'chiefly out of boredom, and really meant no harm';[65] very different from Flanders. By late 1918 the army medical service was attempting to remove the term 'shell shock' (and its negative connotations) from the lexicon, they wanted the condition registered as a nervous disorder. The Director of Medical Services in the IEF recorded that there were moves in France for the term to be 'absolutely done away with' and that if this was also done in Italy then:

---

62   Greenwell, *Infant in Arms*, p.129.
63   J.C. Dunn, *The War the Infantry Knew 1914-1919* (London, 1994), p.372.
64   Holmes, *Tommy*, p.485.
65   Acland, Private Papers, p.108.

Cases of undoubted shell shock without any visible wound in future will be transferred from one Medical Unit to another as N.Y.D.N. [Not Yet Diagnosed (nervous)[66]], accompanied by a full medical history of the case. The final diagnosis resting with the authorities in England. By this means *the term shell shock will be absolutely abolished in this theatre of war.* [My italics]

The renaming of the condition did not stop the phrase becoming synonymous with artillery shelling in the First World War. Nor, in public mythology, did it prevent it becoming a much greater legacy of the war than it actually was – that is not to downplay the seriousness for those who did suffer. Mitchell's history, drawn up after the war when the new phraseology was in use, categorises these cases under the heading 'Functional diseases of the nervous system (including neurasthesia and shell shock)'.

In war men get sick in conditions which are difficult for the medical services to treat them, and others get killed. Having said that, there were demonstrable and quantifiable differences between the Western and Italian Fronts in the illnesses the men were exposed to and the wounds suffered by battle casualties. 'There is not the slightest need for you to worry about me. I have not been in so safe a place for over a year';[67] this view by one young officer will suffice to represent many of the letters home from members of the IEF – they knew they were safer, and could expect to survive. As a consequence the medical services in Italy found themselves dealing much more with sickness than with battle wounds. Of the men deployed to the BEF 56% became combat casualties, in the IEF the figure was 4.76%.[68] In fact Italy had the lowest ratio of casualties to men deployed of all the theatres of the war, as the following table demonstrates.

Table 3: Casualties for each man deployed by theatre[69]

Theatre	Casualties	Men deployed
France	5	9
Dardanelles	2	9
Mesopotamia	2	12.5
Other Theatres	1	10.5
Salonika	1	12
East Africa	1	12
Egypt	1	15
Italy	1	21

66   Macpherson, *Medical Services Vol. 3*, p.vii.
67   Eberle, Private Papers, 22 November 1917.
68   TNA: WO 394/12, p.149.
69   TNA: WO 394/12, report 29, p.149.

The casualty statistics, as well as the data in the history of the medical services, bear out the proposition that the conditions on the Western Front should not be taken as the paradigm for the war as it was experienced by all British soldiers. The differences shown between the battle casualties in France and Italy can be attributed to the fact that battle wounds in France were caused mainly by 'instruments of war', whereas those in Italy came largely from 'accidental' causes, which this book argues were rock splinters. The reduced level of military activity on the Italian Front in 1918 (compared to Flanders), together with the lower intensity of the Austrian barrages, were also significant factors. As regards diseases, the men of the IEF suffered more from enteric and dysentery, probably because of the lower standards of public health in Italy than France, and they also had to contend with malaria in the south of the country. However, like France, the biggest disease challenge was the outbreak of influenza which killed millions of people across Europe, civilians as well as military. Second only to influenza, in terms of hospital admissions, was Venereal Disease. Avoidable, yet somehow unavoidable, the rate of infection across British troops in Italy was higher than that in France in 1918. It has to be said that the medical services in Italy did a good job for battle and non-battle casualties, but they could not maintain the health of the troops on their own; they required the cooperation of the fighting units. While the DMS could provide bathing facilities and distribute instructions on the prevention of dysentery and VD, commanding officers were responsible for ensuring that their men availed themselves of the baths and took the recommended preventative measures against disease.

5

Maintaining morale: "Football was played during the morning"

'Morale is excellent'; Captain Hardie, the official censor, used this phrase to begin one of his reports on the IEF, but this could only ever be a subjective assessment of the mood and spirit of a largely conscripted military formation, whose everyday routine was governed by the exigencies of the service, backed up by the constraints of military discipline. Army commanders, from Haig down, believed that 'high' morale was essential when it came to combat, but how to measure it; how could a commander differentiate between units, or trace a single unit's level of morale over time?

Many of the men in the IEF had been in the army for a period of two to three years, and had taken part in combat during their time on the Western Front. Now, transported to a quieter part of the war, the challenge for their officers and NCOs was to maintain their military efficiency when the necessity for doing so seemed of less relevance to the troops. In his report on the early months of the IEF in Italy, based on men's comments in their letters home, Hardie declared that they were 'war-weary', 'fed up' and that there was 'a growing intensity of longing for Peace'.[1] That sentiment is not to be wondered at. The soldiers wanted to go home, and in the main they were civilians who had been conscripted into an army life which did not come naturally to them. But being 'fed up' does not automatically imply low morale. In a letter to his brother, Lamin put a slightly different spin on the attitude of himself and his mates; 'I hope this year sees the finish of the war, but I think that the enemy is more fed up than we are'.[2] Hardie convinced himself that his analysis of the men's comments allowed him to 'feel the pulse of the Army',[3] a rather pompous claim given that the troops knew that their letters were subject to censorship, and that it was wise to be cautious what they committed to paper. However, as Hardie based his claim on the contents of 'green envelopes' the difference between these and other letters should be made clear. Normally a soldier's letter home was subject to censorship by one of his

1   Hardie, Private Papers, report for February-July 1918.
2   Lamin, *Letters*, p.147.
3   Hardie, Private Papers, report 1916.

regimental officers, and most were opened. This reading of the letters was resented by the writer – 'an activity which I never regarded with favour'[4] – and it was considered as a 'tiresome fatigue'[5] by the officers. The authorities recognised the lack of privacy inherent in this system and introduced the 'green envelopes' as a way of alleviating some of the resentment. The 'greens' were rationed, one per man per fortnight, on the grounds that being scarce, they would not be abused. The soldier was 'on trust' not to write anything militarily sensitive and in exchange the 'green' would not be censored by his regimental officer, but it could be opened – on a sampling basis – further back up the line; and that is where Hardie came into the picture. However, knowing that the letters still stood a chance of being opened, and not wanting to lose his ration of 'greens' (they were regarded as a privilege which could be removed for disciplinary offences) the contents still needed to be treated with a 'health warning', if statements on a unit's morale were to be drawn from them. To take one example: In September 1917 Hardie submitted a report including a comment on the morale of the troops in France, this was based on an analysis of 4,552 green envelopes. In his sample only 21 men made direct references to 'war-weariness' which he translated as a 'weakening of moral' of less than 0.46% – to quote such a small change is akin to giving the senior commanders what they wanted to hear. However, on the basis of these numbers Hardie went on to inform the War Cabinet that; 'The British troops in France are very cheerful and determined, *and that the love of fighting has eradicated the peace-time habit of grousing*'.[6] [My italics]

To draw the conclusion that the soldiers had a 'love of fighting' was preposterous, and they certainly did not hold back on their grousing, either in France or Italy. The morale of an army formation, 'the moral component of fighting power', is difficult to quantify; 'It can neither be counted and costed, nor can it be accurately assessed through drill books, training manuals or pamphlets on doctrine'.[7] Gary Sheffield[8] also pointed out that the mood of the men should not be confused with their spirit (their resolve); their mood could vary daily with such mundane matters as the weather or the jam in the ration pack, while their spirit could remain steady and was dependent on many, often long-term, factors. An excerpt from Hardie's report in January 1917 (with the BEF) demonstrates how he characterised the mood and grousing of the men to his senior commanders, albeit with a very obvious 'positive spin':

At times he [the soldier] curses the Kaiser, the weather, the mud, the frost, the work, the food – but he curses with a cheeriness which shows that his grumbling and animosity, even against "old Bill", are little more than skin-deep, without

4   Gladden, *Piave*, p.103.
5   Carrington, *Soldier from the Wars Returning*, p.160.
6   TNA: CAB 24/26, Cabinet Minutes and Papers; 2001-2100, report 13 September 1917.
7   Holmes, *Tommy*, p.489.
8   Sheffield, *Officer-Man Relations*, pp.64-5.

any real bitterness or mistrust. Amid the noise and horror, shells, filth mud, gas, frost, and suffering, a man who is a cold, wet, dog-tired, lice-bitten, mud-clad object of misery cannot be expected to find that "all is for the best in the best of all possible worlds". The wonder is that so many of them do.[9]

While morale may have been difficult to measure objectively, there were things that commanders believed could be a drag on men's spirit – home leave and the regularity of mail – while others could improve it, largely by improving team spirit. Most soldiers acknowledged that their strongest loyalty was to their mates and the 'family' unit to which they belonged, usually a platoon, possibly the company, and sometimes their battalion. Rarely did men relate closely to their Division; it was too large at approximately 10,000 troops. In today's world of instant communication it is hard to understand the limited view that the ordinary soldier had of the war around him, consequently the commanders put a lot of effort into bolstering 'esprit de corps' within the smaller groups to which the men could relate. The unit war diaries are replete with entries regarding inter-unit sports, shooting, and 'Interior Economy' competitions, as well as encouraging the formation of concert groups to provide entertainment. In his excellent book on troop morale in the First World War John Fuller made the point that troop commanders faced similar problems, whichever part of the world they found themselves in:

> The strains on morale might be to some extent different in theatres other than the Western Front, with casualties generally lighter, and the problems of boredom, isolation, and maintaining a sense of purpose rather greater. However, the backgrounds of the men did not vary between theatres, and the varying problems of morale drew forth a remarkable and illuminating uniformity of response.[10]

There is a second reason for examining the activities put in place to maintain morale and that is to put some flesh on the bones of what the men did when they were not in the front-line. Part of the myth of the war is that the soldiers spent much of their time in forward positions, defending themselves against the enemy – that is simply not correct. Charles Carrington estimated that he was less than a third of a year in positions that could be described as 'under fire', the rest was spent some few hours march from the front, or a long way back in rest and training areas.[11] For the ordinary soldier, one of his main memories was being constantly 'buggered about'. In the words of one novelist 'the true image of bloody War' was 'the eternal waiting'.[12] The same point

9   Hardie, Private Papers, report January 1917.
10   J.G. Fuller, *Troop Morale and Popular Culture in the British and Dominion Armies 1914-1918* (Oxford, 1990), p.5.
11   Todman, *The Great War*. pp.4-5.
12   Ford, *Parade's End*, p.569.

was picked up by Thomas Weber in his history of Adolf Hitler's unit, the German List Regiment; 'most men spent far more of their time 'waiting'. Boredom was a more common feeling among the men of Hitler's regiment than either acute excitement or horror'.[13] The soldiers' experience of the war, whether on the Western or Italian Fronts, cannot be fully understood without some knowledge of what happened out of the trenches, it is not enough to concentrate on what Fuller called the 'surreal and fantastic world' of the front-line. Much of what he termed the 'surreal' world in which the soldiers lived has come to us through the popular novels of writers such as Pat Barker's *Regeneration* trilogy, and Sebastian Faulks's *Birdsong*. These books, with their common themes of men shot at dawn, horror, death and waste, tended to reflect 'the dominant myths of the culture that produced them. In repeating them, of course, they reinforced their power'.[14] Norman Gladden was in the battles at Messines, the Menin Road and Passchendaele, but it was not until June 1918 in Italy, 'nearly two years after I first went to France, [that] I had my first shot at the enemy. On the Western Front, even in an offensive, one rarely saw him until he was a prisoner'.[15] The same point was made by A.P. Herbert (who had seen action at Gallipoli, the Somme and Passchendaele) in his novel *The Secret Battle*: 'In France, apart from full-dress attacks, an infantryman may live for many months without once firing his rifle, or running the remotest risk of death by a rifle bullet'.[16] While the focus of many historians has been on the military action, to understand the lives of the soldiers we must pull back and look at the things which affected his motivation and the steps the authorities took to influence them.

If there was one topic that affected morale more than any other it was Home Leave, it was a constant theme in the men's letters home; where they were in the rota, when they might get home and what might occur to spoil their chances. As the censor phrased it in one of his reports, 'Blighty is the lodestar of their lives'.[17] Glad as they were to be in Italy, on a quiet front and away from the hell of Flanders, the soldiers recognised that the increased distance would lessen the opportunity to get home. Gladden was not unusual, and so serves as an example; after eight months in France with no home leave, and now on his way to Italy he knew that '[his] turn obviously lay too far ahead for me to derive much anticipatory pleasure' from the thought of leave. A researcher reading private papers at the Imperial War Museum soon comes to agree with Hardie's summary of the issue:

> The Army lives for leave; talks and writes of leave; thinks and dreams of leave. Nothing tends more to the encouragement of good Morale [*sic*] than a free

---

13   T. Weber, *Hitler's First War. Adolf Hitler, the Men of the List Regiment, and the First World War* (Oxford, 2010), pp.133-4.

14   Todman, *The Great War*, p.160.

15   Gladden, *Piave*, p.122.

16   A.P. Herbert, *The Secret Battle. A Tragedy of the First World War* (Barnsley, 2009), pp.42-3.

17   Hardie, Private Papers, report early 1917.

flow of leave; nothing is more conducive to grousing and despondency than its prolonged delay.[18]

If home leave had been at a premium in France, it was even more problematic in Italy. The only transportation was by train (in the cattle trucks they had experienced on the way down to Italy) on a journey which typically took five days each way. A photograph in the IWM archive[19] shows 18 men standing by one of these salubrious '*wagons-lit*', all smiling as they wait to depart – comfort or no, leave was leave. The letters and memoirs of those in the IEF bear testament to the few opportunities they had to get home to their families, and the strains this put on their personal relationships; in a sense the fact that the Italian Front was quiet only exacerbated the problem – "if there isn't much fighting, why can't I have time to go home?" Hugh Dalton, the young artillery officer who had arrived with the guns in mid-1917, noted in his memoir that soldiers in his battery had been 'without home leave for nineteen months', he went on to ask the same question as all soldiers; why could leave to England only be granted in special cases? With cynical tongue-in-cheek he explained that the reasons were given in circulars 'written by Staff officers of high rank, who had frequent opportunities of informing themselves of the realities of the situation, while visiting London'.[20] Dalton, like other regimental officers, resented the special privileges enjoyed by those on the Staff, although he recognised that he got more leave than the men.

The paucity of home leave is pointed out by Hardie in two examples from letters written by men of the IEF; one soldier knew to the day how long since he had last seen his wife, it had been "20 months and 7 days without a leave"; while another reminded his wife that it was 'very near three years since I last saw you'.[21] Men who had waited for leave while in France now found that they had to start all over again in Italy. While 'the gilded Staff' (Dalton's words) could rationalise the infrequent leave, the men's officers had twinges of guilt when they considered the differential treatment between themselves and their men. Carrington stated that while his turn for leave came round four times, this was 'twice what I should have got [if] I had been a private soldier'.[22] In the same vein Captain James Dible, a medical officer with the IEF, thought it inexcusable that he should get leave every 'six or seven months: the man gets his on an average of once in fifteen to nineteen months'.[23] Gary Sheffield and Richard Holmes have both written extensively on the British Army in World War One and a point which comes across from both is the paternal attitude displayed by young officers towards the welfare of their men. That concern of the junior officer towards the troops under him is demonstrated by Dible's reaction to one soldier's letter which he has had to read as

---

18   Hardie, Private Papers, report for October 1918, p.8.
19   IWM: Q 26117.
20   Dalton, *British Guns in Italy*, p.136.
21   Hardie, Private Papers, report October-January 1918.
22   Carrington, *Soldier from the Wars Returning*, p.168.
23   IWM: Doc. 10927, J.H.. Dible, *Private Papers, Part 1*, p.179.

the man's censor. The soldier complained to his family that: 'Here am I without leave for fourteen months while my officer has been home three times in the last eighteen', causing Dible to comment that 'the soldier must be a saint to watch the officer who refuses his leave after thirteen months, take his own every three or four'.[24]

Apart from drink, one way that the soldier could express his annoyance with the leave system was through the very popular 'Trench Journals', the best known of which is the *Wipers Times*. Written and produced by the men they were an outlet for frustrations and grousing, things could be written in the journal which, if said openly to an officer or NCO, might well have led to disciplinary proceedings – they were an irreverent comment on aspects of life in the army. The Worcestershire Regiment in Italy produced *The Old Firm Unlimited* which asked 'Who devised the present leave allotment, according to which the last man to go will wait until 1930?' The journals mocked the opportunity that leave taken in Italy – seen by the authorities as a substitute for home leave – might offer for playing the tourist, recommending that they might 'Rush Round Ruined Rome', 'Meander at Monte' or 'Mope at Marostica'. When Gladden did finally get a pass for leave in England he was 'almost speechless with joy'.[25] But some of the men believed that if they took leave in England then there was a risk that the authorities would divert them to France on their return journey, rather than allow them to proceed to the quiet of Italy. Hardie cited two such examples in his report in July 1918: 'I'd rather stay out here an [*sic*] forfeit all leave than go back there again. I've seen quite as much as I want to see of that country. But, here, things are very different. It's like one long holiday'; and the second one 'to tell you the truth none of us are in a hurry for leave as we might get dumped to France, a lot of the men here have not been on leave for 18 months and it is a bit of a job to get them to go'. These were minority views but they give an indication of how much safer the soldiers felt themselves to be in Italy, compared with the Western Front, that they were prepared to forgo home leave rather than risk redeployment to France.

Although the trench journals may have written a little cynically of the advantages of leave in Italy, some of the men did take the opportunity to visit cities like Venice and Rome. However, even leave within the country was granted less frequently than might be expected. Cassar stated that 'leave was *freely granted* to such centres as Rome, Padua and Venice'.[26] [My italics.] That may have been the case for officers but the accounts and letters of ordinary soldiers do not really support the statement. Such trips, as a break in routine, would have been news to include in letters home, yet Walton does not mention any, nor does Lambert. Skirth was granted permission to visit Rome, after the armistice, but he was then lucky enough to have this converted to home leave. Gladden had a day pass to Verona, but again this was after the war had ended. Another with an opportunity for some free days in an Italian city was Lamin,

---

24   Dible, Private Papers, pp.180-1.
25   Gladden, *Piave*, p.146.
26   Cassar, *The Forgotten Front*, p.118.

but that was not until February 1919; he described Venice as 'one of the wonderfulest [*sic*] cities in Italy [...] We put up at the Grand Canal Hotel, and we was [*sic*] alright'.[27] It is unlikely that if the others had made similar trips, that they would have made no mention of them to their families, visiting these places was so far removed from the life at home that they would have been news, if not something to boast about.

Soldiers on leave, especially if that was taken in Italy rather than at home, might have been tempted to drink too much and seek out the company of prostitutes – the need to counter those urges may have influenced the army when it set up a rest camp at Sermione on the shore of Lake Garda. To accommodate the camp two large hotels and some abandoned villas were hired in the town; in the words of the official historian these allowed the men 'to idle their time away in bathing, fishing and taking trips by motor launch, with open-air concerts and a theatre to amuse them in the evening'.[28] The description does not sound likely to have fired the men's enthusiasm, although some who had visited did write positively of their stay; 'a marvellous leave, I think the troops deserve it [the old hotel] and the lads were very grateful to those who arranged it';[29] while Hardie recorded one as writing that he had 'had the time of my life'.[30] On the other hand Gladden, in a rather prim style, reminds us that soldiers, prostitutes and venereal disease frequently found a way of coming together; at Sermione the men were 'too effusively welcomed by the ladies of the town, [who] were soon furnishing an excessive number of patients for the army hospitals'.[31] The camp at Sermione also provides the researcher with the opportunity to see how different historical sources can treat the same subject. Dalton was a young officer who spent time at the camp and wrote his memoir shortly after the war, in 1919. Edmonds, the Official Historian, was a Brigadier who had spent no time at Sermione and wrote his history of the Italian campaign in 1949. Edmonds's picture of the camp gives the establishment view of what was on offer:

> The men staying there were under no description of discipline. Leave was also granted to Rome, Florence, Naples, Pompeii and Venice, where arrangements were made to show the sights to the visiting troops.[32]

Dalton's recollection, set down shortly after the war, was quite different:

> A series of rules was drawn up, that none of us might be led into any avoidable temptation. All towns within reach, Milan, Verona, Mantua, Brescia, Peschiera, were placed out of bounds. So, too, were some of the larger villages on the shores

27   Lamin, *Letters*, p.183.
28   Edmonds, *Italy*, pp.174-5.
29   IWM: Doc. 11465, H. Warner, *Private Papers*.
30   Hardie, Private Papers, report February-July 1918.
31   Gladden, *Piave*, p.109.
32   Edmonds, *Italy*, p.175.

of the lake. The hours during which alcoholic liquor might be obtained, either in the Hotels or in the Cafes of Sermione, were narrowly limited. Beer was strictly rationed.[33]

It is difficult to believe that the two writers were describing the same place although Dalton did also go on to say that the place was 'wonderfully beautiful' and the ground was 'thickly carpeted with wild mint and thyme'.

More than any other, there was one time of the year that was guaranteed to bring home to the men the distance they were from home and the separation from their families, and that was Christmas. The majority of the men of the IEF had to spend two Christmas seasons in Italy, one at war and one after the armistice; many would also have had at least one in France. Most units went out of their way to provide a celebration for the men. For troops used to the routine of army fare they would have relished the large festive lunch that the cooks invariably produced, followed by sports and a fair amount to drink. Although the meal was cooked by the Army Catering Corps, contributions also came from other sources. The Italian Touring Club distributed Christmas gifts to '75 officers and 500 Other Ranks of XI Corps' on 24 December 1917. Also the British Red Cross (BRC), who had been in Italy since 1915, was generous to the troops in 1917 and 1918, supplying them with turkeys which the men had to pluck themselves. The BRC gets little mention in the military histories, but it had been represented in Italy throughout the war, and its help was especially appreciated at Christmas; they supplied 'funds to provide turkeys, fruit etc. [...] for the patients' of some of the hospitals;[34] at 24 CCS they 'provided 22 turkeys for patients' dinners, also money for fruit and a present for each patient';[35] while 39 CCS which had purchased its own turkeys would have 'the amount for them refunded by the Red Cross'. All of these units, for which the BRC provided either turkeys or funds, were in the rear, support areas. The war diaries of the forward area battalions make no mention of the BRC contributing to their Christmas meals. The festivities enjoyed by the men in Italy were similar to those which would also have been on-going behind the front in France, and the diary of the 8th York & Lancaster battalion will serve as an example for them all:

Xmas Day. At 7.0 am the battalion awoke and wished each other a 'Merry Xmas Day'. All were busy putting finishing touches to decorations, etc. At 10:30 am a Church Service was held in B Coy [sic, company] billet by the Rev. Maynard. The battalion sat down at 12:30 noon to enjoy its Xmas Dinner. Each company had a room apart in its own billet which was decorated – no place being available for a whole battalion. The men thoroughly enjoyed their meal which composed

33   Dalton, *British Guns in Italy*, p.137.
34   TNA: WO 95/4198, December 1918.
35   TNA: WO 95/4207, war diary 24 CCS, December 1918.

of: Pork, Beef, potatoes, vegetable, Xmas pudding, beer and rum punch. At 2:30 pm an inter-Coy. football match was played. At 7:30 pm a concert was held in B Coy. billet which was enjoyed by all ranks. Lights out at 10:0 pm.[36]

Christmas was a special time and one when the families at home and the troops abroad would have had particular cause to regret their separation, but for men who had been away for upwards of three years, with only infrequent visits home, staying in touch with loved ones was vitally important for morale. And that is as true today for soldiers as it was then. Television footage has frequently shown helicopters re-supplying troops in forward bases in Afghanistan, and among the most important cargo is the mail – even with mobile phones, email and social media, physical mail (snail-mail) is a great morale booster. In spite of the upheaval of deployment from Flanders to Italy, the post was in place surprisingly quickly and operating regularly, which reflected the level of importance accorded it by the army authorities. The service was intermittent for the first four or five weeks, but Vere Cotton, a young officer, was very harsh with his comment of 23 November (only about three weeks after arriving) as he and others relied on it for the supply of English newspapers, and so for news of the war:

The so-called mail service is beneath contempt. The last papers (English) we have seen are November 9th, and but for about one small paragraph in the Italian papers daily we know no more about the war than the inhabitants of Greenland.[37]

When the British took part in the assault across the River Piave in October 1918, which resulted in the Austrian armistice, Cotton was running a training school. Out of touch with events he commented to his mother that; 'As you will have seen from the papers, this front has at last woken up a bit and scrapping has become general, *so I am told*. As a matter of fact I know probably less about it than you do'.[38] [My italics] The post, and the newspapers, was vital in an age before modern communications. George Walton, who either wrote letters or postcards almost every day (army routine permitting), let his family know in mid-December that 'the post seems to be in regular order now'.[39] Using the dates on letters sent to Harry Lamin, and his reference to them in his replies, it is possible to see that the mail was taking approximately one week from family to soldier. Given that the train took five days it is fair to say that once up and running, the postal service was effective, and quick enough for the soldiers to stay abreast of family news. But grousing was almost a competitive sport in the army, and some would still be complaining in January 1918: 'Why is it that newspapers

36   TNA: WO 95/4240, 8 York & Lancs, 25 December 1917.
37   Cotton, Private Papers, Part 2, p.245.
38   Cotton, Private Papers, Part 3, p.190.
39   Walton, postcard, 15 December 1917.

from London always arrive here in four, sometimes three days, while letters invariably take from five to seven days, and sometimes longer'.[40] The real message behind
this 'gripe' is the importance that the soldiers placed on the regular delivery of mail;
it was up there with home leave as a morale issue that commanders had to pay attention to. Because the mail system was liable to interruptions, especially if the men's
units moved their physical location, soldiers devised their own systems to keep track
of the correct sequence of letters, so knowing if they had missed any. Walton and his
family used letters of the alphabet, each mail item taking the next letter in sequence;
on 15 December 1917 he wrote that he had received E and G (so he and the family
knew he had not received 'F'), and again on 14 March 1918, by which time they had
started another round of the alphabet, 'received F and G yesterday'. As well as keeping
track of the sequence of the mail, soldiers were also keen that their families should
not worry unnecessarily if unit movements caused a gap in the post received at home;
'May write again this week but do not get alarmed if stoppage of letters occurs again'.[41]
A constant theme of soldiers' letters home was a wish to reassure the family that the
man was alright and that nothing sinister should be read into a break in the stream
of letters.

I am very grateful to Clare Pilkington, the grand-daughter of George Walton, who
I met on a battlefield tour of Italy. Clare gave me transcripts of the 111 postcards that
her grandfather had sent from Italy between 12 November 1917 and 23 December
1918, and permission to use them as I saw fit in this book. Walton was not alone in
making great use of postcards, they were quick to write, easily available in local towns
and also in the soldiers' unit canteens. Two types of picture-postcard were particularly
popular with the men; some were in a series such as flowers or birds while others,
probably the most used, had photos or drawings of Italian towns, buildings or scenes.
For men who had travelled little, and their families even less, these vignettes of Italian
life were a form of armchair tourism. Walton had a young son and so he enjoyed
trying to get complete sets of cards for him and his wife; 'This is the 1st [*sic*] of a new
series I have got, the majority roses. Not sufficient of an expert to classify them'.[42]
Those cards with photos or drawings of towns that soldiers had either been billeted in,
or visited, served to make closer connection between the man in Italy and the family
at home. Walton again: '[Milan] Supposed to be one of the prettiest cathedrals in the
world'; and a later card, 'This is the village where I went to see about buying you a good
scarf'. Ronald Skirth also sent picture cards to his girlfriend, one of them showing
the building he had stayed in, 'San Martino, near Vicenza, northern Italy. My first
"residence" on Italian soil. January 1918. Casa Bianca marked with an "X"'.[43]

40   Hardies, Private Papers, report January 1918.
41   Walton, postcard, 30 April 1918.
42   Walton, postcard, 6 May 1918.
43   Barrett, (ed.), Reluctant Tommy, p.139.

Important as the mail system was for delivering news from home, it could also deliver those small reminders of life in Blighty which were more difficult (if not impossible) to find in Italy; items such as favourite foods, books, clean socks, soap and cigarettes. Cakes were important, as they could be shared with friends, but the men would also ask for many small things that could relieve the boredom of eating the same food over and over again – what the modern army calls 'menu fatigue'. The repetitive nature of the content of army meals was summed up by Skirth's comment on the jam in their ration packs, supplied by a firm called Ticklers:

> One of the Great War's minor unsolved mysteries is where Ticklers got all their plums and apples from! I was in the war for 2 1/2 years and never saw any 'issue' jam that wasn't plum and apple – and I never met any long-serving soldier who did either.[44]

The contents of food parcels were especially valued by the troops, as they were 'tangible indications of love and support'[45] from the wives and mothers who had packed them. The sharing of food parcels was part of the bonding that went on within small groups, although the soldiers are unlikely to have called it 'bonding'. Gladden writes of a typical delivery to a man in his billet:

> All over Britain at that time motherly women, lonely women, hiding an endless heart-ache, were for ever packing with loving fingers those carefully thought-out parcels to the front. We each looked forward to our own especial package and none was more welcomed than the budget of good things that came regularly from that poor Bradford home [of his friend], put together at who knows what sacrifice in those poverty-stricken times.[46]

Even though the men knew that there was food rationing at home they would still ask for special treats that they could not get in the field, and which would relieve the boredom of eating the same food, day after day. Lamin was particularly fond of tinned salmon, and at least three of his letters express his pleasure at being sent some; 'the salmon was alright and tasted a treat'.[47] While tinned salmon stood a good chance of surviving the journey to Italy in one piece, the contents of some food parcels never stood a chance; 'the tomatoes, the woodbines and the chocolate was [sic] all in one, and was it butter that you put in the parcel?'[48] In this example the family member meant well, but sending tomatoes to Italy shows how little they knew back home

---

44   Skirth, Private Papers, Vol. 3, p.172.
45   R. Duffett, *Beyond the Ration*, p.460.
46   Gladden, *Piave*, p.99.
47   Lamin, *Letters*, p.123.
48   Hardie, Private Papers, report January 1918.

about the country in which their loved one was fighting, or the fragility of the fruit – butter and cigarettes was also an unfortunate combination in a hot climate. If there was one commodity which, if scarce, could seriously affect the mood of the troops it was tobacco; almost any group photograph of soldiers will show a very large proportion of them smoking, and any shortage of 'fags' would be the cause of a great deal of grousing. If the men could not get cigarettes they would smoke tea leaves 'with apparent enjoyment'[49] and so there is little wonder that many of the men's letters home asked for tobacco to supplement what they could buy through their local canteens. The soldiers' nicotine craving, especially when it was hard to come by, was a fertile topic for the cynical trench journals. The Fifth Glo'ster had a spoof 'Letter from Italy' in which the soldier tells his wife that 'I should like some fags as soon as you can get them. We cannot get fags for love or money, dear wife, out here so please send them to me as soon as possible'.[50] Although Italian tobacco could be had, it was considered very inferior to British products but, when needs must:

> News that a few Italian cigarettes were obtainable in a distant village led to an immediate rush of hundreds of men. Cheap Italian cigarettes need to be smoked for this latter fact to be fully appreciated![51]

One of Edward Brittain's letters from Italy to his sister Vera demonstrates how young regimental officers were sufficiently concerned about their men that some used their own money to buy cigarettes for the troops at Christmas. In December 1917 Brittain 'sent for cigarettes for the men hoping they would arrive by Xmas; 4500 arrived the night before last which enabled us to give 25 to each man. It was impossible to get cigarettes of any sort here until quite recently'.[52]

To enable the men to buy postcards, cigarettes, soap and other small items the army had established Expeditionary Force Canteens (EFC). The EFCs were effectively the fore-runner of the NAAFI[53], and were organised centrally rather than by individual units. However, as EFCs tended to be in rear and rest areas, battalions usually set up their own 'tuck-shop', under the charge of a junior officer. These outlets sold items of food, postcards, writing paper, soap and a multitude of other small 'luxuries' that made the men's lives that little bit more bearable. The larger EFCs were very popular with the troops. Gladden describes visiting two which were 'stocked with English food of all kinds',[54] and by the end of the war there were 26 in Italy and 284 in France.[55] The IEF was particularly well served as with only 4% of the

49   Gladden, Piave, p.98.
50   Fifth Glo'ster, July 1918.
51   Lambert, Over the Top, p.103.
52   Bishop and Bostridge, (eds.), Lost Generation, p.388.
53   The Navy, Army and Air Force Institutes (NAAFI) started in 1921.
54   Gladden, Piave, p.100.
55   TNA: WO 95/394/11, report 26, December 1918.

troop numbers in the BEF, Italy had 8% of all official canteens. On top of that the soldiers in the IEF seem to have been bigger spenders than their BEF colleagues, as they put across the EFC counters the Sterling equivalent of 6% of the money spent in France. The greater density of EFCs in Italy than France may reflect the recognition by the authorities that the soldier in the IEF had less opportunity to buy what he needed in the local communities than his BEF colleagues. But, well served as they were by EFCs, it was the battalion and unit canteens that would be most visited by the men, and which could be a headache for the young officer 'volunteered' to run it. Graham Greenwell had that responsibility at one point in France and recorded being told by his Colonel to:

> buy the food for all the canteens in the regiment – a most frightful job, [...] I am now frantically trying to make the accounts balance – an impossible task, as I have been catering for about six different sets of men, with millions of different articles from Beecham's Pills to bloater paste.[56]

The urge to supplement the army diet is not something unique to the soldiers of World War One. Patrick Hennessey was a young officer in Afghanistan and after spending a week in a forward Patrol Base he describes 'cramming junk food in the NAAFI, coming back up on the sugar high with the sickening combo of blue Gatorade, ice-cream and toffee popcorn'.[57]

Communicating with his loved ones at home kept the soldier in touch with family news and allowed him to reassure them that he was still alive and well. This vital link was maintained by (infrequent) leave passes and an effective letter and parcel service between Britain and Italy. Important as these were for the morale of the troops they needed to be supplemented by activities which would keep the men fit, strengthen team spirit and maintain their motivation to be militarily effective if they were called on to go into combat. Most men would not have wanted to fight; they were conscripts who would rather have been at home. However, when asked why they fought most replied that they did it 'for their mates', they did not want to let them down, or to be thought to have done so. Ian Bellany described the soldier's situation in terms of the 'prisoner's dilemma'.[58] If everyone 'did his bit' then there was a good chance that the whole force would do well. On the other hand the individual could rationalise that his own contribution was minuscule, compared to the whole, and if he avoided risk it would have no discernible effect on the total endeavour. On the other hand, if he did pull his weight he increased his chance of injury or death. But, if one individual thought that way, so could the whole force; it was the job of the men's officers and NCOs to instil

56 Greenwell, *Infant in Arms*, p.66.
57 P. Hennessey, *The Junior Officers' Reading Club. Killing Time and Fighting Wars* (London, 2009), p.194.
58 I. Bellany, 'Men at War: The Sources of Morale', *RUSI Journal*, Vol. 148 (2003), pp.58-62.

in the troops the notion that they should all 'pull their weight'. Therefore concentrating on the individual as part of a small team was the focus of all the IEF inter-unit competitions, many of which, but not all, were based on sport. Demographics dictated that the majority of the ordinary soldiers were working-class men from the industrial cities, and the sport which they had grown up with was football; requiring only a ball and something to designate goal-posts it could be played anywhere, at any time, and all knew the rules – or enough to make a game. Italians also knew the game, having had city football clubs since the 1890s, so it is not surprising that 'internationals' were staged between the IEF and their ally. One side effect of these competitions was that the British Tommy, at least for the 90 minutes of a match, might drop his unflattering opinion of the Italians as fighters. On 13 March 1918 a game was played between No. 9 CCS and 17th Group *Aerosteric* [sic] *Italiana*, this 'exceedingly friendly and fast game resulted in the Italians winning by 3-2'.[59] Honours were evened the following week when the Italians lost 0-3.

Useful as the internationals were for inter-ally cooperation and understanding, the main focus was on competitions between British units. Without a doubt, within the IEF, football was *the* inter-unit sport, promoting rivalry and *esprit de corps*. Competitions were held at all levels, from company upwards, and as long as there was a spare patch of ground and a ball, there was a chance of a game; the 9th York and Lancaster battalion, en-route to relieve an Italian unit on the Montello, stopped to play a game.[60] Commanding officers were very keen to foster this competitive spirit, so much so that the COs of two battalions privately covered the expense of leasing a field near Azignano to allow the men to play sport.[61] Football was regarded as an essential tool in the maintenance of the men's morale, as well as keeping them fit and providing an outlet for their energy and frustration. The extent to which the sport played an important role in the life of the soldier was summarised by Sandilands in his 1925 history of the 23rd Division:

> The present generation must always wonder how the British Army continued to exist before the introduction of football. Nowadays to throw a football to a British soldier is like giving a bone to a dog; it will keep him content for hours, and ease his mind of the horrors and hardships he has endured.[62]

But sport had another beneficial effect, where it involved officers and ordinary soldiers it allowed a level of physical contact and verbal abuse that would not have been permitted under normal off-the-field discipline. Although many of the young officers had come from schools where rugby, rather than soccer, was the main sport,

---

59   TNA: WO 95/4207, war diary 9 CCS, 13 March 1918.
60   Lamin, *Letters*, p.107.
61   TNA: WO 95/4240, war diaries of 9th York & Lancs, 1-12 May 1918.
62   Sandilands, *The 23rd Division*, p.232.

it did not catch on with the men. There are few references to the game in unit war diaries within the IEF. One exception to this was the 2nd Gordon Highlanders who recorded playing a game against 35 Brigade RFA at Christmas, 1917. As far as the ordinary soldiers were concerned, rugby was an officers' sport which had little place in their working-class upbringing; it 'occupied a distant second place compared to the popularity of soccer with troops on active service'.[63]

Competitive sport was all about team identity and loyalty, and that could be accomplished through spectating as well as by participation; turning out to cheer (and jeer) was a big part of the event. And it was not all about the 'beautiful game'; although boxing pitted one man against another each represented a unit and so become *their* man. Boxing was, and still is, popular in the armed services, with regular inter-service competitions today between the Navy, Army and Air Force. The atmosphere at these events is shown in an IWM photograph[64] of an open-air boxing match taking place in Italy in September 1918; hundreds of men in uniform crowding around the ring to cheer on their man. But sports did not all have to be about serious competition, there could be a large element of fun and humour, especially when events included; Tug of War; 'mop fighting' (jousting with wet floor mops); and 'tilting at the bucket' (getting a wooden pole through a hole in a bucket while being pushed along in a wheel-barrow).[65] While sport was important for morale, it could also help to relieve tension; the Gordon Highlanders were on stand-by to support the front-line during the Austrian attack in June, but were not required to go forward – they were stood down and 'the Battalion had one hours [*sic*] physical training and sports'.[66] In an earlier chapter the point was made that personal hygiene and tidiness were important in fighting disease, as well as engendering pride in personal discipline – why not also make some of this competitive? Many of the war diaries have references to 'Interior Economy' competitions – roughly translated as tidiness, cleanliness and efficiency. Examples from the 23rd Division war diaries are competitions 'for the improvement of cook-houses, horse lines, etc'. In the Field Artillery saddlery and harness were polished and judged, infantry units held regular duels on the rifle range to win cups for the best shooting while regimental bands, especially 'pipers and drummers' were sent to play in Rome for a week in March and in Bologna for three days in December 1918. Officers and NCOs put a lot of time and effort into organising a variety of competitions to keep the men occupied and maintain a high level of morale, but sports and 'interior economy' were not the only weapons in the fight to keep spirits up.

One of the tools in the armoury of the British soldier in his battle against boredom, mindless fatigues and the pettiness of military discipline was humour; he could use it

63   T. Collins, 'English Rugby Union and the First World War', *Historical Journal*, Vol. 45, (2002), p.805.
64   IWM: Q 25828.
65   TNA: WO 95/4224, war diary 2nd Gordon Highlanders, 3 September 1918.
66   TNA: WO 95/4224.

to mock his own situation, but if done properly, he could also poke fun at his officers and those who were running the war. One example that has already been mentioned is the trench journal which allowed the editorial teams to express the frustrations of the ordinary soldiers. The decision to allow these publications was a brave one as it did not take a genius to realise that they would take aim at many aspects of army routine, all of which were governed by identifiable officers or NCOs, a point alluded to by the foreword to the first edition of *The Old Firm*;[67]

> We sincerely hope that our thinly veiled personal allusions will cause no offence in any quarter, as most certainly none is intended. Pure fun without malice has been our aim, and if any think himself aggrieved we cordially invite him to take his revenge by contributing to future numbers.

Within their pages the journals could poke fun at senior officers with a level of impunity. Although officers and their men shared many hardships in the front-line, there was still a huge gap between them; for example, officers had 'batmen', or servants, who 'did' for them even in the dugouts; Blackadder's servant, Baldrick, probably being the best known. The men would have seen the humour – and hopefully the officers would too – in a question posed by *The Old Firm*; 'Whether the Officer's servant receives extra pay in proportion to the number of times he comes in and says, "Now Sir, you really must get up"'.

Popular as the journals were, the real hit with the troops were the concert parties and mobile cinemas, both of which allowed the men to be entertained in large groups. The music hall and slap-stick comedy films had been popular forms of entertainment before the war started, and were relatively easy to deliver to the troops in their rest areas. One officer, with a tongue in cheek reference to the quietness of the Italian Front, wrote home that if he were to be asked 'Daddy, what did you do in the great War?' he would be able to answer 'I went to see Charlie Chaplin on the Movies'.[68] But the biggest hit with the men was not the mobile cinema but the concert groups, which were almost universally praised in letters, memoirs and war diaries. Modern readers have to remember that at that time there was no television, entertainment – except for vinyl records and the cinema – was live, the music hall was enormously popular with its comedy and singing and this formed the model for the divisional concert groups. These groups were drawn from the soldiers within a division, and there were always some who had a penchant for acting, singing and performing on some form of stage. They made their own costumes, men played female parts, and they would mock the war, themselves and the powers that be. The authorities quickly realised how popular the troupes were with the men, war diaries frequently refer to performances being 'full', and these were not just occasional shows. The concert groups were so well

---

67   *The Old Firm*, February 1918.
68   Cotton, *Private Papers*, Part 2, p.76.

supported by the authorities and the men that they became effectively permanent units within the divisions, with 250 or more concerts a year by each group. The three divisions who were in Italy all through 1918 each had their own concert group, which toured through the rest areas and hospitals; 7 Division, the 'What Nots'; 23 Division, 'The Dumps' and 48 Division the 'Curios'. Their popularity was enormous, drawing appreciative comments in war diaries – 'a really excellent show'[69] – and memoirs – a 'rollocking show'.[70] Lambert describes a show given on the Asiago plateau by the 'What Nots' who may well have arrived at their venue as they did in Figure 5.1,[71] on the back of a farm wagon drawn by two horses. As the units were mobile their theatre was often an outdoor stage, with little in the way of sets or changing rooms – but let Lambert set the scene:

> The "What Nots" made up in full view of the audience. Men in fearsome baggy trousers and khaki tunics were dabbing vivid paint on their faces between puffs at cigarettes, and the 'girl' of the party, in pink stockings, satin petticoat, and army shirt, was alternately putting on garments and taking long draughts of beer from a mess tin.

The men loved it, even though the cast and audience were soaked in a rainstorm. Lambert goes on to give an insight into the 'sex starved' environment in which cast and spectators lived where, after the show, the performers' sodden garments were hung on a line to dry; 'Quite a crowd gathered round two pairs of silk stockings, a satin petticoat, three dresses and a pair of corsets. They were a strange sight in that Eve-less horrible place'.[72] There is little doubt, from all the soldiers' reminiscences, that unit cohesion benefited from these concerts, but there was one way in which they differed from the music halls of Blighty; they did not go in for jingoism. Back home the halls were full of calls to 'beat the Hun', a sentiment that grated with soldiers when they were home on leave, especially as it was voiced most strongly by women and old men who were unlikely to have to fight. For the men of the IEF the concert parties met a number of needs; they allowed for whole units to appreciate an evening's entertainment together, they were a vehicle for the cast to express the soldiers' frustrations in a way that was humorous and safe from disciplinary action, and they were to some extent a link with the world back in Blighty, where audiences could go out of an evening just to have a good time and escape the daily routine.

The soldiers of the IEF had the advantage over their comrades on the Western Front that they had a much higher chance of surviving the war. However, the safer environment carried with it the risk of boredom and frustration – what is the point of

69   TNA: WO 95/4224, 2nd Gordon Highlanders, June 1918.
70   Gladden, *Piave*, p.88.
71   IWM: Q 25915.
72   Lambert, *Over the Top*, p.175.

Figure 5.1 "The What Nots" 7th Divisional Concert Party. Tressino, September 1918.
(© Imperial War Museum Q 25915)

practicing assaults if you don't do any – which unit commanders took steps to combat. At the heart of the army's efforts to maintain morale was its paternalistic approach to leadership, an ethos drummed into the young officers during their training (as it still is today), and which they then took with them to the front-line. This was not an easy role for a platoon or company officer, many in their late-teens and frequently younger (with less life experience) than the men they commanded; the recent books by Lewis-Stempel and Moore-Bic give an excellent background to the war as experienced by these young men. Once the IEF was established in Italy it was the responsibility of the regimental officers, together with their unit NCOs, to focus on the 'hygiene'[73] factors essential to the maintenance of group morale; mail, food, physical activity, entertainment and home leave. In Italy, in spite of some early complaints, the men were as well served by the postal service as those in France, although distance made it slower, it was regular and dependable. Humour provided a safety valve for frustrations with the army in general, and the war in particular. On deployment to Italy the divisions took with them the trench journals, concert troupes and cinemas which they had established in France, all of which provided humorous alternatives to the soldier's inveterate love of grousing, although it could never replace it. This tradition continues

73   A term used by Fredrick Herzberg in *The Motivation to Work* (New York, 1959) for understanding the factors important in employee satisfaction and motivation.

today (though with a twist to take account of modern technologies) in the form of squaddies in Afghanistan producing 'spoof' Christmas videos on You Tube. Sport was the biggest outlet for the energy and competitive spirit of the men.

With the Italian Front being quieter than that in France and Flanders there was a greater need for activities to occupy the troops, and more opportunity for them to participate. Inter-unit competitions were strongly promoted by Commanding Officers, some of whom donated cups as prizes (General Shoubridge was one, as was the Italian General, Luca Montuori), some even leased sports grounds at their own expense. But, by far the biggest morale issue that commanders had to contend with was the paucity of home leave, for which time taken off in Italy was seen as no substitute. The distance from the UK, together with the slow journey time and lack of sufficient transport, made it a different problem from that in France. According to Nigel Jones 'It was possible for an officer [in France] to receive his ticket of leave at dawn in the trenches and to be watching a popular show such as Chu Chin Chow in London that same evening';[74] but not if he was based in Italy. To his credit Lord Cavan recognised the potential this had to influence morale and the need to try to improve it, but that would have presented operational problems for his force. In August 1918 he informed the War Office that if the IEF could have been taken out of the line then, he would have 'at once ask[ed] for facilities to send 1600 [men] a week, and so try and clear off our arrears'.[75] At that time he had no idea that the Italians might decide to attack the Austrians in October, and so he believed that the war would continue into 1919. Circumstances changed, as is described in Chapter Eight, and Cavan did not have the opportunity to pursue his suggestion. Although the mood of the soldiers varied during 1918, as their letters and memoirs record, their morale remained good. Although they were tired of the war, and many would have been in their fourth year, they expressed the belief that they had to 'stick it out' until Germany was beaten, if only to honour those of their comrades who had died: 'Just think what an insult it would be to all the lads who have gone west'.[76] In October 1918 two divisions of the IEF spearheaded the assault against the Austrians across the river Piave, while the third drove north from the Asiago. In these two assaults the British soldiers demonstrated that their morale, difficult and subjective though it was to measure, was high and translated into a keen fighting spirit and the defeat of the Austrians.

74   N. Jones, 'Living and dying in the trenches', First World War supplement, *Sunday Telegraph*, 1 June 2014, p.5.
75   TNA: WO 106/852, memo to CIGS, 1 August 1918.
76   Hardie, *Private Papers*, 12 February 1918.

6

Crime and punishment:
"In war kid-glove methods cannot always be employed"

Discipline is a central tenet of a military force, and the need for it takes on a particular significance when the men who make up that formation are called on to hold themselves in readiness to kill others. Enforcing discipline on a citizen army, formed mainly of conscripts, heightens the challenge for those in authority. When a man joined the British army, whether as a volunteer or as a conscript, he became subject to a legal code under which, 'in all times and in all places' his conduct – as an officer as much as an ordinary soldier – would be 'regulated by military law'.[1] As we will see, soldiers' actions could be subject to different interpretations, leading to different sentences for what was ostensibly the same crime. To the military authorities good morale (and so fighting spirit) was synonymous with good discipline; the latter had to be enforced to ensure the former. In the same way, if morale dropped then the argument was made that discipline would suffer; whether the consequent tightening of discipline would actually result in a natural increase in morale is probably a moot point.

Because of the presumed tight relationship between the level of indiscipline in a unit, and its morale, the number of courts martial held each month was taken to be an indicator of the quality of leadership of that unit's officers. It was natural then that commanders assessed their performance against the weekly and monthly reports submitted to Divisional, Corps and Army headquarters; were there more or less in any month, and how did that compare with other similar formations? Discipline, as measured by these trial statistics, came to be a measure of morale, leadership and fighting efficiency. This chapter will highlight differences between the BEF and the IEF in the way in which disciplinary cases were handled, and the sentences awarded. In that analysis we need to be cognisant of the fact that the officers were aware that they were also being judged on the way in which they upheld discipline – harsh sentences could be a consequence of a commander feeling that he had to be seen to be addressing 'morale', rather than the offence itself requiring a stiff penalty. Sadly, some of those

---

1   Holmes, *Tommy*, p.555 – cites Manual of Military Law.

soldiers who were executed, while found guilty of the offence, were condemned to death because the discipline of the man's unit was felt to be in need of improvement – had he been in a different battalion he might have lived.

Illness and indiscipline were considered to be interrelated; an increase in the former indicating a possible downturn in the latter. But these assumptions are too simplistic. According to one historian[2] the IEF sickness rate, together with the large number of courts martial trials in the first quarter of 1918, was 'probably a symptom of crumbling morale'. That analysis does not account for the fact that when the influenza epidemic reached its summer peak in June, three times the illness rate of January, and the number of trials was down to half of the January total – the causal link is looking thin. The difficulty inherent in attempting to draw a direct correlation between illness, disciplinary returns and morale (let alone 'fighting spirit' and leadership) is demonstrated by comparing the British Fifth Army on the Western Front with the IEF. For this exercise I am grateful for the data provided in David Englander's article, *Discipline and Moral in the British army.*[3] When the German army launched Operation Michael on 21 March 1918 my grandfather became one of the 21,000 British POWs captured that day; General Sir Hubert Gough's Fifth Army had just experienced their own Caporetto. The German breakthrough has been widely attributed to a failure in morale among Gough's troops, possibly caused by high casualty rates in the previous year's fighting – Gough was consequently relieved of command. In the three months prior to the German assault Fifth Army had averaged 1.28 courts martial, per month, per 1,000 men; this was a large increase on the 0.82 average for the months of September, October and November. Reviewing these reports after the events of 21 March would have allowed the British collapse to be attributed to poor morale, which of course was down to poor leadership, so Gough had to go. No doubt this was partly true but the dense fog at the time of the assault, allied to the implementation of storm-troop tactics (which allowed for rapid penetration of the British front-line), also played a massive part in the German success.

In the same months that Fifth Army's measure of courts martial climbed to 1.28, the newly deployed IEF recorded a figure of 2.57. Applying the same logic, this figure indicated that the men who were writing to tell their families how pleased they were to escape the hell of Flanders, had a morale 'quotient' that was half that of those still suffering on the Western Front. In June 1918 the IEF had its first taste of full-scale action when the Austrians attacked their positions on the Asiago plateau. In the three months prior to the assault the IEF recorded 2.21 trials per month, per 1,000 men; down from earlier in the year but still a lot higher than Fifth Army just prior to its retreat. The IEF, in spite of being seriously affected in May and June by the influenza epidemic, withstood the Austrian attack and by the end of the second day was back

2   G. Oram, 'Pious Perjury: Discipline and Morale in the British Force in Italy, 1918-1918', *War in History*, 9 (2002), p.430.
3   Englander, *Discipline and morale in the British army*, pp.134-5.

in possession of all the ground lost during the assault. The lowered fighting spirit which such a high trial count might have implied did not manifest itself. Similarly, in the three months prior to their participation in the Allied drive across the River Piave, which resulted in Austrian capitulation, the 'discipline measure' for the IEF stood at 1.66. Again this was down on the similar figure for earlier in the year, but it was still appreciably higher than Gough's Army had recorded before morale failure 'caused' their collapse and retreat. By contrast, Cavan's troops fought extremely well in October 1918, with their advance outstripping that of the Italians on both flanks of the IEF. On five of the months between April and December 1917, Fifth Army returned a trial figure per month below 1.0; the IEF signally failed to get their number down to that of Gough's army for the whole time that they were in Italy. On the raw numbers used in this comparative study the IEF should have had morale much lower than that of Fifth Army when it was overwhelmed by the Germans in March 1918. On the contrary, however, Cavan's men showed great fighting spirit (admittedly against Austrians and not Germans, but you can only fight the enemy in front of you) when called on to do so in June and October 1918. Assessing an army's morale, or the leadership qualities of its commanders, is not something which can simply be reduced to a table of comparative statistics, a point which Englander summed up well:

> More needs to be known about generals as decision-takers, and about how the information that was available to them was organized, read and understood, before sound judgements can be reached.[4]

It is as true today as it was in the First World War that one of the biggest shocks for the man who moves from 'civvy street' to the army is the disciplinary regime. As a civilian, provided that a man does not commit a criminal offence, he can go about his business without the fear of his freedom of action being restricted for a petty misdemeanour. Once he 'joins up' that all changes. After an interval of a hundred years the offences for which a soldier could be disciplined often seem trivial, the punishments unduly harsh, and while some of the men undoubtedly saw the application of justice as 'arbitrary',[5] there was 'due process'. The process may have seemed summary, and subject to the interpretation of the officer hearing the case, but Lambert was exaggerating when he said that they 'always convicted the men'.[6] The court martial records have many instances of soldiers being arraigned before a board, tried and then found 'not guilty'.

Although the *Army Act*, *Kings Regulations* and the *Manual of Military Law* all enshrined the code of discipline to be followed by the soldiers and their officers, there was considerable scope for the way in which it was applied in individual cases. Charles

4   Englander, *Discipline and Morale of the British army*, p.134.
5   Gladden, *Piave*, p.11.
6   Lambert, *Over the Top*, pp.71-2.

Carrington, in Italy after the armistice, was in a situation where eight men refused to obey an order to go on parade; the war was over and men were no longer prepared to jump when told to. The following day the men were brought before him for discipli- nary action, he could have charged them with 'refusing to obey an order' which would have resulted in them all being court martialled, instead he used the offence of 'neglect of duty' for which they all did an extra guard-duty, no court martial was involved and honour was restored all round.[7] As Carrington's example demonstrates, the way in which justice was applied could appear to be inconsistent, depending on the individual preferring the charge. It was also the case that the sentence could vary according to the forum in which the man was tried. Although the seriousness of some offences (e.g. Desertion) might dictate that they be heard by a Court Martial, many might be brought before the man's Company Commander, his Battalion Commander or a Court Martial. In the first two cases the offence was dealt with 'within the family', and a note was made on the soldier's service record. Unfortunately about half of these were destroyed by a bomb in World War Two, and there is no database of the charges heard and sentences passed in these 'orderly room' hearings. An analysis of those records which did survive is unlikely to happen because of the sheer size of the task; there are approximately 2.8 million of them on 15,000 micro-films in the National Archives,[8] but for individual families researching their grandfather's war they add a little colour to the picture and show how similar offences were often dealt with differ- ently. Sergeant Henry Davenport serves as an example as his service record survived the bombing. He was with the 9th Battalion of the York and Lancaster Regiment in Italy and was killed in the Austrian assault on 15 June 1918. His service record (in Kew) shows that while a private in France in 1915 he went before his company commander on 27 May. Davenport was charged with being 'absent from 9.30pm till apprehended by civil police at Mexborough at 2pm (16 hours 30 mins)' for which he was awarded '3 days CB' [confined to barracks] and a forfeit of 3 days' pay. In this case Davenport was obviously on home leave, and appears to have been late getting back to base. The same offence in France could have resulted in a court martial. A day later, 28 May, he was 'drunk on Staff Parade whilst a defaulter' and again, because he was in England and not France, he was treated leniently; his record shows that he was 'admonished' and given a further 3 days CB. Both misdemeanours were dealt with 'in the family' with no serious blot against his character. On 18 December (by now he had been promoted to Sergeant) and only a month after arriving in Italy, the court martial registers show that Davenport was tried for drunkenness and found to be 'not guilty'.[9] Had the charge been upheld the consequences would have been much worse than 3 days CB as by then he was an NCO with the responsibility that held to set an example to the men under him. Based on the many other examples in the registers of

---

7   Carrington, *Soldier from the Wars Returning*, p.246.
8   W. Spencer, *Army Service Records of the First World War* (Trowbridge, 2001), pp.1-3.
9   TNA: WO 213/18.

Sergeants tried for being drunk it is most probable that he would have been reduced in rank to Corporal, together with a reduction in pay and loss of privileges. But offences could not only be dealt with differentially, they could also be wiped out if the man subsequently received a bravery award, such as in the case of Private Worthington, 9th Battalion of the York and Lancaster Regiment. Previously sentenced to three years Penal Servitude (suspended under the Suspension of Sentences Act) he was awarded the Military Medal for gallantry in November 1917. As a result the General Officer Commanding remitted his sentence of incarceration.[10]

At this point, as with the earlier chapter on medical services, it is necessary to explain some of the issues that the disciplinary records present to the researcher. Mention has been made of the World War Two bomb which hit the archive storage building in 1940, as a result of this fire only around 3 million of 7 million enlistment records survived. Unless technology provides a solution, the 15,000 micro-films on which these are held are unlikely to be reproduced in a format that would allow easy manipulation of the hand-written data they contain. As a result, the 'orderly room' cases heard by company and battalion commanders (by a long way, the majority of disciplinary cases), are effectively unavailable to the researcher. Because of this it is only those misdemeanours that resulted in a court martial (the WO 213 series of registers in the National Archives) which form a useable body of data. Before outlining the information held within the registers it should be pointed out that, except in the case of the 346 men who were executed, these are not complete court files. For World War One the WO 213 series consists of some 30 registers, each with approximately 4,000 line entries, one for every court martial trial. Across a double page different columns indicate what the man was charged with, and the sentence delivered; there is no detail on the circumstances surrounding the offence or who it was brought by. Some crimes have no 'column heading' in the register, and so are deemed to be 'miscellaneous'. In those circumstances where a man is charged with multiple crimes (e.g drunkenness and insubordination), but possibly only found guilty of one of them, various notations are used which the researcher becomes used to, but are a level of detail not needed in this book. The registers held in Kew were compiled in the War Office (WO) from the court martial returns submitted monthly from the various theatre headquarters. As a consequence the trial details are entered in the month received at the WO, not the month of the offence. In many cases the two events are between three and six months apart. Some researchers have compiled their data based on the month received (it is more complicated and time consuming to separate them by trial month) which results in a false picture of when the indiscipline was occurring. Also, trials specify the geographic area where they were held, but again caution is needed. In the case of the IEF the majority state 'Italy' as the theatre, but there are many, particularly for rear area troops, where the base at which the trial was held is used; for example Arquata and Taranto. These detail points, as well as the separating of combat from

---

10   TNA: WO 95/4240, war diary 9th York & Lancs, November 1917.

non-combat units, are important as they go some way to explain why the information in this chapter may vary from that of others[11] who have attempted to consolidate the IEF court martial data from some 40,000 line entries in the WO 213 series, for the period November 1917 to December 1918.

Although the court martial cases overwhelmingly involved ordinary soldiers, it would be wrong to assume that officers did not also find themselves answering to military justice. In Italy 49 officers were called to account and tried before a court martial, but four of them took place at Taranto some months before the main deployment of the IEF. True to the hierarchical nature of the army, the officers' trials were recorded in a separate register from that of the soldiers, TNA WO 90/8, making it easier to compile the data. Between November 1917 and the end of 1918 there were 45 cases related to Italy, but care has to be taken before drawing conclusions from them. Of the 45, four had their sentences 'not confirmed' when the trial papers went to higher authorities for review, and a further six were acquitted, leaving 35 who were found to be guilty. Not surprisingly given the age of many of these young officers, and the responsibility they were called on to bear, the majority of the trials, 28, involved drunkenness; Lieutenant Johnson was court marshalled twice in January 1918 for being drunk, once in Genoa and once in Arquata, with the second offence leading to his dismissal. 13 of those guilty of over-imbibing received a severe reprimand. This may seem more lenient than the sentence that might have been handed to an ordinary soldier (many were given Field Punishment) but it would have been a career limiting judgement for an officer. In the 45 cases mentioned, 26 were for offences which took place in the rear or rest areas (Genoa, Arquata, Taranto and Faenza), and 22 were committed by officers not belonging to front-line infantry units. The distinction is important. In his article on the discipline of the IEF Gerard Oram cites the case against Lieutenant Aitken for a 'self-inflicted wound' as being 'indicative of low morale'.[12] While that may be the case if the wound was from a firearm, the army also considered VD as 'self-inflicted', and the court martial record gives no detail as to the cause of Aitken's wound. Oram states that 'morale in the force was crumbling', that the trial of officers in Italy was a 'rarity' (there were 45) and that the court martial of Aitken and two other officers was 'significant'. However, the two other officers were both sentenced in Taranto for drunkenness. Given that this port was the point of departure for Egypt and Salonika it is quite possible that neither of them was part of the IEF. Morale of the fighting troops is hard enough to 'measure', but before attempting to do so the relevant data for combat and non-combat troops must be kept separate.

As has been stated above, the British troops in Italy were subject to military discipline, however the Italian authorities also claimed jurisdiction in those cases where a soldier committed a civil offence. Although the Italians pursued their claim for

11   G. Oram, *'What alternative punishment is there?' Military Executions during World War One*, PhD thesis (Open University, 2000) and Oram, *Pious Perjury.*
12   Oram, *Pious Perjury*, p.420.

the whole period that the IEF was in their country, the British refused to recognise it based on the agreement signed by Brigadier Crowe and General Carlo Porro in May 1917. The document produced by these two officers specified the arrangements to be put in place in the event of a deployment of British troops to Italy. On the last page, under the heading <u>Discipline</u> it was quite specific; 'The British Authorities will deal with all offences committed by British troops, whether against British or Italian subjects'.[13] Unfortunately, as Plumer pointed out to the War Office in January 1918, this clause was left in abeyance as the Italians would not accept it on the grounds that it was 'contrary to the laws of Italy'.[14] In his letter Plumer pointed out that the Italians were dealing differently with the French. In August 1917 it was agreed by the Italian Minister of Foreign Affairs (Sidney Sonnino) that 'any offence committed by members of the French Army are [sic] to be tried by French Military Courts'; here Italian law did not appear to stand in the way of an agreement with the French. The British Ambassador in Rome was directed to take up the issue with the Italian government as it was 'very unfriendly of the Italians not to place our soldiers in the same position [as the French]'. It was made clear to the Italians that Britain was seeking the same conditions as had been granted to the French, which were the same as those in place for the BEF. For some reason the Italians appeared to have a blind spot over their differential treatment of their two allies; they proposed that the British should have jurisdiction but only over an 'active army in territory in which operations are carried on'.[15] This was unacceptable to the War Office as it excluded those soldiers away from the front, it was different from the treatment extended to the French, and did not accord with the agreement that the British had for their troops in France. As of August 1918 the issue was still unresolved and the 42 courts martial held in 1918 for an 'offence against inhabitant' – which the Italians would have wanted to come under their jurisdiction – were dealt with by the British military authorities. In 1943, when Brigadier Edmonds was collecting material for his Official History of the war in Italy, he received a letter explaining how British officers had worked around these jurisdictional issues:

> We got over this trouble in the one or two cases which we had of offences against the population by trying them quickly before our own Field General Courts Martials, [sic] and sending them to France. When the Italians asked for them to be produced (which was never until 3 weeks or a month after the offence had been committed) we replied "that we had dealt with the matter and the man had been sent to France and was no longer under the jurisdiction of the Commander-in-Chief in Italy". This and several other examples we had shows that a long time [sic] it took with correspondence with the Italians on any question.[16]

13   TNA: CAB 45/83, Plans for the movement of a British force to Italy, 7 May 1917, p.9.
14   TNA: FO 371/3229, memo from Plumer 9 January 1918.
15   TNA: FO 371/3229, telegram from Rodd, 16 April 1918.
16   TNA: CAB 45/84, Letter from P.E. Longmore to Edmonds, 21 July 1943.

The jurisdictional problem should have been dealt with quickly by the Italians, in line with the agreement of May 1917. By failing to put in place the same agreement for both the British and the French they merely succeeded in annoying an ally, to no real purpose. And for all that, the number of incidents was quite small. The 42 cases of 'offence against inhabitant' recorded in 1918 constituted only 1.6 per cent of the court martial trials in the IEF, a little higher than the equivalent figure for France of just 1 per cent. The WO 213 series gives no details of what the soldier might have done to the 'inhabitant', but two of the cases in February must have been serious as the soldiers were both sentenced to five years imprisonment. With so many young men a long way from home, a large proportion of whom would have been looking for sex with local women, it is difficult to believe that none of the offences would have been for rape, but we have no way of knowing from the limited information in the registers. Gladden described a scene that possibly ended that way. In February 1918, following a pay-parade, some of the men had too much to drink and when a country-woman 'wandered into the lower billet' some of them took advantage of the opportunity, with one of them attempting to 'embrace her', she resisted: 'In the scuffle they had fallen to the ground. The others had appeared on the scene and men had become lustful beasts struggling over her prostrate body'.[17] The account reads as though a rape may well have followed, but the court martial registers show no record for a man of the 11th Northumberland Fusiliers, Gladden's unit, being charged with an 'offence against inhabitant' around that time.

Although the limited way in which the data was entered into the registers leaves us with no specific evidence that any of the soldiers were guilty of rape – and it would be a surprise if it had not happened – they are more revealing regarding homosexual activity. Sex acts between men was against the law in England, as well as being a military offence – termed 'Indecency'. The conditions under which men lived in a war zone would have put pressures on their relationships with their mates which would not have existed within units at home. The strains of combat, the reliance each man had on his comrades, the close confines of army billets and the lack of female companionship, would all have played their part. Carrington describes the close affinity he had with the men of his platoon, but the feeling was not sexual; 'I was in love with my platoon. The whole of my affection and concern was for the forty Yorkshire miners, collectively and severally, with whom my life was so unexpectedly linked'.[18] While the records show that 'indecency' certainly did exist, it was not on a scale where it was noticed by all. Richard Aldington, in his book *Death of a Hero*, wrote that he never saw any signs of sodomy, nor heard of anything to make him believe it existed. He then qualified this statement; 'However, I was with the fighting troops. I can't answer for what went on behind the lines'.[19] And the number of cases brought to a court

17 Gladden, *Piave*, p.65.
18 Carrington, *Soldier from the Wars Returning*, p.76.
19 Aldington, *Death of a Hero*, p.26.

martial, across the whole of the British army was relatively small – only 57 between October 1917 and the end of September 1918. Some cases may have been heard by the Company or Battalion commanders, but that is unlikely, given that it was considered a serious crime in the close confines of barrack rooms. Although the total number of cases was small, a disproportionate percentage took place in Italy. Across the British army indecency constituted only 0.14% of the total number of courts martial trials, while in Italy, for the slightly shorter period of January to October 1918, the figure was 0.5%. Once again the picture changes, and clarifies, if the combat and rear echelon troops are detailed separately. Of the 11 cases of indecency in Italy, one was in the Royal Field Artillery (RFA), one in the Army Medical Corps, and one each in the 5th and 41st Divisions – combat troops – while the other seven were accounted for by members of the British West Indies (BWI) Regiment who were based at Taranto.

If one thing was going to get the British soldier into more trouble with the authorities than anything else, it was drink. Resourceful as ever, and undeterred by exhortations and regulations, the men found ways to get hold of drink, even if it was 'corrosive acid sold by Italian Banditti'.[20] A drunken soldier in a trench, or with a loaded weapon, was a liability, but drink could also result in them being disobedient or insubordinate to an officer or NCO while 'in their cups', with every likelihood of being hauled up on a charge. The records demonstrate that many of the men on a drink related charge were also there for one or other of these consequential offences. But the fact that many of the men sought out cheap alcohol, which they took in quantities that were not good for them, should have been no surprise. Many had been in the war for between two and four years, trips home to their family were infrequent, they were increasingly tired of army life and they just wanted it to be over. With a relatively quiet front, and a consequent reluctance to see the point of much of the army's pedantic routine, drink allowed some escape until drunkenness took over and the man was then disciplined. In the four months from December 1917 to March 1918 drink was a factor in 44% of the courts martial trials in the IEF, a figure which fell to 19% by the last quarter of the year, obviously some of the counter-measures had worked. Only a month after the IEF's arrival in Italy Plumer found it necessary to issue a General Order[21] putting bars and restaurants out of bounds, except between the hours of noon till 2 pm, and from six until eight in the evening, but it also stipulated what could and could not be imbibed:

> The purchase or acceptance of alcohol and champagne is forbidden. Only beer and red and white wine may be purchased, and must be consumed on the premises. The removal of beer or other liquor for consumption elsewhere is prohibited.

20   *The Old Firm*, December 1918 edition.
21   TNA: WO 95/4197, GRO 38, 15 December 1917.

It was almost impossible for the Military Police to enforce such an edict. The reference to champagne might seem out of place when laying down what an ordinary soldier might drink, but not so. The only soldier executed in Italy – in 1919, after the armistice – had been drinking two bottles of that sparkling product, prior to murdering one of his colleagues. Although the court records leave us no explanation of the peak in drink related trials in the early months of 1918, we can indulge in some conjecture. Christmas and New Year are traditionally a time when soldiers would have drunk more, but that may have been exacerbated by the relief at being on a quiet front after the dreadful experience of Flanders. Some even felt a sense of guilt at being removed from the 'real' war, especially during the German offensive in Flanders in March 1918; Gladden wrote of some men's frustration at being 'cut off in Italy from the rest of the world',[22] while another soldier felt 'hopelessly out of it with such big things going on in France'.[23]

The point has already been made that army authorities regarded disciplinary statistics as a guide to a unit's level of morale, and as drunkenness figured heavily in those statistics it would have influenced that presumed indicator of fighting spirit and quality of leadership. In the three months prior to Fifth Army's collapse in March 1918 its average strength per month was 205,000, with 130 men convicted for being drunk in that period. The IEF, in the three months before the Austrian June offensive, had an average strength of 87,000 of whom 282 were guilty of drunkenness. If the numbers are adjusted to take account of the difference in strength between the two formations, then the IEF was getting drunk at five times the rate of the Fifth Army. Excessive drinking was either a major problem among the British soldiers in Italy, or a man could more easily be accused and convicted of the offence in order to try to control it. The official record demonstrates that in 1918 the trials for drunkenness in the IEF, as a percentage of all trials in the country, was twice as high as the similar number for the British army as a whole.

Table 4: Comparison of drinking offences in IEF with those in British Army

	1 Jan–31 March 1918	*1 April–30 June 1918*	*1 Oct–31 Dec 1918*
Drink as % of all trials in British Army abroad	18%	16%	9%
IEF drink trials as % of all British Army drink trials	21.6%	10.8%	13%
IEF drink trials as % of all trials in IEF	44%	33%	18.8%

22   Gladden, *Piave*, p.97.
23   Hardie, Private Papers, report for February-July 1918.

We come back again to the question of how strong the correlation might be between indiscipline and morale and the answer has to be "it's hard to say". The figures quoted for the British army as a whole make no distinction between front and rear echelon troops, nor indeed do those for Fifth Army, and yet it is the morale of the soldier in the forward trenches which is of primary importance; as was demonstrated on 21 March 1918. If the final test of morale is the ability to stand and fight in defence and to go forward in attack then, however bad the disciplinary record of the IEF appears, their morale held during the Austrian attack in June and their own advance in October 1918.

For those men who were tried by courts martial, and then found guilty, consequences naturally followed. The sentences available to the boards who sat on these trials included the ultimate penalty, death by firing squad, but we will leave this until last. For those soldiers who stood, hatless, before their company or battalion commanders, the penalties were designed primarily to cause inconvenience to the man and act as a deterrent; confined to barracks, extra guard duty, work parties, fatigues, and defaulters' drill parades. Sentences handed down by courts martial were more severe, and came from a more restricted set of options; imprisonment, field punishment, loss of pay, reduction in rank and, rarely, death. The remainder of this chapter will set out ways in which the offence a man was charged with in the IEF could differ from that in France, and that sentences could also be varied to take account of the different circumstances in Italy. In some regards IEF commanders were more lenient in interpreting the charge, but could then be more severe with some of the punishments. In the same way that courts in England could sentence a man to imprisonment, so their military equivalents had access to military prisons. The sentences could vary from a few months up to ten years, and often carried the rider that they were to be with 'hard labour'. While there were military detention centres in France and Britain which were designed to hold men for these periods of time, they were not available in Italy. As a consequence, men needing immediate incarceration would have to be sent out of the country. But the picture is not so clear cut. In 1915 the Suspension of Sentences Act came into being. The aim of the Act was to prevent men from wilfully committing a military offence with the aim of having themselves removed from active service. With the Suspension Act a man's conviction would stand, but his term of imprisonment was suspended until hostilities ceased. Obviously for military commanders this meant that the guilty men were still available for duty but, as Geoff Barr pointed out it acted as a 'get out of jail card', they could continue handing out stiff prison sentences without the risk of losing the men: 'Officers and senior NCOs were still able to administer their rigid system of discipline, but now the men knew that being sentenced to prison was more difficult'.[24] Because the soldier would serve no immediate penalty there would be little beneficial effect on discipline – and the soldier could place a reasonable bet that,

---

24 G. Barr, *Military Discipline. Policing the 1st Australian Force 1914-1920.* http://books. google.co.uk/books, last accessed 15 March 2012.

once the war was over, there was little real likelihood of him going to prison for some military misdemeanour in a foreign country.

For the commander in the field the answer was 'commutation'; award the punishment of imprisonment, but then commute this to some other sentence which could be served in theatre – usually field punishment (discussed in detail below). By this means the issues raised by the Suspension of Sentences Act were circumvented, punishment was awarded and served, and the man was available for duty in his unit. This 'work-around' would seem to have been particularly in favour in Italy as a partial solution to their lack of local prison facilities. Between 1 October 1917 and 30 September 1918 there were 41,668 trials of British soldiers, outside the United Kingdom.[25] For a similar period, 1 January to 31 November 1918, the IEF recorded 2,184 courts martial.[26]

Table 5: Imprisonment and Field Punishment comparison[27]

	British Army UK & Abroad	IEF
Total trials	41668	2184
Imprisonment	8515 (20.4%)	430 (19.7%) [252 (11.5%) after accounting for commuted sentences.]
Commuted imprisonment		178
Field Punishment No. 1	17972	1245
Field Punishment No. 2	4123	93
Total Field Punishment	22095	1338

The trial statistics for the army as a whole do not record how many of the sentences for imprisonment were commuted to some other punishment, but the confirmed total for those sent to some form of detention was 8,515 – 20.4% of those tried. This contrasts with the IEF. An analysis of all the individual entries in the courts martial registers for the Italian Front shows that while 430 men were given the punishment of imprisonment, 252 of these had their sentence commuted. As a result the number sent to detention was reduced from 19.7% of offenders to 11.5%; the IEF imprisonment rate was a little over half of that of the army as a whole. But if the authorities in Italy were effectively substituting something else for imprisonment, what was it?

The confirmed sentence most frequently handed down following a court martial was Field Punishment (FP). It was intended to humiliate the delinquent soldier, and

25   TNA: WO 93/50, *Extracts from the Statistics of the military effort of the British Empire during the Great War 1914-1920.*
26   TNA: WO 213/19-26.
27   Data taken from WO 93/50 and also extrapolated from WO 213/19-26.

was criticised by many at the time for just that reason. Richard Holmes reminds us that flogging was only abolished in the British Army (for those on active service), in 1881, and not until 1907 in military prisons.[28] Hanging was still on the statute books in Britain and physical punishment was deemed necessary by many who had been brought up in the old Regular Army. But first, what was Field Punishment? It came in two forms which, in true army style, were designated as Field Punishment No. 1 (FP1) and Field Punishment No. 2 (FP2). FP1 required that the soldier suffer loss of pay, lose the privilege of 'green envelopes' and the rum ration for the period of the sentence, and go to the bottom of the leave roster. To achieve the humiliation objective he should be tied to a fixed object, often a fence or a wheel, for a period not to exceed two hours in any day, for no more than 21 days in all and for no more than three days out of four; this meant that a court had to pass a 28 day sentence in order to achieve 21 days of confinement. During the period that he was not physically restrained the man was made to work as if he were on 'hard labour'. With FP2 the punishment was the same, except that the two hours tied to the wheel, post or fence was omitted; it lacked the public humiliation of FP1. It quickly becomes obvious when studying the courts martial registers, that a very large percentage of the FP1 verdicts were for more than 28 days, frequently up to 90, which is at variance with the stated limit; why so? A letter from Lloyd George,[29] who was Secretary of State for War, to his counterparts in Italy and France asked them for details of punishments used in their armies which might be equivalent to the British use of FP1. On this letter there is a handwritten note correcting the 28 day limit and stating that while this was the maximum that could be 'inflicted by a Commanding Officer', a court martial could impose a sentence of up to three months. This point has been missed by many historians who constantly cite the 28 day limit. The Italians, especially when Cadorna was Commander-in-Chief, had a particularly harsh disciplinary regime (including decimation), but both they and the French replied saying that they had nothing similar in their penal code, and that such restraint could only be used in exceptional circumstances – the British regime was harsher than that of its allies. In his letter Lloyd George stated that the reasons for the use of FP were twofold. First it avoided keeping the soldier away from duty 'as would be involved by an equally severe sentence of imprisonment'; second, it required fewer men to guard the prisoners. Both of these points support the probable justification in the IEF for the commutation of prison sentences as it solved the problem of lack of prison facilities as well as not losing the man from duty.

With its history of using physical punishment on soldiers it is not surprising that some senior officers believed strongly in its retention. In a comment to the 1902 inquiry into the continuing use of field punishment, Colonel St. Clair gave it as his belief that in the Boer War it had 'utterly failed in its object as an efficient substitute for 'flogging''. In paragraph 39 of the inquiry report the board felt, reluctantly, that all other

28   Holmes, *Tommy*, p.558.
29   TNA: WO 32/5460, letter from Lloyd George, 21 November 1916.

punishments, save corporal punishment, had failed to meet disciplinary requirements and in their view flogging should be reintroduced on active service for acts punishable by death under the Army Act, but with the number of lashes limited to 25.[30] As we know, the lash did not come back. But it was not only senior commanders who wanted stern punishment. Ordinary soldiers of the regular army were also asked to give their views; one stated that without FP1 as an alternative to imprisonment then some men would commit crimes simply so that they could go to prison and be removed from the line, but if prison had to be used, it should not be in England where the men might get home. In the account of his time in Flanders, Gladden makes the telling point that, from the perspective of a conscripted man whose freedom of action is bound about by Army regulations, 'prison sentences really matter only in a free world'.[31] A Colour Sergeant Grove told the board that; 'With regard to No. 2 field imprisonment, that is no use at all. The man only does fatigues, and his comrades have to wait on him, giving him his meals and so on'. Field Punishment No. 1, while it removed a man's privileges, was primarily intended to humiliate him; 'Field imprisonment when carried out publicly is degrading, but again if carried out where other soldiers cannot see it, loses its effect as deterrent'.[32] This view was in line with that of Haig who believed that two of the indispensable elements of punishment were; '(i) the infliction of physical discomfort' and '(ii) the stimulation of the sense of shame'.[33] As we shall see, field punishment became the fall back verdict for the majority of trials in the IEF, but it was not supposed to be that way. While Carrington was to write after the war, possibly naively, that it was not handed out other than for 'a serious military offence, such as neglect of duty that endangered the line',[34] Lieutenant General Sir Thomas Morland was closer to the mark in his written note to the enquiry into this form of punishment; it 'should not be awarded for cases of drunkenness and overstaying leave, as has been the tendency during the present campaign'.[35] In April 1918, while Carrington was with the IEF, there were some 120 courts martial involving drunkenness and in almost 80 of them the sentence was field punishment; it is difficult to see how he could have been unaware of them, and the fact that it was awarded for offences which often did not 'endanger the line'.

While many men were sentenced to FP1, most of them for more than 14 days, it is surprising that it is hardly mentioned in any of the soldiers' letters – it is possible that they did not want families to know how some of their mates were treated – although some memoirs written years after the war do cover it. From today's standpoint the punishment is overly degrading, but not all of those affected took that view; Captain

30 TNA: WO 32/4512, Report of the Committee on Punishment on Active Service, p.11.
31 Gladden, *Ypres*, p.28.
32 TNA: WO 32/4512, Lt. Col. Granet, p.17.
33 TNA: WO 32/5461, Enquiry into Field Punishment No. 1, memo from Haig, 4 December 1916.
34 Carrington, *Soldier from the Wars Returning*, p.171.
35 TNA: WO 32/5461, memo, 8 May 1919.

Gameson, while a medical officer in France, had to inspect a prisoner to ensure that the sentence was not affecting the man's health:

> Had to inspect one of our men who was strapped to the wheel of a G.S. Wagon undergoing Field Punishment No. 1. Often heard of this F.P. No. 1 business but have never seen it in action before. Part of one's job was to make sure that the victim's bonds were not too tight, and that he was not likely to collapse. *In point of fact he was grinning broadly.*[36] [My italics]

Of course, this could just have been bravado on the soldier's part, or the men may have been less censorious of the practice than we now feel they should have been. Did a working-class background inure the troops to a treatment that we would deem completely unacceptable? In *The British Working Man in Arms* John Bourne argued that these men, many of whom were labourers or manual workers from the industrial cities, were 'not unpromising military material' because they were used to physical discomfort, had low levels of expectation, and were 'comfortable with the idea of hierarchy and knew their place within it'.[37] Such a generalisation would not have applied to men like Gladden, a permanent civil servant with the Post Office before he joined in 1915, who regarded kit inspections as 'like children playing shops'. For those who came from office jobs, or middle-class positions of responsibility, army routines and punishments were the 'sort of childish pettiness that made the army so unattractive to anyone with the least sensitiveness or independence of mind'.[38] Whether the men did or did not accept field punishment as just one more difference between civvy street and army life, there were those at home who spoke out against it; it was labelled as 'crucifixion' by those who wished to see it done away with.

The term crucifixion was a useful one for the opponents of the punishment; it drew immediate pictures in the minds of those who heard or read it, but was it valid? In the files at the National Archives there is one which contains drawings of the approved way in which a soldier should be restrained when undergoing FP1. This clearly shows that the arms should not be spread, they should be at the man's side or behind him, but that was not always the case in practice. Robert Graves described a man 'spreadeagled' with his wrists and ankles tied to a wheel 'in the form of an X',[39] while Carrington stated that although he had heard of such cases, 'this I never saw in the Army'.[40] But crucifixion had a resonance with the campaigners against it, many using newspapers to make their views known to Lloyd George. A Mrs. Ingham denounced the practice

---

36 Gameson, Private Papers, p.11.
37 J. Bourne, 'The British Working Man in Arms', in H. Cecil and P. Liddle (eds.), *Facing Armageddon* (London, 1996), p.348.
38 Gladden, *Piave*, p.143.
39 Graves, *Goodbye*, p.147.
40 Carrington, *Soldier from the Wars Returning*, p.171.

as 'German Kultur' while Mr. Roy Horniman used the *Evening Standard* for a jingo-istic outburst:

> Had I been told that I should live to see the day when Englishmen would tie their fellow-citizens in an agonising position for hours, day after day, like carrion to a gallows, I should have called that man a liar; I should have answered that there did not live the Englishman who would not sooner face a firing party than commit such a treachery on our manhood, and on our liberties.[41]

While the writer was probably safe in the knowledge that he would neither have to serve time in the army, nor risk a firing squad, the campaign did gain traction because of the emotive use of the descriptor, crucifixion. The issue was addressed by Haig in a letter to the Secretary of State for war in December 1916; the punishment would stay, but the perception of it had to be changed.

> It is suggested that descriptions and possibly drawings of men tied up with their arms extended may have aroused prejudice owing to the unfortunate use of the term "crucifixion" as a simile in this connection, and I therefore, think that the definition should be such as to exclude this position.[42]

Haig's acknowledgement of public distaste for the way in which field punishment was perceived appears a little grudging, but then he was a firm believer in its use: 'I am quite certain that it would not have been possible to maintain the high standard of discipline in the British Army in France if Field Punishment No. 1 had been non-existent'.[43] In his opinion, if field punishment were not available to commanders, then 'recourse to the death penalty would have to become more frequent'. This statement implies that Haig would have been prepared to execute men for the less serious crimes, which carried a sentence of field punishment, if that option were to be abolished.

The courts martial registers allow us to see the extent to which the penalty was embraced by commanders in the British Army abroad, and in Italy particularly. Between October 1917 and September 1918, 53% of all trials in the army outside of the UK resulted in a sentence of field punishment; in Italy the figure was higher at 61%.[44] There is a case for arguing that, as with the death sentence (to be covered later), the IEF adopted a different sentencing policy to the BEF over the use of field punishment. Throughout the army there was an increasing tendency to hand down sentences of FP1 and FP2, in 1916/17 these had accounted for 48% of punishments, growing to 53% in 1917/18. This growth is likely to have resulted from the introduction of

---

41   TNA: WO 32/5460, letter from Horniman to the Evening Standard, 13 December 1916.
42   TNA: WO 32/5460, memo from Haig, 4 December 1916.
43   Englander, *Discipline and morale in the British army*, p.132.
44   The figure for the IEF is for January to November ,1918.

the Suspension of Sentences Act, but it may also demonstrate a desire to be seen to be dealing toughly with indiscipline. The table below outlines the split between the use of FP1 and FP2 across all theatres, and compares this with that in the IEF. In Italy FP1 is used almost to the exclusion of the lesser option. It is difficult not to see the 93% use of FP1 as other than a determined policy to crack down on discipline, together with the commutation of prison sentences in favour of field punishment, for the reasons already suggested.

Table 6: Comparison of the use of FP1 between the IEF and other theatres

	1916/17		1917/18	
	FP1	FP2	FP1	FP2
All theatres	79%	21%	81%	19%
IEF			93%	7%

However, the propensity to use FP1 (almost exclusively) was not the only pointer towards a tightening of the disciplinary regime in Cavan's IEF, the period for which a soldier would serve the sentence also increased. In July 1918 there were 110 trials which resulted in a sentence of FP1. Of those soldiers, 87 (or 79%) received terms greater than 28 days, with 35 of the men suffering the humiliation for the maximum period of 90 days. More to the point, the percentage awarded FP1 for the full three months had increased from 18.5% in January to 32% in July. With the war coming to an end, there was a marked tendency in the IEF to avoid charging men with offences that might carry the death sentence (as we shall see below) as well as sentences of imprisonment. To counter any charge that they might be softening in their position on discipline, a harsh stance on Field Punishment showed that commanders in Italy wished to be seen to 'crack the whip'.

Another of the crimes which demonstrates the value of looking behind the raw statistics is theft and here again the picture is different between those in the front-line and those who made up the support services at the various depots. These rear echelon units provided essential services to the fighting battalions, but that role could also provide the opportunity for petty larceny – food, clothing and equipment which could be sold on to local civilians. Being in the rear also meant working in depots that were close to local civilian populations, so providing more access to drink and local women, many of whom were employed by the army as labour in those supply bases. All of this put temptation in the way of soldiers, many of whom were bored with their role as 'labour'. A case in point was the British West Indies (BWI) Regiment which had the worst disciplinary record of any of the British units in Italy. The men were coloured and had joined up to fight but they found themselves being used as labourers and were subjected to racial discrimination – the British army at that time, as well as most 'ordinary' people, saw little wrong in drawing distinctions between 'white' and 'native'

races. The War Office did not want black West Indians to be used in combat formations against whites; they also questioned their fighting qualities on the basis of their
colour. In the opinion of the WO, if they had to be used (and the King was in favour
of doing so), then it should be in a hot climate, not France. The BWI was sent initially
to Egypt, before its relocation to Italy to work in the docks at Taranto, primarily
as stevedores. In true chauvinist style the accommodation and hospital facilities for
these men from the Caribbean were segregated from those used by white soldiers.[45] It
should not be surprising that men, who had volunteered to fight for King and Empire,
and then found themselves used as dock labourers on account of their colour, should
vent their frustration through indiscipline. A December 1917 report declared that the
BWI were not 'doing satisfactorily. They show a strong disinclination to work, and
do not seem to pay much attention to their officers or NCOs'.[46] In February 1918 the
Taranto Commandant (who at one time said they were 'only niggers'[47]) requested that
they should be replaced by Italian labour, but he was refused and was sent another
3,000 BWI instead. Racial discrimination was not likely to engender good discipline.
Of the 110 trials mentioned above, which resulted in FP1, 13 were for the full three
month sentence, and of these 11 came from the BWI. In 1918 the number of courts
martial among the West Indians was out of all proportion to other units in the IEF.
In July of that year, although they only constituted 3.5% of the British troops, they
managed to account for 17% of that month's trials; in December, when an increase
in their numbers had taken the BWI to 9% of the IEF, their trials had increased to
22% of the British total. An analysis of the disciplinary record of the IEF needs to
highlight the distorting effect that units like the BWI can have. The point is made
with an extreme example. In December 1918 there were 48 convictions in the IEF for
mutiny, evidence (one might conclude) for a serious breakdown in morale among the
British troops in Italy, following the end of the war. Not so; 47 of the men were from
the BWI, they were a long way from the fighting front, subjected to colour prejudice
and wanting to return to their Caribbean islands.

In the last 30 years the most controversial aspect of the harsh discipline under
which the men served has been the use of the death penalty. This book is not the
place to argue for or against the sentence as it was implemented in the British Army
in the First World War. Hanging was still in use in Britain for crimes of murder, and
we should be careful of judging the penalties awarded for offences carried out against
military law, a century ago, in a time of war. Death by firing squad is no longer available to a court martial board – and a good thing too – but it was in the Great War,
and 346 soldiers were executed. The rest of this chapter will review those situations
in which a man could be sentenced to death, and how the British Army in Italy took
a different stance from the BEF towards the awesome penalty of condemning a man

45   Macpherson, *Medical Services Vol. 3*, p.329.
46   TNA: WO 95/4255, Taranto Base: Commandant. War diary, 29 December 1917.
47   Starling and Lee, *No Labour, No Battle*, p.246.

to be shot by his colleagues. One of the myths of the war is that impressionable young men, half out of their mind from shell-shock, were hauled before kangaroo courts and then executed for cowardice. Of the 3,076 death sentences passed, 346 (or 11%) were carried out; in 89% of those cases where the court martial board decided that a firing squad was appropriate the review process commuted the sentence. Due process ensured that these men were not shot. Also, 'cowardice'; contrary to urban myth only 18 of the 346 were executed for cowardice, the vast majority, 266 (including two officers), were shot for desertion. As Corns and Hughes-Wilson[48] point out in their study of British military executions, some of the early cases of cowardice would have been dealt with as desertion later in the war. One reason for this was that 'cowardice' was a very subjective term, while desertion (with the need to prove 'intent') was more objective; there was more room for error when returning a guilty verdict for cowardice than for one of desertion. As a result of a campaign by the families of some of those executed men, a pardon was granted in 2006 to those shot for desertion or cowardice. As a consequence, these men are memorialised twice; they have a headstone in a CWGC war cemetery as well as an individual wooden stake with their name on it, as part of the 'Shot at Dawn' memorial in the National Arboretum. Those men who stayed at their post, until killed by the enemy, have only a headstone or their name carved on a memorial to the missing. Following the granting of the pardon Andrew Mackinlay, Labour MP for Thurrock, made the kind of statement that perpetuates a myth and distorts history: "All the courts martial were flawed. People did not have a chance to produce evidence or call witnesses."[49]

Military law, as we have stated, granted courts martial the authority to recommend that a man be shot by firing squad for a number of offences (often with the proviso that the man was 'on active service') which did not carry a death penalty in civilian life. While a murderer could be hung in London, or shot in Flanders, to be caught asleep at one's desk in the City might lead to the sack, but in a trench it was deemed a capital offence. In the last 11 months of the war 55 British soldiers were executed. In Italy 17 trials resulted in a verdict of death, but only one man was shot and that was for murder, after the war had finished. It would seem from the statistics that a more lenient, or at least different, approach was taken towards the use of the extreme penalty. An analysis of the way in which capital offences were treated within the IEF will demonstrate that this was the case. In the public mind the man who was shot at dawn was there because he was accused of cowardice, a situation poignantly caught by Kipling:

> I could not look on Death, which being known,
> Men led me to him, blindfold and alone.[50]

48   Corns and Hughes-Wilson, *Blindfold and Alone*, pp.176-7.
49   R. Norton-Taylor, 'Executed WW1 soldiers to be given pardon', *The Guardian*, 16 August 2006, www.theguardian.com last accessed 24 June 2014.
50   J. Silkin, *The Penguin Book of First World War Poetry* (London, 1996), p.135.

But as mentioned above, the judgement of cowardice is a very subjective one. Lord Moran, a medical officer in France during the war, holder of the Military Medal as well as being Winston Churchill's doctor, wrote an acclaimed book on the subject of courage, in which he argued that this quality is not inexhaustible:

> Courage is will-power, whereof no man has an unlimited stock; [...] A man's courage is his capital and he is always spending. The call on the bank may be only the daily drain of the front line or it may be a sudden draft which threatens to close the account.[51]

Although the British front in Italy was much quieter than that in France and Flanders, as the casualty statistics demonstrate, there were still men being killed and wounded and although the fear of death was not as keen, it was still there; there was still, to use Moran's phrase, a 'daily drain'. The subjective element in a charge of cowardice (how close is the man to 'closing his account'?) is highlighted by Corns and Hughes-Wilson:

> Is the soldier, swallowing, white-faced, hands shaking and wetting his trousers before dashing over the top of a trench into the angry bullets of a machine gun scared? Is he exhibiting fear? Is this cowardice?[52]

If the man stays in the trench while the others take up the attack, should he be charged as a coward or with 'refusing to obey an order'? The latter would be easier to prove. Although the IEF saw relatively little action, they had a disproportionate number of men charged with cowardice. Of the 91 trials – among all British troops abroad – for this offence between October 1917 and the end of September 1918, 11 (12% of the total) were from the IEF, although their strength would have indicated a share of only 5%. As always, the devil is in the detail. Seven of the men were charged in June, the month in which the Austrians launched their short assault against the British lines on the Asiago, and this may have been the trigger for the offences. However, four of the men were all from one battalion, and all occurred on the 7 June, a week before the Austrian attack. Although charged with cowardice, all four were convicted for 'quitting' their post, a charge which commonly resulted in a period of FP1 within the IEF. Also, of the remaining three from that month, one was found not guilty, another was sentenced for disobedience while the charge against the third was upheld, but the man was given five years imprisonment rather than death.

The tendency to change the offence for which a man was convicted, from one which carried the death penalty, to one for which it was not required, can be tracked through the IEF court martial statistics. If a sentry was not at his post when the duty officer or

---

51   Lord Moran, *The Anatomy of Courage* (London, 1945), p.xxii.
52   Corns and Hughes-Wilson, *Blindfold and Alone,* p.48.

NCO made his rounds (he might have gone to the toilet) or he was asleep at his post, then he ran the risk of a death sentence. After all, it was his job to remain alert and raise the alarm should the enemy approach the trench system. In Italy only one man was condemned, for 'quitting his post', but this was commuted to a year of imprisonment with hard labour. Although nearly 70 men were tried for being asleep at their post, or for quitting it, the majority received periods of field punishment – no fun, but much better than a firing squad. Some of those accused were rear-echelon troops, and so the court could treat them as not being on active service. Officers and NCOs would often have turned a blind eye, recognising that in many cases the sleeping man was not putting the lives of his mates in peril, he was simply exhausted; a well-timed cough, or stamping of the foot, could waken the sleeping sentry and avoid placing him on a charge. Just such a situation was recorded by Max Plowman. Although he was a subaltern in France, the anecdote was no doubt familiar to junior officers inspecting the trenches at night in Italy.

> Half an hour afterwards I go back to find him sitting where I left him, only now fast asleep. [...] Ignorant, insensitive, snoring lump – let him stay there. Of course I ought to haul him up before the C.O., and perhaps get him shot for sleeping on duty. But what's the good? Besides, I don't want the trouble ...'[53]

The incident described points up the fact that the courts martial records only give us a partial picture of the state of discipline in the British units. There are likely to have been many such instances of junior officers and NCOs having some sympathy for the soldiers under their care, and so either looking the other way, or having the man brought up before his company or battalion commander, so avoiding a full-blown court martial (and being invisible to later researchers).

By far the largest single defaulter group who received a death sentence was those accused of desertion; a little over 2,000, of whom 266 were executed. Within the IEF 17 men were under threat of facing a firing squad, 12 of them for desertion, but only one suffered the extreme penalty. Private Albert Denny of the BWI – that regiment again – was shot in 1919 for murder, a crime for which he could have been hung in England. In 1918, within the British Army outside of the UK, 43 men were shot for desertion, while none were executed in Italy; was there a more lenient approach to the death penalty in the IEF than in other theatres? Here again the researcher faces the problem of insufficient evidence to draw firm conclusions. The court papers for the 12 men who were tried for desertion are no longer available, we cannot see the case against them, the grounds used by the courts martial boards for commuting these sentences, nor at what level the recommendation was made for commutation. Only in those cases where the man was shot are all the documents still available. This is a shame on two levels. First is the lack of documentation available to the researcher on

---

53   M. Plowman, *A Subaltern on the Somme* (New York, 1928), p.85.

the charge and how it was dealt with, unless he was shot. Second, in the absence of any evidence to the contrary, critics can perpetuate the view that these were all kangaroo courts with no process, and in which the soldier could not put forward a defence. There is no doubt that a reading of the documentation, in the cases where the man was executed, shows that evidence was limited, few witnesses were called, and justice was swift. However, courts martial boards were constituted according to military law and, contrary to Andrew Macinlay, the man could call witnesses and defend himself; the fact that some did not is another issue. Patently, in the case of the twelve men of the IEF who were tried for desertion, something worked correctly as their sentences were commuted.

British military law recognised two separate offences where a soldier was not where he was supposed to be, one was 'absence' and the other was 'desertion'. For a charge of desertion to stand it was necessary to convince the board that the man had the 'intent' of not returning to military duty, or that he had deliberately avoided a particular activity so as to absent himself from active service. Merely being absent from his post did not make a man a deserter. However, if he was later found to be in civilian clothes, or without his military equipment, then these could be grounds for proving that he intended to desert. The distance from Italy to England could also be used as a defence that the man did not intend to remain away from his unit; it was much harder to make his way home from here than from France. What we can see from the courts martial registers is that there was a marked tendency in the IEF to 'downgrade' many of the charges of desertion to one of 'Guilty of Absence' (GoA). By so doing the court turned the offence from a capital to a non-capital crime. An analysis of the WO 213 registers (from 18 – 30) shows that 60% of those charged in Italy with desertion had the offence downgraded to GoA. The corresponding figure for the British Army as a whole was 44%.[54] In the majority of cases, those who were found guilty of desertion were handed down severe terms of imprisonment, while those whose cases were changed to GoA received substantial periods of Field Punishment No.1. When those offences which potentially carried the death sentence are considered, it does appear that the authorities within the IEF had determined to forego capital punishment. To ensure that this was not interpreted by the troops as 'going soft' on discipline, long periods of FP1 were more harshly employed than in the rest of the British Army.

What this chapter has demonstrated is that although the soldiers of the IEF and the rest of the British Army were governed by the same military regulations, enforcement of them did vary between theatres. Gerald Oram, in his study of the British military executions carried out in World War One,[55] reveals how the sentencing was also inconsistent between divisions in the Regular, New and Territorial armies. Discipline tended to be more harshly meted out to Regulars (whose commanders felt that they needed to maintain old army standards), than to Territorials. The latter's 'citizen

---

54   This figure is calculated from data in TNA: WO 394/6 p.642.
55   Oram, *What alternative punishment is there?*

soldiers' resented the enforcement of regulations and directives which they considered to be petty and pointless, especially when many of the men had voluntarily signed up to fight. The problem for the researcher, highlighted earlier in this chapter, is the nature of the documentary evidence. Sadly, the only group for which a full record of trial proceedings exists is the 346 men who were executed. For the hundreds of thousands who committed such cardinal sins as being on parade with a dirty belt-buckle, or failing to clean their rifle, there is no equivalent to the Courts Martial registers. For those whose service records survived the bombing of the Second World War, there may be a note of these minor misdemeanours in the microfiche films at the National Archive – a study of these would be a mammoth task. The only data which allows a comparative study of discipline between theatres of the war and different military units is that related to the court martial trials. The idiosyncratic way in which the information on separate cases has been entered in these registers, and the care needed in interpreting them, has been noted in this chapter. Notwithstanding these limitations, they can be used to draw conclusions on the enforcement of discipline in the IEF, compared with that in France. Commanders in Italy were prepared to pass death sentences, but (except in one post-armistice case of murder) these were all commuted. In contrast the last man to face the firing squad in France, for the military offence of cowardice (two others were later shot for the civil offence of murder), was executed on 7 November 1918 – just four days before the war ended. The ultimate penalty was most frequently awarded in cases of desertion, but here again a difference is noticeable in the IEF. A soldier in Italy was more likely to be found 'Guilty of Absence', a lesser charge than that of desertion, than his colleagues in the BEF. Imprisonment, frequently for many years and with hard labour, was problematic in Italy (a lack of facilities) and so was more likely to be commuted to Field Punishment. Divisional and Battalion commanders were conscious of the way in which their seniors equated an excess of minor disciplinary infractions with declining morale – the fix for which was to 'stiffen' sentences and make individual examples; *'pour encourager les autres'*. The regime in Italy – no death sentences, guilty of absence in place of desertion and commutation of imprisonment – might have been interpreted at Headquarters as lax. The Courts Martial registers show that the corrective was a much harsher use of Field Punishment No. 1 in Italy than in France. The conclusion can reasonably be drawn that the enforcement of discipline within the IEF, given the standards of the day, the circumstances of war, and the fact that many men were serving under the duress of conscription, was stern but fair.

7

The Austrian attack, June 1918:
"It was exciting when they came over the top"

If the war was going to be brought to a successful conclusion then the British and French were convinced that this would be on the Western Front, against the Germans. However, Haig and Foch would be at pains in 1918 to encourage the Italians (now commanded by Diaz) to launch their own offensives. It was hoped that these would be coordinated with those in France and Flanders, to prevent Austrian divisions being sent westwards to assist the Germans. The apparent unwillingness of Diaz to fall-in with these requests would harden the view of the British and the French that the Italians were fighting their own separate war, and that they would only take the military initiative when Italian – rather than allied – objectives would be met. However, the IEF (and the newly formed Royal Air Force) would take part in two major actions in 1918. The first, in June, was to turn back a two-pronged Austrian attack around Asiago and also across the River Piave; the second was as part of the Italian assault in late October, which history records as the battle of Vittorio Veneto. The result was the collapse of the Austrians and their signing of an armistice a week before the Germans. The British contribution to these June and October battles is the subject of this chapter, but it is not the intent that this book should describe them in great detail, that has been done successfully by those authors mentioned in previous chapters. This chapter will address some of the issues which arose from the June and October actions; the ignoring of this front by most British histories of the war; and the way in which Italian histories have downplayed the British contribution to Vittorio Veneto.

The priority afforded to the Western Front by the War Office would affect the IEF from the time that it was deployed until the October armistice; the fluctuating fortunes of the Allies in France resulted in changes to the number of British divisions in Italy, which then had a knock-on effect on who commanded the force. The initial British contribution was set at two 'good divisions' under the command of a 'good man'[1] Lieutenant-General the Earl of Cavan (henceforth Cavan), commanding

---

1   Edmonds, *Italy*, p.59.

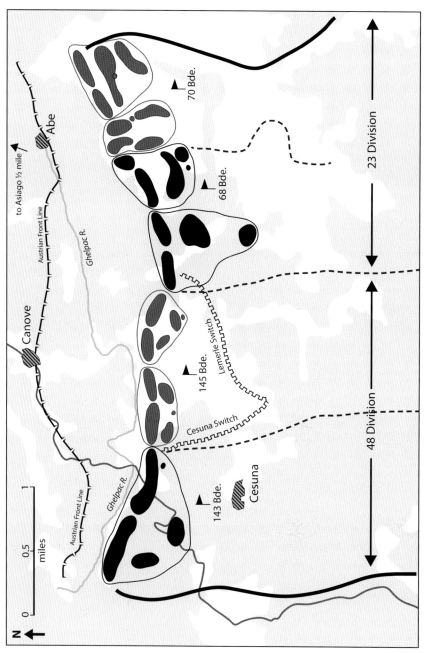

Map 2 The British front on the Asiago, 15 June. 48 Divn. on the left with only six companies in the line; 23 Divn. on the right with eight companies in forward positions.

XIV Corps was chosen. Cavan, then a Major-General, had led the Guards Division at the battle of Loos in September 1915. Well thought of by Haig, he came close to replacing General Sir Hubert Gough after the collapse of Fifth Army in March 1918; after the war he took over as Chief of the Imperial General Staff from Sir Henry Wilson. Considered to be something of a 'thruster', the man sent to command the IEF appeared to have the credentials for the job, however, the official historian would later refer to him as 'bone from the neck up'.[2] For a few days the question of command in Italy became entangled with the replacement of Cadorna, the setting up of the Supreme War Council, the establishment of a General Reserve and unification of military command in one *Generalisimo*. On 2 November 1917 it was suggested that pressure would be brought to bear on the Italians to accept the authority of the French General Pétain;[3] on 3 November Lloyd George was said to be trying to persuade Haig to take supreme command on the Italian Front and that he would 'force this on [the] French and Italians'.[4] While neither of these came to pass, they demonstrate the arrogance of the British towards their southern ally. As was the case with Haig when he took command of the BEF, Cavan was directed to comply with the orders of the Italian Comando Supremo but he should also act as an 'independent commander' reporting directly to Robertson (as CIGS) on operational matters;[5] he should not accept orders that would cause him to use his expeditionary force against British interests. As the French had decided to send more than two divisions, the British felt that they could not allow themselves to be out-done and assigned two more as well. This larger force required a more senior commander and it was decided that Cavan would remain in Italy, but would now be subordinate to General Sir Herbert Plumer. Rotund and heavily moustached (in photographs he looked the archetypal 'Colonel Blimp'), Plumer was one of the most successful of the British commanders, especially after his recent victory over the Germans at Messines Ridge in June 1917. With Plumer only a matter of days into his command in Italy, Robertson was making clear to him his frustration with the need to divert troops from Flanders. He told Plumer that those which had been deployed were 'not to be regarded as a permanency, but very much as a temporary measure only'. The deteriorating situation in France in February and March 1918 required Italy to take a back seat and Plumer, with two divisions, returned to the Western Front and handed command of the IEF back to Cavan. But, let us return to November 1917 and the arrival of the IEF.

While the British troops de-trained around Mantua the ally they had come to support was being hard-pressed by the Austrians in the mountains between the rivers Piave and Brenta, in the vicinity of the high points of Mt. Tomba and Mt. Fenera. As further Austrian attacks were expected on that part of the front the Montello

---

2   Carrington, *Soldier from the Wars Returning*, p.226.
3   Woodward, *Robertson*, memo Maurice to Delmé-Radcliffe, 2 November 1917, p.250.
4   Woodward, *Robertson*, memo Maurice to Delmé-Radcliffe, 3 November 1917, p.250.
5   TNA: WO 79/67, Private Papers of Earl of Cavan. Memo from CIGS, 28 October 1917.

was chosen as the concentration area for the IEF; a position that would be 'within supporting distance should a serious attack develop'.[6] The River Piave, the new defensive line behind which the Italians would stand to prevent any further advance by the Austrians, flows out from the foothills of the Alps and onto the north Venetian Plain. On its way southeast, towards the Adriatic, it comes up against the large, oval-shaped, high ground that is the Montello. This feature, which rises gently to around 800 feet, diverts the course of the Piave and causes it to narrow as it flows around the north-eastern slope of the hill. Orientated north-east to south-west, the Montello is some seven miles long and three and a half miles wide, with a gently undulating top. Although it lay close to the river its rising slope allowed the British trenches to be dug well above the water table (an opportunity not afforded them in Flanders), with a good view out towards the Austrian positions. The Piave, with its flow broken by numerous small islands and shingle banks, was not a single stream; it was fast flowing (especially after storms or snow melt) and in many places was very wide. On this front the British and enemy trenches were anywhere between one and two thousand yards apart, the whole geography so different from that on which they had fought in France and Flanders. The distance between the opposing troops was 'so wide that the men in the trenches were immune from sniping or ordinary machine-gun fire'.[7] This separation reduced the daily casualty count that had been such a feature of their life before Italy and, as was pointed out to Edmonds while he was researching the *Official History*:

> What must be appreciated is the difference between the warfare in Italy and France. In the former you hardly appreciated a war was on & [sic] one always motored up to the front line (I should have been sorry to have attempted it in France).[8]

While this comment reflected the views of many of the men as they compared their experience on the Western Front with that in Italy, it was also typical of how the British tended to judge the whole of the war in Italy. They had not been a part of the bitter two and a half years of fighting in the mountains above the Isonzo, and so they discounted it as being similar to the experience of the IEF in 1917-18. Some figures from the history of the 23rd Division will serve to demonstrate how different the war the unit experienced on the two fronts was. In December 1917 the division had only 31 Other Ranks killed, with one officer and 88 soldiers wounded, then in January 1918 the casualties dropped to a total of 47, of whom seven were fatal. In those two

---

6   TNA: WO 79/67, Operation Order No.1, 23 November 1917.
7   A.H. Hussey and D.S. Inman, *The Fifth Division in the Great War* (London, 1921), p.204.
8   TNA: CAB 45/84, letter from G.W. Howard to Edmonds, 30 August 1943.

Figure 7.1 British trenches on the banks of the Piave on the Montello.
(© Imperial War Museum Q 26053)

months there were only 167 casualties. Contrast that with the division's last 11 days in Flanders when they recorded 1,229, of which 275 were fatal.[9]

Although the front was 'quiet', it was not inactive; British commanders considered it necessary to pursue aggressive trench raids and patrols in order to 'dominate' the enemy and to collect intelligence on the opposing forces. Frequently this would be achieved by capturing Austrian prisoners who would be brought back into the British lines. However, not all the troops (or indeed all regimental officers) agreed with the need for these raids, which were ordered by Staff Officers from their more sheltered headquarters some miles from the front. In spite of the official line that troops should adopt an aggressive stance towards the enemy, many units preferred an unofficial policy of 'live and let live'[10] towards those in the opposing trenches – examples can be found in the IEF and the Italian units, as well as those on the Western Front. Units had learnt that if they only fired back when they had been fired on, then the opposing side was likely to adopt the same stance. According to Thomas Weber the practice was

9   Sandilands, *The 23rd Division*, pp.227 & 209.
10   Ashworth, *Trench Warfare*.

even indulged in by Hitler's regiment, and that it was 'endemic all along the Western Front'.[11] Unfortunately for the men, just as sickness and discipline returns were considered a measure of a unit's morale, so the number and effectiveness of trench raids and patrols were taken as indicators of their 'fighting spirit' and of the leadership of their officers. In the terminology of the war, units which did not encourage regular raids and patrols exhibited a 'trench habit', they had become 'sticky', and this should be eradicated as 'the whole value of the trench raid to the battalion commander lies in the effect it has in maintaining the *morale* of the men'.[12] [Emphasis in the original.] For the troops of the IEF becoming 'non-sticky' would involve spending time in the icy, strong-flowing, waters of the Piave while wearing full uniform and carrying rifles and equipment – frighteningly, many would have been non-swimmers. Those ordering the raids may have considered them necessary (while not having to go themselves), but Gladden probably spoke for many when he wrote that he was 'not filled with any particular joy at being thus chosen [to participate]'. However, having met no Austrian opposition, and returning safe, though cold and wet, he did admit to 'a certain pride at having been chosen for a mission just a little out of the ordinary run of things, a sort of vote of confidence that we were the types that could make it'.[13] One detects a grudging acknowledgement that maybe raids did increase morale and spirit after all.

From the time of their arrival in November 1917, until the end of March 1918, the troops of the IEF spent most of their time improving their defensive positions, sending out periodic trench raids and training when they returned to the rest areas some miles behind the lines. However, the make-up of the IEF, its commander and the defensive positions it would occupy were about to change; German divisions had been transferred from the Russian to the Western Front (following the Bolshevik revolution), as well as six more from the Italian Front. On the 21 March the Germans launched their *Kaiserschlacht*, causing the retreat of Gough's Fifth Army (and the capture of my grandfather). The concern over the German troop movements led Foch to call for four divisions to be returned from Italy (two each from the British and French deployments) to help offset the expected German numerical superiority in France. Arrangements were put in place for the 5th and 41st divisions to leave the IEF, without any consultation with the Italians. To make this decision unilaterally was contrary to the formal procedure which required that such a move should be agreed via the Inter-Allied Superior Council; the failure to abide by the agreement led to a protest from the Italian Prime Minister.[14] It was acknowledged in the War Cabinet that the removal of these divisions should have been dealt with by the agreed process but as the British government had sent them to Italy 'on their own initiative' they

11   Weber, *Hitler's First War*, pp.85-6.
12   Sandilands, *The 23rd Division*, p.58.
13   Gladden, *Piave*, p.51.
14   TNA: CAB 23/5, minutes of War Cabinet 351, 21 February 1918.

would be 'perfectly within their rights in recalling the Divisions'.[15] Back in October 1917, when the movement orders were sent out to deploy the IEF, Lloyd George had told Sir William Robertson that by helping the Italians Britain would be in a position to 'dictate' to them. Now, with the unilateral decision to withdraw two divisions to France, they could also be ignored. When Italians heard of the proposed move they voiced their opposition. In an attempt to slow or postpone the move, Diaz stated that as he had received no instructions from his government he could provide no transport. The Italian Foreign Minister, Sonnino, in conversation with General Smuts, had claimed that 'Austrian divisions were pouring in on the Italian Front' and that 'if a big attack came and the Italians failed, they would say that we [Britain & France] had deserted them, and the blame would be put upon us'.[16] Once again the Italians were perceived as ignoring the big picture of the war in favour of scaremongering with unsubstantiated claims of Austrian numerical superiority. Cavan and General Paul Maistre (the French commander in Italy), believed that Diaz regarded Austrian strength on his front 'in far too pessimistic terms'.[17] Gloom laden statements by the Italians worked contrary to the effect intended by those making them, they smacked of an unwillingness to bear their share of the war (again, discounting previous Italian losses), and as Sir Arthur Nicholson put it, 'British and American opinion is more important at this stage of the war than Italian opinion'.[18] In spite of the opposition of Diaz, and Sonnino's statement that their removal meant that Italy had been 'deserted', the official report which came out later on the battle of Vittorio Veneto stated that those British troop numbers had been 'sensibly diminished'. In this there was no hint of 'desertion' or betrayal by their ally, instead an impression of Italian acquiescence in a move which reduced the fighting troops in Italy, but did not prevent their winning a glorious victory at Vittorio Veneto. After the war Italian historians were at pains to present the battle as a glorious feat of Italian arms, it was important that Italy should be seen to have triumphed as much as possible on their own. Any suggestion that British and French help had been either important or necessary would dilute the picture that Fascist historians would wish to paint of a resurgent Italian militarism. However the Italians would later represent the reduction in British troop numbers, the situation in France took precedence over Italy – whether the Italians agreed or not. Consequently by 1 April the 5th and 41st Divisions had left, as had Generals Plumer and Fayolle, to be replaced by Cavan and Maistre, the latter a veteran of Verdun.

At the same time as the IEF lost the two divisions, those remaining were moved from their positions on the Montello to the mountains of the Asiago. Once again the British troops would find themselves in an environment that was radically different

15   TNA: CAB 23/5, minutes of War Cabinet 347, 15 February 1918.
16   TNA: CAB 23/5, minutes of War CAbinet 357, 1 March 1918.
17   K. Jeffery (ed.), *The Military Correspondence of Field Marshal Sir Henry Wilson 1918-1922* (London, 1985), Rawlinson to Wilson, 22 March 1918, p.30.
18   TNA: FO 371/3230, *Italy:1918*, memo 42599, 2 March 1918.

from their Flanders experience; mountain combat was not a part of their training, and they would need to take some lessons from their ally. Even today, in a modern tour bus, the drive from Calvene up the steep southern side of the Asiago plateau is quite thrilling. The narrow road is one long series of hairpin bends, with a tremendous view back over the Venetian Plain and the River Astico. For the troops it meant a hard five-hour route march, with ten minute breaks every hour, to reach the top. Once the men had gained the plateau they found themselves on terrain that varied between 1,200 to 1,400 meters above sea level. However, there were large open areas, as at the base at Granezza, though much of it was heavily wooded, covered with rocks, and swathed in mist even in July; at least it was on the day this author visited. The forward trenches lay some five kilometres north of the steep climb which had tested the men's fitness. These front-line positions were in the tree-line which formed the transition between the open plain on which lay the small town of Asiago and the Austrian lines, behind them was a steep 200 metres climb through the woods to the plateau above. As on the Montello the distance between the opposing trenches was about a kilometre, with the small river Ghelpac in between them. For those modern-day battlefield tourists who wish to clamber down the front slope of the British position, there are still signs of the original trenches, blasted and hammered out of the rock using Italian *perforatrici*.[19] As one engineer officer put it, 'explosives are an invaluable aid to field engineering in the mountain areas'.[20]

Not only the trenches, but the dugouts in which the men lived had to be hewn from solid rock, unlike Flanders where they were scooped out of the earth. One result of blasting into the rock face on the forward slope was that the entrance to the dugouts faced no man's land, and left the entrances vulnerable to shelling. Most students of the war will be familiar with the pattern of trenches on the Western Front; a 'zig-zag' front-line serviced by similarly shaped communication trenches coming up from the rear areas. In this way the soldiers were below ground level as they approached and occupied the forward areas. The slope of the ground and the solid rock made this impractical for the troops on the Asiago; Edmonds says they were 'judged unnecessary in the wooded sector',[21] where the trees were supposed to provide cover. Instead of communication trenches, woodland paths wound down the forward slope from the top of the plateau, to the trenches at the bottom. The men using them might have felt themselves to be sitting targets, and Gladden wrote that he felt 'particularly exposed on the hillsides, where there was no trench cover'.[22] In fact the dense trees hid the troops' movement and made them difficult to see from the Austrian positions. In these circumstances it was time for the British to take lessons from their ally.

19   Trevelyan, *Italy's War*, p.159.
20   J. Ure, 'The Warwickshire (Mountain Brigade)', *Journal of the Western Front Association*, 53 (1998), pp.25-29.
21   Edmonds, *Italy*, pp.168-70.
22   Gladden, *Piave*, p.91.

Figure 7.2 View towards Asiago from British front-line trench positions on the Asiago plateau. (© J. Dillon)

They learnt that as well as tree cover, the exposed paths could be further camouflaged by erecting canvas screens and wooden fences along the side facing the Austrians. These were built some two to three metres high and made it extremely difficult for the Austrians to detect movement along the tracks. An example of this technique is shown in Figure 7.3 from the IWM archive.[23]

When the units of the IEF had been in France and Flanders they had been used to a system of defence which allowed for a deep front. This was achieved through the use of forward, support and reserve trenches, with hundreds of yards between the three lines, allowing troops to fall back rather than be overwhelmed in the first attack. The geography of the plateau precluded this approach. Behind the men in the forward trenches in the tree line was the 200 metres slope to the plateau, with a second line of trenches part of the way up. This formed a very narrow forward defensive position. With the very steep drop to the Venetian Plain on the southern side of the plateau, if the Austrians drove the IEF back from the forward slope then they would have had to fall back all the way to Vicenza before establishing a holding line. With no depth to the position held by the British they could not allow themselves to be over-run. If they did then the IEF would be fighting 'with its back to a wall, or, more literally,

23   IWM: HU 057552.

Figure 7.3
Austrian troops move a wounded
man. The screens are visible behind
them – similar screens were used
by the British and Italians. (©
Imperial War Museum HU 57552)

to a chasm'.[24] A visitor today can see how any retreat would have quickly turned to
a rout. While the terrain on the plateau would have allowed some units to provide
rear-guard cover, the steep southern slope would have caused chaos. It would have
resembled the later retreat of the British from Crete in 1941; driven southwards across
the Askyphou plain the British, Australian and New Zealand troops then had to
descend the precipitous slope to the village of Sphakia and the sea. Before leaving the
geography of the plateau, it is worth mentioning one more challenge that the British
had not anticipated. The hairpin bends on the road made the British supply vehicles
almost unsuitable. The Italians had to supply them with hundreds of short-wheelbase
Fiat trucks which could negotiate the sharp bends, and which drew praise from the
IEF soldiers who had to drive them. In terms of equipment needed for fighting in the
mountains, the British had lessons to learn from the Italians.

The 8,000 yards of front to be held by the IEF was deemed by the British to have
become 'stagnant', in their view the Italians had adopted a 'live and let live' philosophy,
an attitude which some British units were also guilty of. With just a hint of arrogance
the 23 Division history stated that; 'The continuous harassing fire of artillery, the

24 Sandilands, *The 23rd Division*, p.237.

Figure 7.4 Rocky terrain in which the British had their front-line trenches. (© J. Dillon)

perpetual action of patrols, and the frequent minor enterprises, which had become habitual in France and Flanders, had been unknown on this front'.[25] Just as the icy water of the Piave should not stop raids and patrols, so the ice, snow and mountainous terrain of the Asiago would not be allowed to get in the way of aggressive patrolling; 'a policy of passive defence was not followed'. Austrian occupancy of any of the abandoned houses and farms in the one to two kilometres of ground that separated the two armies 'could not be countenanced'. Lieutenant-Colonel Sandilands' history of his division has that smack of pompous chauvinism with which the British sometimes regarded their ally. Convinced that the Italians had done no real fighting he went on to comment that; 'Things were beginning to stir on the Asiago plateau, and the enemy, if he had been in any doubt before, now realised that there had been changes in the mountains'.[26]

The British were not specialist mountain troops, so why were they (together with the French) sent to Asiago? In February 1918 the French commander, General Fayolle, had proposed an offensive in the Trentino, which had been favourably received by

25   Sandilands, *The 23rd Division*, p.237.
26   Sandilands, *The 23rd Division*, p.245.

Diaz. The rationale behind it was that any future advance by the Italians across the Piave, to recover territory held by the Austrians, would leave its flank and rear threatened by the Austrians above Asiago. To counter that eventuality the Austrians would have to be driven back in the north. Cavan, an advocate of offensive action and its positive effect on an army's 'fighting spirit', gave it as his opinion that it would also 'raise the Italian moral[e]' to see the Allies pushing forward against the Austrians.[27] In their new positions on the Asiago the British section of the front was on the right of the Italian X Corps, and would be held with two divisions at the front and the third in reserve. On the British right were the French, who in turn had the Italian XIII Corps on their right flank; all were part of General Montuori's newly formed Italian Sixth Army. The offensive suggested by Fayolle was subject to a number of changes and the cause of a large amount of frustration between the Allies. Before he was recalled to France, Fayolle had planned on an attacking force of 25 divisions; 5 British and 2 Italian under Plumer; 4 French and 6 Italian under Maistre; 2 French and 6 Italian under an Italian commander.[28] However, with events in France having led to the reduction of the Anglo-French force in Italy, only 17 divisions were available for the assault and the IEF would be commanded by Cavan instead of Plumer. But the assault was not to be. Instead the proposal became a shuttlecock, bashed around between one start date and another, until strong rumours of the Austrians' own attack in June caused its cancellation. Cavan was in favour of the plan, but believed that it should be carried out 'by May 1st at [the] latest', and the objectives should be scaled back commensurate with the reduction in the number of divisions.[29] As ever, plans laid in Italy were hostage to events in France and to the continuing Italian tendency to exaggerate the number of Austrian troops that they believed were arraigned against them. In London, following Haig's "backs to the Wall" Order of the Day during the continuing German offensive in France, Wilson (CIGS) telegraphed Cavan to express doubts over the proposed attack from the Asiago. Wilson told Cavan that the attack should only go ahead if he (Cavan) was sure that it would involve a low cost in casualties and 'lead in the long run to economy of men'.[30] The IEF would not be allowed to call on France for any reinforcements or 'refills' for any casualties, the Western Front took priority. Cavan, ever eager to push an attack, also had his hopes dashed by Diaz who was similarly concerned to economise on troops; at a meeting between the two on 15 April the offensive was postponed.

In the decision over whether or not to attack the Austrians from the Asiago, Diaz and Cavan came at it from different start-points; both had been Corps commanders but Diaz was now C-in-C of all his nation's armies, including an international force – an Eisenhower and Montgomery situation, though on a rather smaller scale. Cavan,

27   TNA: WO 106/852, memo from Cavan to CIGS, 2 April 1918.
28   Edmonds, *Italy*, pp.158-9.
29   TNA: WO 106/852, memo from Cavan to CIGS, 2 April 1918.
30   Edmonds, *Italy*, pp.175-6.

the ex-Guards divisional commander, had the independent command of an expeditionary force which he was keen to use in attack; Diaz had command of an army that had recently suffered a humiliating defeat, he could not afford to use it recklessly. Cavan believed the Austrians were a 'poor' enemy who did not respond to British raids; 'our patrols are absolute masters of the broad "no Man's Land" and a good deal of reconnaissance takes place there in broad daylight unmolested'.[31] As well as an assured belief in the superiority of the British soldier over the Austrian he tended to discount any of the intelligence that convinced Diaz that the Austrians were planning their own attack on the Asiago; he could not 'discover any real evidence from photographs or daily reconnaissance to show that a big offensive is imminent in the immediate future'. But they were, as he would discover on 15 June. One historian has stated that, during these early months of 1918, Diaz 'cautiously husbanded his military strength, *rejecting Allied pleas for action* to relieve pressure on the Western Front in June and July 1918'.[32] [My italics.] It was the mixed messages from the Italian commanders that were causing British frustration. Cavan's IEF was part of the Italian Sixth Army and its commander, Montuori, was giving Cavan to believe that just such an attack was on the cards. On 1 May Montuori told his corps commanders that 'the elements of doubt [regarding the planned offensive] had to a considerable extend disappeared and that the offensive might be considered as *highly probable*'.[33] [My italics.] By 16 May Cavan informed Wilson that Montuori had warned the units under his command to be ready by the 31st of that month to launch an attack 'on whatever day the Comando Supremo decided'.[34] Diaz may have been rejecting Allied pleas, but his staff appeared to be planning otherwise. The Italians were not likely to 'reject' Allied requests for coordinated attacks if they were in fact planning one, as Montuori led Cavan to believe. On the other hand, if he had ruled out the possibility of any offensive then he would appear not to have been in control of his army commanders, who were apparently still planning one.

At the end of May it was still Cavan's view that an allied assault from the Asiago was likely: 'The situation as described in my last letter still holds good, viz., that we are to be ready to take the offensive by 31st instant'.[35] In Cavan's opinion, while his preference for an attack appeared to be going ahead, he was unimpressed with the way in which it was being planned. He considered Italian planning to be 'frothy', and with too much reliance that 'it will be alright on the day'. But, while Diaz had an army to lose, Cavan only had three divisions in the game and was dismissive of Italian fears; as he told Wilson, 'My fear is that the dread of an Austrian offensive may paralyse the preparations for our offensive'.

31   TNA: WO 106/852, memo from Cavan to CIGS, 24 April 1918.
32   Gooch, *Morale and Discipline*, p.445.
33   Edmonds, *Italy*, p.177.
34   TNA: WO 106/852, memo from Cavan to CIGS, 16 May 1918.
35   TNA: WO 106/852, memo from Cavan to CIGS, 25 May 1918.

In his first independent command Cavan betrayed an over-eagerness to 'get at' the enemy, even to the exclusion of intelligence that might have warranted more caution, and which was being taken seriously by Montuori. Cavan's exasperation with his Italian counterparts is obvious in his memos to Wilson; by the 27 May 'There [had] been a kaleidoscopic change in the Italian situation in the last 24 hours, and I cannot deny that I am disappointed at the attitude adopted'. Cavan did not accept that the information available at that time, especially aerial reconnaissance, necessarily led to the conclusion that there was an impending Austrian offensive. But, as he acknowledged, it mattered more what the Italians thought; 'the fact remains that the Italians [especially Montuori] do accept it [the aerial reconnaissance]. The ASIAGO [sic] offensive is definitely postponed'.[36] As well as aerial photography, information also came from Austrian prisoners and deserters. In one comic incident 'three Austrian officers entered the British lines, accompanied by their servants carrying their portmanteaus'.[37] The details gleaned from captured Austrians led the Italians and British to believe that the assault (when it came) would not be against the British line; that would only be subjected to an artillery bombardment. Because of the messages he was getting from Montuori, Cavan was now in the awkward position of planning for an offensive any time after the 31 May, while at the same time preparing to receive an artillery bombardment on his own line and give support to the Italians on his flank who would be attacked by the Austrians. He was not impressed. The guns and troops which had been put in place for the Allied assault from the Asiago were now repositioned to face the attack that Diaz expected across the Piave, as a result Cavan told Wilson that the offensive 'cannot now be undertaken at short notice'. A month later he would apparently forget having made this comment. Cavan was an Italophile, and he did an excellent job of commanding Tenth Army in October, but he could still take a chauvinistic view of Italian concerns over possible German troop movements to support Austria: 'Commanders talk with bated breath of the presence of German Divisions. Of this they have I think little or no evidence. The attitude is bad for moral[e]'. For all that he wished to launch an attack from the Asiago, Cavan was wrong in his dismissal of the intelligence available to the Italians. The Austrians were planning their own two-pronged offensive, one against the positions on the River Piave, the other against those on the Asiago (see Map 2). Diaz was right to be concerned, had the Austrians prevailed on the Asiago then his northern flank would have been turned and the enemy would have been on his rear at the Piave.

At this point we should quickly review the position held by the British units on the Asiago. Their line stretched for some 8,000 yards, with the front-line trenches at the bottom of the northern slope of the plateau where it joined the flatter ground of the Asiago plain. In front of them, to their right, was the small town of Asiago

36   TNA: WO 106/852, memo from Cavan to CIGS, 27 May 1918.
37   J.F. Gathorne-Hardy, 'A summary of the Campaign in Italy, and an account of the Battle of Vittorio Veneto', *Army Quarterly* Vol.3 (1921), p.26.

and beyond that, a couple of kilometres away, the ground rose again into the Alps. Between the British and Austrian forces meandered the small River Guelpac, its distance from the British being rather more on the right, than on the left, where it ran through a steeper ravine and formed more of a natural barrier for attacking forces. Behind the British were the wood covered slopes that rose some two hundred metres to the plateau, leaving the troops with a relatively narrow defensive line. With three divisions at his disposal Cavan followed traditional practice in having one, the 7th, held back in reserve, while the 48th and 23rd shared the forward area; the 23rd on the right and the 48th on the left of the Corps front.

Although it should not have made any difference to the way in which the battalions were placed in the defensive line it should be noted that 48 Division were occupying the left of the corps front for the first time, previously they had always been on the right. While the terrain was similar to that on the right of the line – rock covered, with a tree-covered slope to the rear of the forward trenches – the division's frontage was quite different. Here the Asiago plain was considerably narrower than on the right, with the River Guelpac close to the British trenches. This terrain difference influenced the approach of the two divisional commanders to the disposition of their troops, which in turn was significant for the way in which they held their lines against the Austrian assault, and for the career of Major-General Fanshawe. Commanders at all levels followed the principle of having part of their available force 'forward', the remainder being held as a reserve which could be utilised as an action developed. To this end Cavan had two of his three divisions on the Asiago plateau – the 48th and the 23rd – with the 7th some miles to the rear in reserve. Each of the forward divisional commanders had two of his three brigades 'up', the third held back in support. Cavan's British Corps held a frontage of 8,000 yards with four brigades (two each from 23rd and 48th divisions), giving each brigade roughly 2,000 yards to defend, depending on the ground they occupied, and that to their front. For those readers who have stuck with the author so far, we come to the salient point. Brigade commanders also divided the force available to them into 'front' and 'rear' units – although those in the support role are actually quite close to the active trenches. Each put two of their three battalions in the front-line positions, but where 145 Brigade (on the right of 48 Division front) had four companies forward (two from each battalion), 143 Brigade on their left was defending its 2,000 yards of front with only two companies. Fanshawe is likely to have approved this 'thinning' of the line on the grounds that the Ghelpac came close to that brigade's trenches and any Austrians trying to cross there would have had to do so under the guns of the defenders. Cavan would later give the reduced manning of these trenches as one of his reasons for removing Fanshawe from command.

We return now to June and the postponed allied attack northwards from the Asiago. As part of the preparation for that assault by the combined British, French and Italian forces, the medical units that would normally have been available on the Asiago had been increased to handle the expected casualties. This move of the medics would prove to have been fortuitous – the British troops were hit by an epidemic which was later

Figure 7.5 A British command post, made of concrete, on the plateau above the front-line trenches. (© J. Dillon)

diagnosed as influenza; 'the scourge of the armies in Europe'.[38] Having the augmented medical facilities close to the front-line enabled the medics to treat those affected by the outbreak more quickly than would otherwise have been the case. This was a lucky-break as contagion rates were high and the fever spread quickly through the divisions just days before the Austrians attacked. In the eight days from 6-11 June (just prior to the assault) the 23rd Division had 1109 men admitted with influenza, and between the 6th and the 15th of the month 1019 were evacuated.[39] In 48 Division the staff officers were particularly badly affected, with one diarist stating that they were 'mown down by mountain fever'.[40] With the medical staff almost overwhelmed, and troops going down like flies, the IEF met its first real test of morale and fighting spirit in the early hours of 15 June.

Cyril Falls, writing in 1966 before the official documents were open to the public, rightly states that the military action on the Asiago plateau in June 1918 'gets very

38   Sandilands, *The 23rd Division*, p.247.
39   TNA: WO 95/4231, data extrapolated from the graph for June admissions.
40   Morshead, *Private Papers*.

little mention in English histories'.[41] That omission has since been rectified in books by Cassar and also John and Eileen Wilks, both written in the 1990s, but since then the histories of the Italian Front have concentrated on the Italians. Thompson's *White War* has no mention of the action on the Asiago other than that Conrad, the Austrian commander on that front, 'was in retreat' on the second day.[42] The most recent history is by John Gooch, but this also gives no more than a passing reference to Cavan's men: 'British and French divisions lost their positions but took them back with immediate counter-attacks'.[43] At 03:00 on 15 June – 'punctual to the minute'[44] – the Austrians opened the bombardment that heralded the start of their offensive. What did surprise the British was that the shelling was followed by a frontal assault on their lines, contrary to Cavan's expectation, and which was passed down to junior commanders. Young Lieutenant Greenwell, with the 1/4th Oxfordshire & Buckinghamshire Light Infantry (1/4 Ox & Bucks), was on the right of the 48th divisional front when the shelling started:

> On the night of the 14th we had warning that something was afoot for the following morning and were consequently to a certain extent prepared. But we were not prepared for what really happened. We never thought the enemy would actually attack on our front and expected only a certain amount of bombardment.[45]

Not far from the Ox & Bucks was Norman Gladden, close to the junction between 23rd and 48th divisions. Warned of the possibility of a gas shelling, he was surprised when the bombardment opened: 'Guns were firing out in front, actually out in front!'[46] His surprise is an indirect reference to how unusual such an event was, and is in marked contrast to his battalion's experience in France and Flanders where such shelling was 'normal'. As well as having been told that intelligence indicated the British line would only receive a bombardment, the men of the IEF believed that the Austrians would avoid their line in favour of the Italians, who they rather arrogantly considered to be 'weaker'. This point is made by Sir Henry Wilson (in his new role as CIGS) to Cavan; 'the Bosche [he included Austrians in this group] will take damn good care not to attack that particular bit of the line, but will fall on the parts of the line held by pure Italians'.[47] Well, he was wrong.

Before reviewing the events that led to the dismissal of Major-General Sir Robert Fanshawe, 48 Division Commander, it is worth mentioning the situation of 23

41   C. Falls, *Caporetto 1917 (London, 1966)*, p.155.
42   Thompson, *White War*, p.345.
43   Gooch, *The Italian Army*, p.280.
44   TNA: WO 79/70 Cavan's notes, p.8.
45   Greenwell, *Infant in Arms*, p.225.
46   Gladden, *Piave*, p.118.
47   Jeffery, *Sir Henry Wilson*, memo from Wilson to Cavan, 29 March 1918, p.33.

Division, who occupied the right of the British line. Here, the Austrians came out of a thick mist, but their attack failed to achieve more than a brief penetration of their line towards the slopes of the San Sisto ridge on the extreme right. At this point the ground was held by the 11th Sherwood Foresters; their battalion commander, Lieutenant-Colonel Charles Hudson, won the Victoria Cross for leading a counter-attack which threw back the Austrians almost as soon as they had got into the British line. While Hudson's name might not be familiar to all, that of Vera Brittain probably is. Her brother, Captain Edward Brittain (awarded the MC for his actions on the first day of the battle of the Somme) was in Hudson's battalion, he also led a counter-attack, but was killed doing so. The divisional history mentions by name some of the men who performed individual acts of bravery, or were killed that day, but there is no mention of Brittain – one would have expected a Captain to be so named. One account of his death is given by Francis MacKay in his detailed guide to the action on the Asiago. During the counter-attack 'he [Brittain] apparently paused to observe the enemy, and was killed, possibly sniped by an Austrian officer'.[48] Richard Holmes puts forward another possible sequence of events which would also account for Brittain not being mentioned in either the divisional or Edmonds' histories. Prior to the battle (according to Holmes) Brittain had been told that his mail had been opened in a random check, and that the provost marshal would be investigating his references to homosexual relationships with private soldiers. For an officer this could be devastating: eight were court-martialled in the war for 'indecency'. Holmes notes that while 'we can never be sure of the circumstances of his death' it could be argued that 'an impossible counter-attack was suicide by proxy'.[49] Whatever were the circumstances of Brittain's death, for most soldiers a battle was often a confusing and chaotic series of events within a small geographic area; most men saw little of what happened beyond their own company trenches.

For historians and researchers the accounts left to us by the men, whether in later biographies or contemporary letters, provide that 'I was there' insight which is so valuable a century later. But they cannot be mistaken for the whole picture. In his official history Edmonds states that what happened on the Asiago was very much a 'battalion commanders' and soldiers' battle', fought in the woods and the clouds; what happened 'can only be pieced together, and the exact relation in time of events, even in adjoining battalion sectors, is not always certain'.[50] Gladden's account of that June day tells us little more than what happened to a small platoon.[51] Similarly, Harry Lamin was in a support company and 'did not have to fire'. His unit was about one kilometre behind the front, on top of the plateau, and his appreciation of the battle was gleaned

48   F. MacKay, *Asiago 15/16 June 1918. Battle in the woods and clouds* (Barnsley, 2001), p.65.
49   R. Holmes, *Soldiers. Army Lives and Loyalties from Recoats to Dusty Warriors* (London, 2011), p.590.
50   Edmonds, *Italy*, p.201.
51   Gladden, *Piave*, pp.118-30.

largely from a visit he made to the front-line the following day 'to have a look when things had quietened down'. Lamin's comments on how he believed the action had gone would have been well received at home; 'them in the front line simply mowed them down and he [the Austrians] got no further than the wire'[52] – no mention of temporary break-throughs and counter-attacks elsewhere on the line. However, he does make a comment which backs up the British command view that the Austrians would attack Italian, rather than British, trenches: 'The prisoners […] thought that they were going to meet the Italians and where [sic] surprised to see our lads in the trenches'. George Walton, whose unit was involved in meeting the attack, made no mention of it in his postcards home, possibly to prevent his family from worrying. On the other hand one soldier in the same brigade as Gladden wrote enthusiastically to his wife of the British defence:

> My word Love, it was exciting when they came over the top for they came in thousands, but they couldn't get through [they did not on this brigade front] – they were running about like rabbits and we were potting away at them. We got lots of prisoners and they were only too pleased to give themselves up.[53]

The Austrians were as tired of the war as any of the British soldiers, and just wanted to go home. Lamin also stated that the prisoners he saw were 'pleased to be made prisoners', they also had 'plenty of money' on them which he and his mates seem to have relieved them of as he tells his brother that 'I am putting an Austrian note in [the letter] I hope you get it'.

On the right of the British front Major-General Sir James Babington's 23rd Division had quickly driven back those Austrians who had managed to penetrate their line, whereas on their left it took somewhat longer for Fanshawe's 48th Division to re-establish its forward positions. Before discussing this division's experience on the 15 June it is worth reiterating five points, all of which are relevant to the events of that day. First, the British criticised the Italians for holding too many men in their forward trenches, and that this was a contributory cause of their defeat at Caporetto. Second, British commanders had been told to expect an artillery bombardment, not a frontal attack; it would be normal to reduce the manning of the trenches during a bombardment to reduce losses, with troops moving forward again as the shelling stopped. Third, following the German breakthrough on Fifth Army's front during the Spring Offensive, General Gough was removed from command. Fourth, Fanshawe's front was held by only six companies, not eight as was the case with 23 Division. Fifth, the British considered themselves to be militarily superior to the Italians. Given points one and two it is not surprising that Fanshawe thinned his front line, employing only three rather than four battalions. The extreme left of the divisional position was held

52   Lamin, *Letters*, p.147.
53   Hardie, *Private Papers*, report for February-July 1918.

not by two battalions, but one, the 1/5 Royal Warwicks; why only one? Their front was more open than that of the units on their right, an enemy attack would be more exposed and the Ghelpac was closer to the British trenches, so any attempt to cross it would have to be done under the Warwicks' guns. There was less tree cover for this battalion so that 'no such cover from view existed, and movement was perilous during daylight'.[54] There were good defensive reasons for having fewer troops in these front-line trenches during an expected bombardment. Fanshawe (who had led his division since May 1915 and had fought at the Somme and Passchendaele) had given thought to how his division might meet an Austrian attack; in Edmonds' opinion the 48th 'was better prepared to meet the attack than the 23rd'.[55]

The 48th had implemented a system of flexible defence, this would allow them to survive the initial bombardment, absorb an enemy break-in, and then utilise troops in the support trenches to drive back the attackers, so preventing a 'break-in' from becoming a much more dangerous 'break-through'. Two trenches in 145 Brigade's area (to the right of the Warwicks) were the key to this plan. The Cesuna 'switch' and Lemerle 'switch', which together formed a semi-circle behind the brigade front, into which a break-in could be drawn and subjected to enfilade fire from this trench system. As there was heavy tree cover to the brigade's front, through which the Austrians could advance under cover, this was considered the most likely point for a possible attack.[56] We should at this point recall that the divisional strength had been considerably reduced by the influenza epidemic, and that this was not restricted to ordinary soldiers; of the division's HQ staff, only Fanshawe and his Intelligence Officer were on duty, two of three infantry brigadiers were absent and half of the infantry battalions on the 15 June were commanded by Majors rather than their normal Lieutenant-Colonels. In spite of this, Fanshawe's defensive plan – which had been twice rehearsed – worked; the Austrian advance was stopped. Because the troops had practiced just such an eventuality, they knew their roles. Small groups of men, cut off from their commanders, sometimes consisting of 'clerks, cooks, orderlies, servants and everyone who could use a rifle',[57] held their ground. On the occasion where it mattered – combat – the fighting spirit and morale of the 48th can be assessed as 'good'. During the day counter-attacks were made, but as they were delivered piecemeal they had only limited success. The following day, however, was much more productive. Fanshawe ordered a concerted assault to be made at 04:30, using troops from all three brigades and by 07:30 the 'whole of the divisional front line was re-occupied, many prisoners being taken and many dead and wounded found on the ground'.[58] Not unnaturally, given the way the attack had gone, 48 Division bore the brunt of the casualties; 53% with 23rd

54   Edmonds, *Italy*, p.169.
55   Edmonds, *Italy*, p.208.
56   For those who wish to follow the action 'blow by blow', see relevant chapters in Wilks, Cassar and Edmonds.
57   Edmonds, *Italy*, p.206.
58   Edmonds, *Italy*, p.215.

having 34% and the rest carried by HQ and 7 Division (who were in support). Many more would probably have died of their wounds but for the fact that the medical units, brought forward for the planned allied offensive, had not been withdrawn when that was postponed.

On 15 June the IEF received its first frontal assault in the Italian theatre. Although unused to fighting in forested and mountainous terrain they had absorbed the attack and within 28 hours all ground gained by the Austrians was back in XIV Corps control. Unfortunately for General Fanshawe, Lord Cavan did not see the day's events in such a positive light and he was removed from divisional command. Charles Carrington, who served under Fanshawe, saw the 15/16 June as 'a brilliant example of flexibility in defence' but for which Fanshawe was 'unjustly' sent home by a Corps commander who was 'an exponent of rigid defence and cramming the front line with troops'; on the personal level, he regarded Cavan as a 'tough fighting soldier, and a charming man'.[59] Carrington regarded Fanshawe's removal as a slight against the division which; 'throughout the war [had] never lost a defensive line or failed to hold its objective, once taken. But on several occasions front line trenches were overrun and retaken by immediate counter-attack'.[60] In other words, the way in which the division dealt with the Austrians was 'business as usual'. But if mistakes were made, were they all Fanshawe's?

We have seen that Cavan and the other commanders had received strong intelligence that the British line would at least be subjected to a heavy artillery bombardment in the early hours of 15 June. While a direct assault was not expected, it could not be discounted, and intelligence rarely gives the whole picture. As this was Cavan's first independent command it is reasonable to assume that he would have wanted to ensure that his lines were as well prepared as possible for the anticipated action. While Fanshawe was organising the counter-attacks to push back the Austrians Cavan visited 48 Division headquarters, he later noted that he did this 'to see if he could be helpful; his presence was encouraging, and he did not interfere with the arrangements which had been made'.[61] However, in the days following, and years later when writing to the official historian, Cavan distanced himself from Fanshawe's troop dispositions to both meet and repel the Austrians. In 1945 he wrote to Edmonds regarding the counter-attacks:

> Privately I think Fanshawe could have 'softened' the pocket with trench mortars for some hours before his first counter attack which was unprepared. I looked at the position from above Magnaboschi in the late evening of 15th and told

59   Carrington, *Soldier from the Wars Returning*, p.226.
60   C. Carrington, 'The Defence of the Cesuna Re-entrant in the Italian Alps by the 48th (South Midland) Division, 15th June 1918. A Study of Minor Tactics in the Defensive' *Army Quarterly*, Vol. XIV (1927), p.307.
61   Edmonds, *Italy*, p.212.

Gathorne-Hardy [his Chief of Staff] that the triangle with apex at CLO [a point on the map] could be well plastered & a counterstroke by reserve Bde. [brigade] Sd. [should] follow, but Fanshawe had already given other orders & a counter-order then Wd. [would] have made confusion'.[62] [underlining in original]

In the event Cavan left Fanshawe to get on with things and his signal sent to CIGS on the 15th giving a summary of the day's events is a little equivocal. He acknowledges that both divisions were seriously undermanned as a result of the influenza epidemic, and that 48 Division held its line 'very thinly':

> This was done for economy in men, and to avoid the destructive bombardment, but I think it was too thin – the result being that in two or three place the enemy was able to get through the wire unopposed.[63]

Fanshawe had avoided the Italian mistake of packing the front-line trench with men when a bombardment was expected; it is difficult to believe that as this was Cavan's first defence of an assault while holding independent command, he would not have been aware of how the line was manned. In a 1921 article for the Army Quarterly he adopted the position of fence-sitter:

> Owing to the situation in France, *the conserving of man-power was all important.* [...] We had also taken the precaution of keeping as many men as possible out of the front lines in order to avoid the bombardment. *In places this latter policy was overdone*, and the temporary success of the enemy in getting through the wire on the British left was due to this cause'.[64] [My emphasis]

Here there is an oblique reference to Fanshawe as the cause, with no responsibility on the part of the C-in-C. In his memo to Sir Henry Wilson, written on the evening of 15 June, there is no indication that a divisional commander might have to be removed. 'There was an anxious half hour about 9.30 a.m., when CESUNA [the trench] might have been captured and a serious breach made in the LEMERLE [trench] defences. Our local commanders showed the better initiative [than the Austrians] and the situation was restored'. However Cavan told Wilson that it was necessary to hold a 'careful enquiry into exact reasons of the break into the 48th Division line, in order that we may benefit in the future, and see how to strengthen our defence'.

On 4 July Fanshawe was removed and his position was taken by Major-General Sir H.B. Walker. Unfortunately Lord Cavan did not publish an autobiography, nor has anyone written a biography of the man who followed Sir Henry Wilson as

---

62   TNA: CAB 45/84, letter from Cavan to Edmonds, 26 June 1945.
63   TNA: WO 106/852, memo from Cavan to CIGS, 15 June 1918.
64   Cavan, *Tactical and Strategic Considerations*, p.15.

CIGS – a project for a future researcher. Why did Cavan, by removing a divisional commander, draw attention to what was only a small break-in (one which could have been serious had it not been contained and repulsed), and which caused no concern to the War Cabinet: 'On the Asiago plateau, where the British troops were engaged, after giving way slightly, we had re-established ourselves'.[65] Cavan was well aware that Haig had removed Gough from command of Fifth Army following the German breakthrough in March – he came close to being Gough's replacement. Did Cavan take Gough's removal as an example of how break-ins were dealt with? British pride may also have played a part. In the months following Caporetto both the French and British had produced reports detailing how they perceived the Italians to have failed to hold the Austrian attack. In the opinion of Franco-British commanders this poor performance was against an enemy who they considered to be less aggressive than the Germans they faced on the Western Front. How embarrassing then to have the Austrians break-in on the British front, even more so when assistance had to be accepted from the Italians; the security of the front 'was assured by the G.O.C. of the Italian 12th Division, on its [143 Brigade] left, offering assistance in any form, in particular suggesting that he should take over eight hundred yards of the extreme left. The offer was accepted, and it enabled more men of the company to be held ready for counter-attack'.[66] Unfortunately the Italian newspapers on 16 June reported that the British line was broken, while the Italian line was intact – not what the British would want to see.

Cavan made a success of his time in Italy and was promoted from Corps to Army command in time for the successful crossing of the Piave in October, where his forces were instrumental in bringing the Austrians to an armistice. However, his treatment of Fanshawe was not his finest hour. Edmonds, in his official history, avoids mentioning the removal of the divisional commander, recording simply that Walker 'had taken over command of 48th Division on 4th July'. In a private note to Carrington in 1944 Edmonds stated that Cavan was 'too stupid to understand elastic defence in depth';[67] a harsh view, but Sheffield, in a review of Edmonds' memoirs, said that the official historian was jealous of the success of his contemporaries and was prone to 'tittle-tattle'.[68] The Austrian attack on the 15 June was not limited to the Asiago. A simultaneous assault was launched by General Boroević across the River Piave. The Austrian crossing was successful and gained a foothold on the west bank, where their progress was held up by the Italians. By the 23 June the Austrians were driven back across the river. The only British involvement in this section of the front was by the Royal Air Force who, having given assistance on the Asiago which drew praise from Cavan, was diverted to the Piave because of the fog and mist in the mountains.

65 TNA: CAB 23/6, minutes of War Cabinet 431, 17 June 1918.
66 Edmonds, *Italy*, p.208.
67 Cassar, *Forgotten Front*, p.164.
68 G. Sheffield, 'War of Words', *BBC History Magazine*, August (2014), p.77.

33 Sopwith Camels supplemented the Italian air force in successfully attacking the bridges, boats and rafts being used by the Austrians to cross the river, so slowing Boroević's progress.[69] In written comments after the war Cavan took issue with the Italian defence on the Piave, in a way which seemed to ignore his own experience on the Asiago; 'only on the Montello did the enemy gain any real success, reserves were required to restore the situation in that place'.[70] No mention here of the break-in on 48 Division front, or Italian assistance to restore it. In a letter to Edmonds in 1945, Cavan made a comment which did not make it into the official history; it was 'simply criminal to let the Austrians cross the Piave there – the best and strongest position on the whole front'.[71] [Emphasis in original.] Although one of the more Italophile of the senior British commanders the view expressed here gives the impression that 'we' did it right, 'they' did it wrong.

69   H.A. Jones, *The War in the Air* (London, 1937), p.284.
70   TNA: WO 79/70, p.9.
71   TNA: CAB 45/84, letter from Cavan to Edmonds, 8 February 1945.

8

British participation in the Battle of Vittorio Veneto:
"A conscious thrill of victory."

After the excitement of June the Italian Front returned to relative quiet, until the final offensive in October. This interim period was labelled 'The Long Pause' by both Edmonds and Cassar. During these months the work done to maintain the morale and physical fitness of the troops would have been particularly important. With the situation improving in France, raising hopes that the war was coming to an end and so allowing the troops to think of going home, it would have been particularly difficult for soldiers to see the relevance of a strict military regime of trench-life, drill and discipline. But it had to be done, the war was not yet finished. The British remained on the Asiago until late September when they returned to the Venetian Plain and the River Piave; at that point they expected to be returned to France while their place was taken by 'tired' divisions from the Western Front. During the months on the plateau, following the June attack, there was little action except for trench raids and patrols which continued to be a part of front-line life. The largest of these took place on the night of 8/9 August, and involved 22 companies. The scale of the operation can be gauged by the fact that there were 204 British casualties and 355 Austrian prisoners taken back to the British lines. But raids were not enough, and Cavan's thoughts quickly returned to the potential for mounting an offensive to the north from the Asiago.

The British commander, together with his French counterpart, General Jean Graziani (he had taken over from Maistre, but should not be confused with the Italian, General Andrea Graziani), pressed Diaz to be allowed to follow up on the withdrawal of the Austrians with an assault towards the Val Sugana. Cavan was 'convinced of the disheartenment of the enemy' and after a 'quiet talk with Graziani' they agreed that if they struck at once (immediately after the 17 June) they would 'seize the big ridge that separates the Asiago plateau from the Val Sugana and threaten Trento'.[1] Understandably, Diaz did not agree with the proposal. The Italian commander had

1   TNA: WO 79/70, Cavan's notes, p.10.

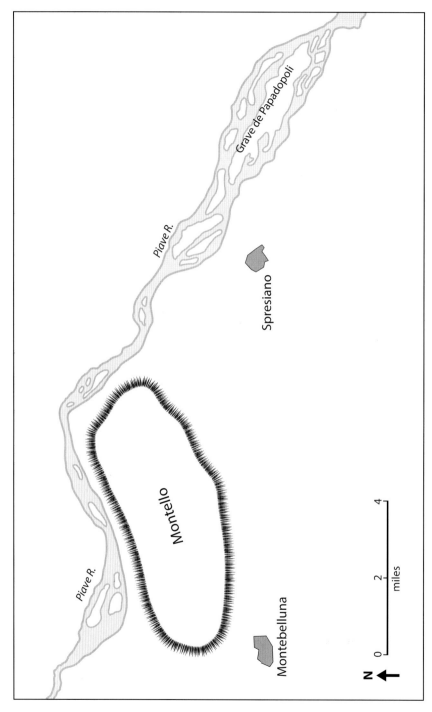

Map 3 The River Piave after it leaves the mountains. The large formation of the Montello is at the top with the river sweeping round to the Grave Di Papadopoli.

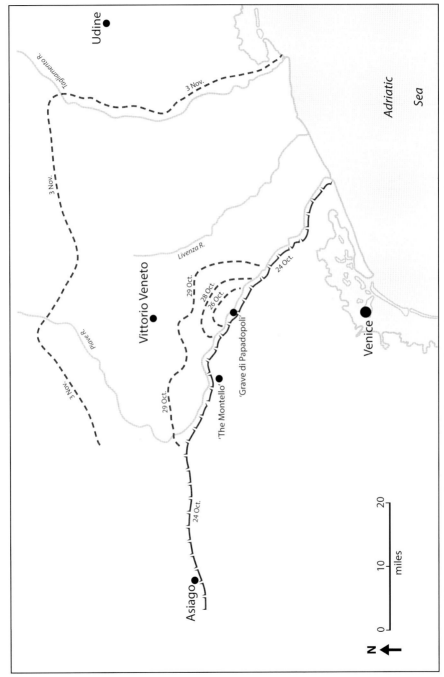

Map 4 The front line on the Piave on 24 October 1918. Across the river are lines showing the advance of the succeeding days.

his hands full, pushing Boroević's Austrians back across the Piave, and did not want the British and French leading a separate assault in the north. In his notes, written some years after the war, Cavan owned to 'feeling a bitter disappointment' at Diaz's decision, which the Italian commander felt was necessary as he claimed to have 'no reserves' and wanted 'to take no risks'. As with Cavan's enthusiasm for an offensive in April/May, the British commander was risking three divisions, but Diaz could lose an army and his country. Cavan was also a little disingenuous in the proposal he was putting to Diaz; he wanted to reinstate the original May assault which 'had been in preparation for weeks previously and was only postponed to await the Austrian attack'.[2] Here he was being less than honest with all the facts. The plan he refers to had included the Italian divisions on either side of the British and French units, but these would not now be advancing, so leaving the flanks of the Franco-British advance exposed. Also, raiding parties which Cavan had already sent out had had to be withdrawn from the villages of Canove and Ambrosini (in front of the British lines) 'on account of the difficulty of supplying them across a wide open No Man's Land'.[3] These supply problems were known to Cavan as he wrote his post-war notes. If the raiding parties had had to be pulled back, then the resupply of a full-blown assault, with exposed flanks, would have been even more problematic, but he makes no reference to this. An even bigger over-sight in his proposal to Diaz, and in his post-war notes, was the comment he had made previously to Wilson when he was annoyed at the postponement of the May offensive, he wrote then that; 'Guns and men intended for this offensive have been withdrawn and *it cannot now be undertaken at short notice*'.[4] [My emphasis.] Cavan, ever the thruster, seemed prepared to overlook the problem of supplying an advance, as well as his previous statement that it could no longer be undertaken. Recognising that the opportunity had been a 'fleeting' one, he then declared 'what is generalship but the power to seize opportunity and take a hazard when the chance offers to do the unexpected'.[5] The intervening years may have influenced this rather self-serving comment; the 'hazard' to which he referred was a demonstrated supply problem, exposed flanks and the withdrawal of artillery. With the Austrians still on the right bank of the Piave, Diaz could not risk a failed attack in the north and the consequent danger this would have posed to his flank and rear. On 29 June the Italian commander announced that 'it had been decided to abandon for the moment all intention to proceed to a general offensive'.[6]

While Diaz had scotched the plan that Cavan had proposed so enthusiastically, Italy could not be divorced from the wider plans of the Allies, even though they were focused on the defeat of Germany on the Western Front. With the unification

2   TNA: WO 79/70, Cavan's notes, p.10.
3   Edmonds, *Italy*, pp.215-6.
4   TNA: WO 106/852, memo from Cavan to Wilson, 27 May 1918.
5   TNA: WO 79/70, Cavan's notes, p.11.
6   Edmonds, *Italy*, p.238.

of command of the Allied armies, General Foch had been invested with the power to co-ordinate the action of the various allies, including the Italian Front. Although Foch could not order Diaz to follow his instructions (the Italian King was the titular Commander-in-Chief of the Italian army), he could strongly recommend a particular proposal,[7] and he wanted an assault to be made by Italy, coordinated with those being undertaken in France and Flanders. Both Foch and Cavan were of the opinion that if an offensive were launched in Italy, then it should be north from the Asiago, rather than east across the Piave. Cavan told the War Cabinet that crossing the Piave would be 'bad strategy, as the moment the Italian Army penetrated to the eastward along the plains, their lines of communication would become menaced from the North'.[8] For Foch the objection was that crossing the Piave 'was not advisable against the well-organized defence of the Austrians'.[9] Both would later be proved wrong.

As was the case in the late summer of 1917 with Cadorna, so now a year later, Diaz declared that an offensive was not possible owing to the numerical superiority of the enemy, and the likelihood of the Germans moving divisions to assist the Austrians. At a meeting in London between Lloyd George and Francesco Nitti,[10] the Italian Finance Minister declared that there were 70 Austrian divisions facing 51 Italian, figures which Cavan and British Military Intelligence disputed; the latter put the Austrian figure at 58 or 59. According to Edmonds the opposing forces in June were 58 Italian divisions (including British and French, as well as 4 from the cavalry) while the Austrians had 55. In October the numbers were 60 for the Italian (Allied) force against 61 Austrian, 'as near as may be, equal'.[11] The constant Italian refrain that their forces were numerically inferior to those of Austria, that the Allies were doing insufficient to provide assistance to Italy and that if Italy fell it would adversely affect the war, was wearing thin with their British and French allies. By this time there was little chance of the Germans moving divisions to the Italian Front, they had enough trouble of their own with the Allied push to victory (the Hundred Days), and the build-up of American forces in Europe. When the final Italian offensive was launched in October the British assessment of the Austrian numbers was found to be more accurate than that of the *Comando Supremo*. Italian shroud waving and doom-laden predictions were having an adverse effect on their allies, who believed that the Italians faced a 'war-weary, ill-fed and ill-equipped' opponent.[12] In September Cavan informed the War Office that while he was 'most anxious to be loyal to Italy' he was

---

7   Edmonds, *Italy*, pp.242-3.
8   TNA: CAB 23/44a, *Committee of Prime Ministers of the Dominions: I.W.C. meetings 19A-36A*, minutes of IWC 26A, 23 July 1918.
9   Edmonds, *Italy*, pp.242-3.
10   TNA: CAB 23/44a, minutes of IWC 26A, 23 July 1918.
11   Edmonds, *Italy*, p.265.
12   Edmonds, *Italy*, p.243.

concerned by Diaz's postponement of 'any decision [on an offensive] from day to day as is now being done'.[13]

The prevarications of the Comando Supremo, in the face of requests from Foch for action on the Italian Front, led the British to decide that their own troops could be better employed in France; if Diaz would not use them, then they could fight Germans elsewhere. On 9 September the War Office ordered that infantry brigades in Italy should be reduced from four to three battalions. This reduction had been implemented on the Western Front at the beginning of the year, but Plumer had successfully argued in February against applying it to the IEF on the grounds that it would have had a 'bad moral effect on the Italians',[14] if they saw British units leaving them to return to France. The September directive from the War Office meant that there were now nine 'surplus' battalions in Italy (approximately 8,000 men) which were transported to France late that month – not what Diaz would have wanted, but necessary as he had 'shown clearly that he was not going to attack'.[15] Keen as he was to see the IEF involved in offensive action in Italy, Cavan recognised the logic of the 'use them or lose them' argument and suggested that, as he had not been made aware of any intended Allied attack on the Italian Front, then his units could be better used elsewhere. To that end Cavan suggested to Wilson (CIGS) that the IEF should transfer 'good fresh divisions to France, which could be replaced by divisions who were tired out'; the War Cabinet on 27 September minuted this as an action that was going ahead. To that end the 7th and 23rd Divisions, in late September, redeployed from the Asiago to the area of the Montello, preparatory to their transfer back to England. To all intents and purposes the British were convinced that the Italians were planning to remain where they were on the Piave for the remainder of 1918. There would eventually be an Italian offensive, including the British troops, but how this came about is not as clear cut as the Italian history of that battle would have us believe.

In his recent history of the Italian Army in World War One, John Gooch speaks up for Diaz's planning of his final offensive. According to Gooch any suggestion that 'the battle of Vittorio Veneto was an extemporisation spatchcocked together to look better than it was, did Italy no favours and started an historical hare running that has been running ever since'.[16] The British official history, together with Cabinet and War Office documents, if they do not give that hare legs, they do back up Cavan's opinion that right up and till the last moment Diaz had no intention of launching an offensive in 1918. In Gooch's account the Italians began preparing plans in late August for a possible attack across the Piave, but to do that Diaz told 'Foch, Pershing and others' that he needed an additional 20 to 25 divisions from the Allies to be successful.[17]

13   TNA: WO 106/852, memo Cavan to CIGS, 3 September 1918.
14   TNA: CAB 23/5, minutes of War Cabinet 340, 7 February 1918.
15   TNA: CAB 23/7, *Cabinet Minutes and Papers; 438-479*, minutes of War Cabinet 479, 27 September 1918.
16   Gooch, *The Italian Army*, Kindle edition, Locn. 6603.
17   Gooch, *The Italian Army*, p.286.

Given the advances at that time on the Western Front, against the Germans, these were troops which he was never going to get, but planning continued within a small group of Italian commanders. The catalyst for a decision to actually do something appears to have been a string of allied successes on the Western Front between 26-28 September. During this period of Allied advance Marshal Foch told the Italian Prime Minister that:

> There is no war without risks. The question today is to know if, with the breakdown in morale and the disorganization of the Austrian army, the Italian Command is ready to run these risks.[18]

The Franco-British successes in France and Flanders, and the possibility of the Central Powers accepting armistice conditions suggested by the American President Wilson, left the Italians with the need to do something. They could not allow the war to end with Austrian troops occupying Italian territory; they needed a military victory and the expulsion of the Austrians. In previous wars Italians had gained territory through the efforts of their allies, rather than their own military prowess, and they were keen that this time that accusation should not be levelled at them. As Gooch summed up the Italian position; they had to 'forestall the dissolution of Austria-Hungary in which Italy had not participated'.[19] In their official history of Vittorio Veneto (in translation in the National Archives at Kew) the *Comando Supremo* was keen to portray a preparation start date for the battle which did not make it appear as though they were being too opportunistic following the recent French victories over the Bulgarians.

> All the details of the secretly prepared operative plan had meanwhile been quickly worked out. On 25th September, *four days before the conclusion of the Bulgarian armistice*, orders were issued for a rapid concentration of troops, artillery and technical services in the sector chosen for the attack, which was no longer the plateau, but on the middle Piave. Vittorio Veneto was to be the first stage in the advance, into which we were going to throw all our forces and all our spirit, in order to win, the victory'.[20] [My emphasis].

If the Italians had been planning an attack for some time then Diaz did a masterful job of keeping his allies in the dark regarding an offensive which Foch had been urging, and in which the Italians would have been keen to show that they were pulling their weight. At the very time that *Comando Supremo* was issuing orders for the concentration of troops, the two British divisions were preparing to go to France

18 Edmonds, *Italy*, p.246.
19 J. Gooch, *Italy during the First World War*, p.161.
20 TNA: WO 106/837, *Report by the Comando Supremo*, (translation), p.11.

to be replaced by tired ones, a decision with which the British War Cabinet concurred two days later. Also, in that month of September, nine 'surplus' British battalions were returned to France. It is difficult to believe that this redeployment would have gone ahead if Foch had been told that they were needed as part of a planned Italian attack in October; one which he had been constantly urging on them. Additionally, if this was not a 'spatchcocked' plan why was the release of the 7th and 23rd divisions, both familiar with Italy, not stopped until two weeks after the 25 September – the date on which the orders were issued 'for a rapid concentration of troops'. It was only on 7 October that 23 Division heard from Cavan that 'a sudden complete change of plan had been made by the *Comando Supremo*', and they were to participate in the attack.[21] Preparing to send these experienced units home, to be replaced by 'tired' ones, would have been a strange thing to do in the final stages of planning an assault to drive the occupiers out of your country. There is little in the planning of the final Italian offensive of the war to gainsay Cavan's early comments that their staff work was 'frothy' and relied on everything being 'alright on the day' – in the event the British would be across the Piave before the Italians, and would have to clear the banks for Diaz's Eighth and Third Armies to make the crossing. The Italian Commander's comments to Delmé-Radcliffe on 28 September,[22] which he knew would be relayed to London, do not have the smack of firm resolve: 'His *intentions* were offensive and he hoped that he would if possible certainly take *some* offensive action'; and 'He [Diaz] thinks it would be imprudent to compromise [the] future by undertaking an offensive which might considerably weaken Italian Army and *produce negligible results*'. [My emphasis.] These statements by the Italian Commander-in-Chief do not completely accord with the claims of the official Italian report that they intended to 'throw all our forces and all our spirit' into something Diaz said might only have negligible results. The hare is still running.

After the battle the Italians wanted it to be seen as a 'game-changer'; the Italian report opens with the statement that 'the decision of the world conflict would be brought about more rapidly by putting the Austrian army *hors de combat*, so as to isolate Germany militarily and force her to surrender' – in other words the Italians wanted to position Vittorio Veneto such that it forced the subsequent German surrender. The Italians needed their win, but many British historians have either ignored events on the Italian Front, or misrepresented them. In his comprehensive account of the war from the perspective of Germany and Austria-Hungary, Watson gives short shrift to this Italian battle:

> On 24 October the Italians had launched a *last-minute offensive* on the South-Western Front in order to position themselves better for the coming peace negotiations. After three days, defending troops of all nationalities had refused to

---

21   Sandilands, *The 23rd Division*, pp.293-4.
22   TNA: WO 106/852, memo from Delmé-Dadcliffe to Wilson, 29 September 1918.

go into the line and on 28 October the imperial authorities had unconditionally requested an armistice.[23] [My emphasis.]

Italy had spent all its war, from May 1915 to October 1917, fighting just the Austro-Hungarian army (though at times that had been reinforced by Germany), for its battle to decide the 'world conflict' to be summed up in two sentences. The (overly patriotic) Andrew Roberts completely ignored Vittorio Veneto with the chauvinistic claim that only the armies 'of the English-speaking peoples were the ones still capable of mounting any kind of offensive in 1918'.[24] Gordon Corrigan (ex-Major from the Gurkha regiment, presenter of TV history programmes and battlefield tour guide) is particularly dismissive in his book on the myths of the Great War:

> This [Vittorio Veneto] again was an unnecessary campaign, initiated by politicians who thought they knew more about waging war than did the professionals, It held down Allied troops who would have been far better employed in France and Flanders. Italy could well have been left on the defensive, but was insistent on taking the offensive in order to capture Trieste, her sole reason for coming into the war in the first place. An offensive could only take place if the Italian armies were stiffened by French and British divisions.[25]

In this statement Corrigan is open to criticism on a number of points. As we have seen in this and previous chapters, Diaz was not only pressured to 'do something' by the politicians; all through 1918 Foch and Cavan were putting to him the need for attacks in Italy which should be coordinated with those on the Western Front. Yes, Trieste was one of Italy's war aims, but that was not the only reason for the offensive – apart from the pressure from Foch, Italy could not end the war with the Austrians occupying Italian territory. Diaz had to push them back from the ground they had taken after Caporetto, before the war ended. Corrigan over-states his argument when he writes that the Italians were only able take the offensive if they were 'stiffened by British and French divisions'. By October 1918 the Austrians were a demoralised army and, unlike at Caporetto, they did not have German divisions alongside them. It may have been harder for the Italians to have won their last battle without Anglo-French assistance (Cavan's army was instrumental, as we will see below), but he is wrong to say that they could not have gained that victory without the help of the Allies. Corrigan, while stating that Trieste was Italy's 'sole reason for coming into the war', ignores the fact that Britain's Foreign Secretary went to great lengths to persuade Italy to join the Entente. The Italians were in the war at the behest of the Allies, as well as to satisfy

23   Watson, *Ring of Steel*, p.543.
24   Roberts, *A History of the English-Speaking Peoples*, p.117.
25   G. Corrigan, *Mud, Blood and Poppycock. Britain and the First World War* (London, 2003), p.320.

their own territorial ambitions. Corrigan is firmly in the camp of those historians who believed that Italian participation was 'more of a hindrance than a help'.[26]

We should return now to the preparation for the final assault. From the British perspective 'no definite orders for an offensive were [...] received [...] till 6th October',[27] and it was only at this point that Diaz appointed Cavan as Army Commander for the newly formed Tenth Army. Of the three British divisions the 48th, still on the Asiago, would become part of the Italian XII Corps, while the 7th and 23rd (those who were originally intended to be replaced by 'tired' units), together with the Italian XI Corps (with Italian 37th and 23rd Divisions), formed XIV Corps in Tenth Army. By the time that the crossing of the Piave was under way Cavan's force would also be augmented with the Italian XVIII Corps (33rd and 56th Divisions). As with the earlier Austrian offensive in June, so with the battle of Vittorio Veneto, readers should look elsewhere for the minutiae of the action in which individual units were involved; Gladden[28] gives an excellent account from the viewpoint of a single soldier, while Crosse[29] does likewise for a division; Edmonds, Sandilands and Cassar all document in detail the action which took place between 24 October and 4 November.

The area of front allocated to Cavan's Tenth Army was approximately nine miles in length, and prominent on its left-centre (facing XIV Corps) was the island of Papadopoli. The *Grave di Papadopoli* (henceforth, Papadopoli) was a major obstruction to the flow of the Piave; some three and a half miles long, and about a mile at its widest, the island was low-lying but was itself surrounded by small sand and gravel islands which completely disrupted the water's flow. Crossing points moved according to the depth and strength of the river's current. To get at the Austrian defences the British would need to cross one stream of the Piave to get to Papadopoli, consolidate their position on the island, then cross the river on its north-east side to make the left bank of the Piave. The mountains of the Asiago district had presented the British with one set of challenges, now they faced another terrain which was very different from that on which they had fought on the Western Front; a surprise attack here would not be easy. Although the men of the IEF had launched small raiding parties across the river during their earlier months on the Montello, a full-scale assault across the gravel banks and Papadopoli – and with the Piave in spate after recent floods – would be a very different kettle of fish. The British would require specialist help to establish pontoon bridges for the crossing, and that assistance (acknowledged by many who were there) would come from the Italian *pontieri*:

26   Corrigan, *Mud, Blood and Poppycock*, p.16.
27   Edmonds, *Italy*, p.249.
28   Gladden, *Piave*, pp.159-204.
29   Crosse, *The Defeat of Austria*.

I think we must give the Italians full marks for their bridging. We could not get the anchors into the river bed to hold the pontoons. The Italians seemed to have the technique for this as after a few throws the anchors seemed to hold.[30]

Cavan was proud to pay tribute to these Italian boatmen 'and their dauntless leader, Captain Odini', when he unveiled their War Memorial at Piacenza in later years. Almost all British accounts of the battle, written by those who were there, give unstinting praise to the *pontieri* and the way in which they transported Cavan's men across the streams to Papadopoli.

By the 26 October the British held their island in the stream and were ready to drive forward against the Austrian defences on the left bank. The enemy lines were behind a concrete 'bund' which formed the left bank of the river; about 10 feet high, six feet wide and with a clear area in front of it, the Bund should have been a difficult position for the British to take. However, as a result of poor placement of machine guns by the defenders, 'it availed the enemy little'[31] and did not prevent the attackers from reaching their first objective on time. Although the Italian battle report stated that the Austrian army maintained a high morale to the end,[32] the British view was that 'they were not enemies of the same quality as the Germans' and that 'neither their discipline, training, nor morale was of the soundest'.[33] Although the British did not rate the Austrians as fighters on a par with the Germans, many of the soldiers' letters drew no distinction between them, they frequently referred to the Austrians as 'Huns', 'Boche' and 'Fritzes'. With Italian armies on both flanks (the Eighth on their left and the Third on their right), Cavan's Tenth Army was part of the wedge which Diaz wanted to drive between the Austrian Sixth Army (to their left front) and the Austrian Isonzo Army (to their right front). The aim was to split the Austrians, reach the transport hubs at Vittorio Veneto and Sacile, and so cut the communication lines of Sixth Army. In a separate attack the Allied forces on the Asiago (including the British 48th Division) would strike northwards into the Trentino. The plan called for the Italian armies on Cavan's flanks to force the Piave at the same time as his Tenth Army, the actuality did not match the intent.

The British line of advance, after crossing the river, was north east to Sacile on the River Livenza then wheeling westwards to the River Tagliamento. During the first phase (to Sacile) the Italian report of the battle stated that it was the duty of the Tenth Army to 'form a defensive flank'[34] for the Italian Eighth Army on their left, but that could only be done if the Italians moved forward. Cavan was well established on the river's left bank on 27 October, but now had to use part of his force to clear that same

30   TNA: CAB 45/84, letter from Lang to Edmonds, 28 September 1945.
31   Edmonds, *Italy*, p.286.
32   TNA: WO 106/837, Italian report of Vittorio Veneto, p.1.
33   Atkinson, *7th Division*, p.472.
34   TNA: WO 106/837, Italian report, p.23.

bank in front of the Italians on both of his flanks to allow them to cross – which they did not do until the night of 28/29 October. The role played by the British in clearing the left bank was acknowledged by the Duke of Aosta (commanding Third Army) directly after the battle; 'If the British had not crossed the Piave, the Italians would not have crossed the Piave. After the war other things will be said'.[35] His last comment was prescient, given the way that the official Italian report recorded events. Cavan's Tenth Army had a head of steam up, and was pushing on aggressively towards its objectives, its flanks 'en l'air'. Meanwhile the Italian Eighth Army, elements of which required Cavan's help to cross the Piave, and which was 'cast to play the principal part' in the battle, 'was not in a position to do so'.[36] As a result, instead of providing flank guard for the Italians, the British XIV Corps was now the 'spearhead of the attack'. After the war Cavan described his exposed position to the official historian:

> I never realised that my Italian Divisions were so sticky [slow] after crossing the river – the reason being that Babington [commanding XIV Corps] and his Divisional Commanders never grumbled – but got steadily on with the job. I realize now, far more clearly than I did then, what a big risk we took in extending the tip of our 'umbrella' with very sketchy flanks – but I do remember clearly, that I gave a special warning about this – when against my first inclination we decided to push on in spite of the failure of the Third Army to cross the Piave on my right and the Eighth on my left.[37]

According to Edmonds this 'spearheading' by the British, and the failure of the Italians to keep up on their flanks, was 'not an outcome that has won much recognition from Italian historians'.[38]

For the veterans among the IEF, those who had previously taken part in the attritional battles of the Western Front, here was another difference from their time in Flanders – a war of movement! After becoming accustomed to static trench warfare Gladden, who was part of the advance, expressed a 'conscious thrill of victory', he was 'no longer afraid' and was happy that 'we now had the novel experience of marching forward into country just evacuated by the enemy'.[39] While the civilians would have been pleased to see the British, the troops would also have had reason to feel satisfied as 'this was the first time since Loos [September 1915] that the 7th Division had had the privilege of finally liberating civilians from the hands of the oppressor'.[40]

While the British divisions of Cavan's XIV Corps were pushing on towards the rivers Livenza and Tagliamento, the 48th, as part of the Sixth Army on the Asiago,

35   TNA: CAB 45/84, Sandilands to Edmonds, 24 August 1945.
36   Edmonds, *Italy*, p.285.
37   TNA: CAB 45/84 Cavan to Edmonds, August 1945.
38   Thompson, *White War*, p.359.
39   Gladden, Piave, pp.192-9.
40   Crosse, *Defeat of Austria*, p.67.

participated in the assault on 1 November up the Val d'Assa towards the Val Sugana and the town of Caldonazzo. This division, which saw its commanding officer removed after the events of 15 June, had not lost its fighting spirit; it became the first British unit in the war to set foot on enemy territory, as opposed to ground occupied by the enemy. Although receiving little recognition, all three British divisions played their part in the military action that ended the war in Italy. Vittorio Veneto also saw the entry of another ally into the war on the Italian Front; the United States of America. Ernest Hemingway's novel (in the genre of autobiografiction[41]) may be the most well-known piece of English writing to come out of the Italian Front, but his countrymen played a very minor part there in late 1918. As Tenth Army pushed towards the Tagliamento the American 332nd Regiment (their only unit in Italy) was placed under Cavan's command. In 1917 Robertson – in his typically blunt style – had commented to Haig that 'it would be a good thing to get some Americans killed and so get the country to take a real interest in the war'.[42] Cavan would probably not have agreed with Robertson's sentiment but he did note that on his front, in 1918, the Americans 'had one man wounded at the Tagliamento & honour was saved'.[43] Histories of the Second World War are replete with British comments on the late entry of the 'Yanks', and the way in which they were better fed and treated, but such sentiments were also expressed by soldiers of the IEF:

> You know, we get rather fed up at times. Anything will do for the British – any old barn or pig-sty & any old front where there is a beaucoup war, but when the Yanks are coming – well, stand back and let them have a go (I don't think). No, instead of wading in & fighting they tour the jolly country – live in posh billets & have a jolly good time.[44]

By the 4 November the Austrians had capitulated and an armistice was signed, a week before the war ended on the Western Front. The Italians had been desperate to achieve a victory over the Austrians before the war ended; they could not afford to go into the peace negotiations with no last battle to their name, and the enemy still occupying Italian territory. Churchill famously stated that history would be kind to him, as he would write it, and the Italians were equally determined that history should see Vittorio Veneto as a glorious feat of Italian arms. In the years after the war, Mussolini's Fascism needed to portray the country as being vigorously militaristic. Vittorio Veneto was to be the rock on which this was based, wiping out the disgrace of Adowa and Caporetto. In that spirit the repulse of the Austrians on the Piave in June was hailed (rather pompously) by *Comando Supremo* as 'the turn in the tide of

---

41   Defined by Stephen Reynolds in 1906 and explained in *RUSI Journal*, Vol. 159, p.108.
42   Woodward, *Robertson*, p.169.
43   TNA: CAB 45/84, Cavan to Edmonds, 18 August 1945.
44   IWM: Doc. GS 0389, W.F. Cresswell, *Private Papers,* letter 14 October 1918.

the world war';[45] – an extraordinary claim and one which would not stand any critical assessment of how that dreadful conflict ended. The arguments over how the battle was represented, and whether or not the Italians gave sufficient credit to their allies, started before the armistice was signed. Immediately following the launch of the final offensive, Cavan had to calm Italian reaction to comments in the French press. The Paris newspapers echoed a sentiment which many had felt when the Italians, in 1915, belatedly entered the war on the side of the Entente – they were 'leaping to the aid of the victors'. The French media took some delight in employing this *leit-motiv* to report Vittorio Veneto; 'at the very moment when Austria is tired, in a state of revolution, and suing for a separate peace, Italy launched her attack'. Whatever the French thought of their southern ally Cavan disagreed in his letter to Sir Henry Wilson, written during the fighting; 'to a sensitive nation this was almost an insult and it was untrue'.[46] In 1963 A.J.P. Taylor chauvinistically dismissed Vittorio Veneto with the comment that 'only on 23 October did the Italians nerve themselves to attack, and even then the most successful advance was by the British army corps under Lord Cavan'.[47] The Italian wish to 'big up' their final battle, not just as a feat of arms, but also as a critical catalyst in the collapse of Germany, and the British resentment that their contribution was not sufficiently acknowledged, may account for the fact that the whole Italian Front gets so little coverage in British histories of the war. Even when the theatre is mentioned, the picture given can be a distorted one; one historian notes that at Vittorio Veneto 'Diaz had 57 divisions under his command including, for the first time, an American contingent'[48] – an American regiment is mentioned (a nod towards Hemingway's novel?) but the much larger British contribution of two divisions, and Cavan's command of a joint Anglo-Italian army group, goes unspoken.

While the Italian account of the final battle says little about the failure of their units to keep up on Cavan's flanks, it is not reticent regarding the 'courage and dash' of their cavalry, which is at variance with the British record. According to the Italians their cavalry, 'debouched into the plain beyond the front of the Tenth Army' on 31 October. On the same day a detachment of light cavalry 'attacked Sacile, which was strongly defended and with *the assistance of British infantry* [my emphasis], took possession of it, after sharp house to house fighting'.[49] This act of derring-do was remembered differently by the British. The 9th Battalion of the York and Lancaster Regiment 'requested, and was granted, permission to force the passage at Sacile and form a bridgehead'.[50] Edmonds is very critical of the Italian version of events:

45   TNA: WO 106/837, report, p.5.
46   TNA: WO 106/852, memo from Cavan to CIGS, 31 October 1918.
47   A.J.P. Taylor, *The First World War* (Harmondsworth, 1963), p.246.
48   K. Robbins, *The First World War* (Oxford, 2002(, p.79.
49   TNA: WO 106/837, report, p.25.
50   Edmonds, *Italy*, p.323.

That any Italian troops were present is not recorded in the British War Diaries. The G.O.C. 23rd Division and other British officers present in Sacile, report that they saw no Italian troops there.[51]

Even Cavan, who was so quick to defend the Italians against the French newspaper article, disputed the Italian account; 'when I arrived at Sacile very shortly after its capture I never heard one word about the action of the Italian Cavalry in the town. Like you [Edmonds] I greatly doubt its accuracy'.[52] Did the Italians feel that they needed to be seen, in the official report, as having some troops ahead of Cavan as he 'spearheaded' the drive to the Tagliamento? In spite of the claims that their cavalry 'debouched' on Cavan's front, Edmonds is categorical, 'no Italian cavalry was on the Tenth Army front'. For the Italians it was important to project their military as having recovered from Caporetto, but for Edmonds the issue of the cavalry at Sacile was an example of their 'one-sided method of writing history' where 'credit is taken for a British feat of arms'.[53] As the official historian he regretted that the Historical Section of the Italian General Staff made no request for 'particulars of the British operations in Italy', unlike their French and German equivalents. As a result Edmonds put his opinion into the official record:

> Italian accounts have not rendered justice to the moral support and sound advice given to the Comando Supremo by Maréchal [sic] Foch, or to the vital assistance given by the French and British troops both in the mountains and on the plains.[54]

The Duke of Aosta has already been noted as having made the prescient comment on the British contribution – 'After the war other things will be said' – but in bidding farewell to Cavan after the war he gave more credit to the contribution of the IEF than was accorded by the Italian report: 'Goodbye General. I am indeed sorry that you are leaving Italy. Without the presence of you and your troops there would have been no victory at Vittorio Veneto'.[55] However the British contribution was portrayed, there was an Allied victory over the Austrians at Vittorio Veneto, and it did lead to the Austrians signing an armistice. As one private soldier summed it up in a letter home; 'we did jolly well & [sic] helped the Austrians to make up their minds & they helped the Huns; so there you are'.[56]

The British troops of the Italian Expeditionary Force saw out the last 12 months of the war, largely free of combat. The Austrian artillery did not bombard their trenches

51 Edmonds, *Italy*, fn.1, p.324.
52 TNA: CAB 45/84, Cavan to Edmonds, August 1945.
53 Edmonds, *Italy*, p.358.
54 Edmonds, *Italy*, p.358.
55 TNA: CAB 45/84, Aosta's words which Cavan agreed Gathorne-Hardy could relate to Edmonds, 1945.
56 Cresswell, *Private Papers*, letter 15 November 1918.

as frequently, or as intensely, as the Germans did in France and Flanders, but to 'keep up fighting spirit', trench-raids and patrols into No Man's Land were still a part of front-line routine – if less so than on the Western Front. The terrain on which the troops fought was very different from their previous experience. In June they defended steep, tree-covered, slopes rather than trenches knee-deep in the mud which is so closely associated with that war. Then, in October they were called on to attack across a wide, fast-flowing, river using the services of Italian boatmen. However, when called on to repel a major Austrian attack, or participate in the final offensive of the war in Italy, the men performed well. All the inter-unit sport, internal economy inspections, trench journals, concert parties and effective postal system, did their part in maintaining the morale of the IEF; when they were required to fight and kill, they did. The Austrian attack on 15 June was beaten back and all ground gained by the enemy was recovered. The Austrians did not try attacking Italy again for the rest of the war. Had Cavan not drawn attention to the transient Austrian success on the front of 48 Division, by the removal of Major-General Fanshawe, it is unlikely that their minor break-in would be remembered. It is to the credit of the men of that division that, reduced in numbers by influenza, they performed as they had rehearsed and had recovered their line within twenty-four hours. In October, having come close to a return to France as a result of Italian vacillation over whether or not to finally attack the Austrians, they found themselves in a war of movement, spearheading the drive to the Tagliamento with their flanks exposed by the slower moving Italians. After their humiliating defeat at Caporetto it was understandable that the Italians would want to make much of the victory at Vittorio Veneto, but their downplaying of the Anglo-British contribution to the battle may partly account for why it receives so little attention in British histories of the war. Or as Cyril Falls put it; he was 'disinclined to harp on Italian official and unofficial depreciation of the part played by allies'.[57]

To the citizen soldiers of the IEF the end of the fighting meant that they were finished with the war and the army's routine, they wanted to return quickly to their families and civilian jobs – unfortunately politics and peace negotiations are rarely that simple. A slow demobilisation process, and Italian irredentist claims to the Adriatic port of Fiume, meant that hundreds of troops had their stay in the country prolonged until late 1919, with some still there well into 1920.

57   Falls, *Caporetto*, p.177.

9

Post-armistice and demobilisation: "It's about time we all got home."

At 3pm on 4 November, a week earlier than on the Western Front, the Austrian armistice took effect and hostilities ceased. As if to prove that the 'fog of war' is more than just a historians turn of phrase, many of the guns had fallen silent a day or two earlier as rumour and confusion spread among opposing troops over when exactly the shooting war should stop. By the time of that final Allied advance on the Italian Front the Austro-Hungarian army, though numerically strong, exhibited poor morale, was short of food and could see that their German allies were suffering a series of defeats in France and Flanders. The Central Powers were collapsing while the British and French were being bolstered by the increasing flow of American divisions, food and 'the stuff of war'. The Allied advance, which resulted in the victory at Vittorio Veneto, demonstrated that the Italian army had recovered from its defeat at Caporetto. For their part, the British forces (under the command of Lord Cavan) could be proud of their role in what the Comando Supremo, with some hyperbole, had called 'the great battle which crowned the heroic efforts of the Italian people with victory'.[1]

With hostilities at an end the troops, not unnaturally, expected demobilisation to happen quickly so that they could get home to their families and civilian employment. Unfortunately wars do not end that simply and bureaucracies do not work that quickly. The process of demobilisation would be a cause of resentment for the troops in Italy as well as elsewhere in the British Army. Those men who had volunteered believed that their commitment to the war ended with the cessation of hostilities, while those who had been conscripted for the duration considered that the armistice concluded their obligation. The reality was more complex, both at the macro and individual levels. The ending of the war presented the politicians with a number of challenges which are frequently overlooked in the histories of that conflict. A war-time army of some four million soldiers had to be quickly reduced to a size commensurate with peace-time conditions, while avoiding the unemployment that might follow from more than three million men re-entering the labour market – one in which women were doing the

---

1   TNA: WO 106/837, report p.34.

men's jobs. Although the armistice brought the conflict to an end it did not remove the continuing need for an army, one of whose functions would be to occupy German and Austrian territory throughout the peace negotiations; but how would soldiers (tired of four years of conflict) be induced to re-enlist?

First, what was the process for demobilisation which caused the soldiers to be so critical? As far as the men were concerned it should have allowed all those who wanted to return home to do so, with priority given to those who had served the longest. For the government it could not be that simple. Although an armistice had been agreed, final peace terms with Germany had not been signed, and until they were the war was not over. This technical point had implications for the soldiers as, until peace was signed, they would only be 'demobilised' and not 'discharged'; this meant that they were liable for recall in the (albeit unlikely) event that hostilities resumed. This need to maintain an army, with its consequent slower than expected return to civilian life, was acknowledged by Lloyd George's secretary in a letter to Sir Henry Wilson in January 1919:

> The Prime Minister has been giving careful personal attention to the speed at which the process of demobilising the army is being maintained. [...] Demobilisation cannot be carried out in any way that would undermine the military strength of Britain until final peace is secure.[2]

In the summer of 1916, with the end of the war still not in sight, the question of how to return millions of conscripted soldiers to civilian life was studied by a Cabinet subcommittee under the chairmanship of Edwin Montagu. He believed that the committee's primary concern was to avoid the mass unemployment which could result from an influx of 'demobbed' soldiers – trained to kill, and so also a possible source of social unrest – into the labour market. The decision was taken that men would be released individually, as opposed to disbanding whole units, and they would be let go 'in accordance with the needs of industry rather than on any other basis, such as length of service';[3] and therein lay the rub. To the soldiers, the only fair system had to allow the release of those who had served longest, before any others went. In order to make the selection under the Montagu terms all the men were classified into five groups, in descending order of priority these were: 'demobilizers', whose release would expedite the release of others; 'pivotal men', whose speedy return would create employment; 'slip men', who had a definite promise of a job when they re-entered civilian life; those who did not have a guaranteed job, but came from an essential industry and so were likely to be speedily employed; all others, depending on the importance of

---

2   Jeffery, *Sir Henry Wilson*, memo from Philip Kerr to Wilson, 8 January, p.75.
3   S.R. Graubard, 'Military Demobilization in Great Britain Following the First World War', *Journal of Modern History*, Vol. 19 (1947, p.298.

their industry to national reconstruction.[4] While it was apparently a very rigid system there was scope within it for giving preference to married men, and those with long service. Unfortunately it was poorly understood by the men, and was not seen by them as fair. It also called for equal treatment to be given to those serving overseas. Again, however, the men in Italy perceived themselves (rightly or wrongly) to be disadvantaged by distance. This point was raised by Cavan to CIGS in December 1918; '[The] Demobilization people are not quite fair to us. [...] At this moment only six men have left Italy!'[5] In true bureaucratic style the five priority groups identified by Montagu's committee were further subdivided into more than 40 'classes'.[6] Captain Greenwell hoped to return to his studies at Oxford when he was released but told his parents that 'Students are "Class 43" on the demobilisation list – the last but one, whereas "gentlemen" are in "Class 37". So it would seem better to be a mere gentleman'.[7] If he was confused, what chance the ordinary infantryman?

As Cavan had noted to Wilson, the demobilisation process in Italy was moving slowly and according to one officer it had not improved much by January 1919:

> Things are drifting a bit now; demobilization has not yet begun except for 'pivotal men' and students [a different viewpoint from Greenwell] and coal miners – and already the labour market is said to be glutted.[8]

For the majority of ordinary soldiers their main concern, now that hostilities were finished, was to get home and into employment, but that was not the case for all of the officers. Many of the junior regimental officers had not joined the army from civilian employment; a large proportion had come direct from schools and universities. Not having worked previous to their army life, some would no doubt have echoed the sentiments of young Charles Carrington who, when faced with demobilisation, was 'a little scared of it and was in no hurry to be thrown out of the nest'.[9] The scale of the demobilisation challenge, just for the IEF, was huge. In broad terms the British in Italy had to reduce from 27 battalions to 10, with a further decrease to only four by early February 1919 – around 75,000 men to be sent home to civilian life. But it was not going smoothly, and led to resentment. In June 1919 Lamin was asking his brother in England to tell him what was going on. 'Write and tell me as soon as you see anything about demob in the papers as we get to know nothing about it out here'.[10] The frustration of the men was compounded by the authorities further restricting home leave, even though the war was effectively over. Men who went on

4   Graubard, *Military Demobilization*, p.298.
5   Jeffery, *Sir Henry Wilson*, letter from Cavan to Wilson, 14 December 1918.
6   W.P. Crozier, 'Demobilization in England', *Atlantic Monthly*, Vol. 123 (1919), pp.275-83.
7   Greenwell, *Infant in Arms*, p.249.
8   Morshead, Private Papers, letter, 4 January 1919.
9   Carrington, *Soldier from the Wars Returning*, p.243.
10   Lamin, *Letters*, p.192.

leave were not returning, believing that with hostilities finished they would not be accused of desertion; 'when a man goes on leave from here he does not return but stops in England'.[11] Others were taking the opportunity while at home to get themselves a job, and so (under the rules) could avoid going back. Lamin, almost a year after the Austrian surrender (and in rather poor English), spoke for many:

> If I could get leave, I could easily get demobed [*sic*] when I got to England but the thing is getting there as there is no leave going from here, only odd ones they are only men for demobilisation, but any way I hope to be home for Christmas [1919].[12]

In fact he did not make it home until early 1920. Resentment at Montagu's system was building up among the men, and one focus for their ire was the miners. As part of the government's reconstruction plan these were essential workers, but they were seen by the troops as 'jumping the queue': 'About all the miners have gone, some which [*sic*] came up in April 1918 have got away'. Lamin's point here is that some of the miners had only served six months of the war. Norman Gladden made a similar point when he noted that 'the dispatch of miners *out of turn* had made us all fed up with the army authorities' and this had 'sparked off trouble with Allied troops in many areas'.[13] [My emphasis] The antipathy towards the release of men who had only served a short time (as demonstrated in Lamin's comment) was not only based on what they regarded to be natural justice, these men also had a definite advantage over the long-timers. Those who had joined the army late were more likely to have retained contact with their employers and so would find it easier to become 'slip men'. The term derived from the 'slip' (a letter or note) which they could obtain from their previous employer to say that they would get their job back – men who had been away for up to four years were unlikely to have this guarantee.

The unfairness of the Montagu system had led to soldiers' protests in England, with up to 10,000 reported as demonstrating at Folkestone in January 1919, leading to the temporary closure of the port. *The Times* reported the men as 'perfectly orderly and respectful' and that their discontent was caused by 'the feeling that they were not all being treated alike'.[14] The article went on to point out that while the men's grievances were understandable, a state of war still existed with 'such a slippery negotiator as Germany' and consequently all the troops could not be released. Although the incident took place in England, not Italy, it did involve a divisional commander from the IEF. Major-General Shoubridge (C.O. 7 Division) was on home leave and was ordered by Sir Henry Wilson to remain in Britain to take command of the situation

11   Lamin, *Letters*, p.200.
12   Lamin, *Letters*, p.204.
13   Gladden, *Piave*, pp.216-8.
14   'Common Sense and Demobilization', *The Times*, 6 January 1919, p.9.

in Folkestone. Shoubridge was sensitive to the complaint in Italy that men returning on leave found excuses to remain at home, he did not want to be tarred with that brush, as Wilson explained to Cavan; '[Shoubridge was] upset at the idea that anyone should think that he has taken advantage of his leave to get himself placed in a billet at home'.[15] Some days previous to the Folkestone incident, at the depot in Arquata, 460 men from the 23rd and 48th divisions refused to turn out on parade when ordered to, a serious breach of discipline which – had conflict not ceased – would have led to serious consequences. In this instance, and it was not unique, the officers warned the men of the seriousness of their disobedience and told them to parade next day. They did, and no further action was taken against them. The base war diary records that the cause of the men's grievance was their belief that they were to be transferred to a Labour Corps, rather than being sent home.[16] In the absence of good information it was only natural that rumours should fill the void.

The most serious instance of a breakdown in discipline within the IEF occurred in this period after the armistice, and involved the British West Indies Regiment based at Taranto. These men from the Caribbean, formed into labour battalions, have been singled out previously on account of their disciplinary record, but there is a case for saying that they were treated more harshly than their white colleagues. In the incident at Arquata (in the previous paragraph), the men – presumably all white – got off lightly. In the case of the BWI, where the men wanted to go home to their tropical islands once the armistice was signed, forty-seven of them were tried for mutiny in December 1918. Most of the men received very harsh sentences of between three and ten years imprisonment with hard labour – and this was after hostilities. In his history of the 23rd Division, Sandilands noted that 'in the treatment these coloured troops had received there had been much that constituted very real grievances'.[17] Within the IEF the officers and NCOs treated occurrences of indiscipline, following the armistice, pragmatically rather than 'by the book'. There was a measure of sympathy for the soldiers' wish to return home, a need not to let situations get out of hand and recognition that, with hostilities over, there was less of a willingness on the part of the men to accept the enforcement of military law.

Britain had never before had to mobilise so many men during a period of conflict, so it is not surprising that the problems of returning them to civilian life, many from points all over the globe, were more complex than had been thought. While the government's concern over a possible dramatic rise in unemployment was legitimate, it later proved to be unfounded. However, the unintended consequence of the unrest and disquiet among the troops, caused by the failure to release first those men who had served the longest, might have been anticipated with a little more thought. But changes were to come. Following the general election in December 1918 Winston

15   Jeffery, *Sir Henry Wilson*, letter to Cavan, 6 January 1919.
16   TNA: WO 95/4254, 29 December 1918.
17   Sandilands, *23rd Division*, p.341.

Churchill became War Minister and made changes to the demobilisation process which addressed this grievance. Army Orders 54 and 55, announced in January 1919, took a lead from the plan adopted by the French which recognised age, length of service and combat experience.[18] The changes brought in by Churchill allowed for the rapid exit of all men except those who had joined the armed forces after 31 December 1915, were under thirty-seven years of age, and had fewer than three wound stripes. It was estimated that by the adoption of these measures Britain would still have an army of 1.3 million men until after the Germans signed the peace. But not everyone was keen to leave the army. Just as Carrington admitted that it would be hard to 'leave the nest', so many ordinary soldiers recognised that they would struggle to find employment, consequently many accepted the improved pay and conditions that Churchill offered to induce them to stay. His Order 56 allowed for additional pay and bounties for those who stayed to man the occupation armies. And the offer worked. Within the IEF Carrington claimed that the inducements allowed them to raise 'a battalion of new regulars [about 800 men] with no difficulty from the ten dwindling units of our Division in Italy'.[19] Introduced to encourage men to re-enlist, the additional money also benefited those who were forced to stay on for many months after the armistice until their release was approved. In April 1919 Lamin told his sister that 'I got 10/6 [ten shillings and sixpence] bonus from Feb 1st so that is about £9.00 to my credit and I have never had so much money while I have been in the army'.[20] His new found wealth, however, was not sufficient to persuade him to serve with the colours any longer than absolutely necessary.

For the troops on the ground demobilisation only took form when they could see men actually leaving, and in spite of the delays and grousing, the first trains started to leave in December; the first left Tavernelle on the 23rd of the month with 1,138 men, the second a week later with a further 1,100 (miners, teachers and instructors) and 40 officers. The ending of the war brought no improvement in travel comfort with the men still being accommodated in 'covered trucks' and the officers in '1st class coaches'.[21] Unfortunately for those who were staying, leave trains were cancelled to allow for a schedule of 'demob' trains; eight left in January 1919 and demobilisation was declared to be 'proceeding satisfactorily at the rate of two or three trains per week'. While many were disappointed that their turn was to be some way off, the process (once it got going) did release men and the IEF was not disadvantaged by distance. By 15 January 1919 almost 10,000 had been sent home, with an average of 650 a day leaving after that, until they had all returned by 15 April 1920 – almost a year and a half after the armistice.[22] And the leaving could be something of an event. In January

18   Graubard, *Military Demobilization*, p.304.
19   Carrington, *Soldier from the Wars Returning*, p.255.
20   Lamin, *Letters*, pp.187-8.
21   TNA: WO 95/4198, war diary of General HQ, 23 December 1918.
22   Edmonds, *Italy*, p.384.

1919 the 8th battalion of the York and Lancaster Regiment was based in Fiume (more on this later) and their war diary records the send-off given to a large number of their mates returning to civilian life:

> The party for demobilization paraded outside the Battalion Billets at 07.00 and marched to the quay, the band playing them down. The party were aboard the SS. Szapary by 07.30, the band playing on the quay until the boat cast off at about 08.40. The crews of H.M.S's Diamond, Sir Thomas Picton and destroyers in port "manned ship" and gave them a rousing send-off, the H.M.S. Diamond's band playing "For auld lang syne."[23]

The draw down in troop numbers presented challenges for those left in command; how to function with the reduced numbers; how to keep the men occupied now that there was no enemy to face; and how to maintain discipline. One of the consequences of a demobilisation process which released individuals rather than units was that the best qualified were frequently the ones who left first, as happened to the 39 CCS:

> Demobilization has now reduced the strength of the Unit in Other Ranks to 72, many of the most efficient NCO's [sic] and men having gone and the demobilisation [sic] of clerks has made the working of the office difficult.[24]

While the war was in progress the soldiers had largely accepted that the routine of life in an army in a combat zone involved long periods of time-wasting and menial chores, but that forbearance was tested after the armistice as men fretted over the need to return home and get back into civilian employment. Lambert's unit was sent to Austria as part of the army of occupation and he records spending much of his time learning to ski and toboggan; fun, possibly, but not his priority at that time. He and his colleagues were seething 'with discontent, seeking to forget the exhausting routine of sentry-go, and the desire for England, by every possible evasion of discipline and furious indulgence in the winter sports'.[25] The journal of the 5th Gloucesters grumbled that 'since the Armistice was signed, our energies have been divided between rolling up barbed wire and other salvage work, education and sport'.[26] Harry Lamin had joined the army late (December 1916), and did not get released until January 1920. He wrote that he was sorry that he would not be home for Christmas 1919 as even the Austrian prisoners they were guarding 'are going home this month'[27] – that must have been particularly galling. While it was frustrating for those who were waiting,

23   TNA: WO 95/4240, war diary 8 York and Lancs, 7 January 1919.
24   TNA: WO 95/4207, 31 January 1919.
25   Lambert, *Over the Top*, p.218.
26   *Fifth Glo'ster*, Issue 25, January 1919.
27   Lamin, *Letters*, p.204.

the process was working and by April 1919 55.5% of all officers and 78.3% of soldiers eligible for demobilisation had re-joined 'civvy-street'. The low unemployment rate of 2.4% in 1919 and 1920 indicates that post-war reconstruction did absorb many of the ex-soldiers into the civilian workforce.[28]

The situation in Italy was no different from that faced by the authorities in France; how to prevent military formations from becoming agglomerations of disaffected men. The change in the soldiers was described by Gladden as one where conditions 'had reduced almost to nothing any loyalty we may have had for the unit, in which we had certainly come to take a great deal of pride'.[29] The chosen solution to this fall in *esprit de corps* was sport, leavened with as full a programme of educational lectures as possible. Officers were asked to give talks on subjects that interested them, or in which they might have some special knowledge. For the men of the 9th York and Lancaster battalion the Reverend Hudson Shaw spoke on 'Civilization's debt to Italy', while others held forth on the 'League of Nations', the 'Colonies', and 'Italian History'. The aim was less to educate, more to fill the soldiers' time. But some lectures were intended to assist their resettlement into civilian life with subjects such as the demobilisation process, Post Office work, shorthand, agriculture, carpentry and the French language.[30] But sport was the big boredom release valve. In December 1918 600 men of the Gordon Highlanders entered a cross-country run; the battalion held football competitions on nine days that month while boxing and shooting competitions took up three days and the chaplain gave a talk on *Macbeth*. Being a Scottish regiment, the Gordons provided classes for the officers and men in highland dancing, though the availability of female partners was not recorded in the war diary. On the other hand the officers at the base depot in Arquata were more fortunate as 'dancing [was] temporarily allowed for Nursing Sisters and V.A.Ds [Voluntary Aid Detachment nurses]'. Quick to take advantage of this relaxation of the rules, a ball was held at the Miramare Hotel with 450 guests. The event was considered a 'great success and appreciated by all present'. The value of the divisional concert party groups was shown in these post-armistice months, as much as during the active phase of the war; the 'Dumps' (23 Division) gave 'nightly performances to crowded houses at the theatre'.[31] The last unit to leave Italy was the 8th Battalion of the York and Lancaster Regiment, on peacekeeping duties in Fiume, but they were not forgotten by the 'What Nots' of 7 Division. The performers gave a series of successful concerts for British and American troops, to which the local Italian population seem to have had the opportunity of attending, as the war diary attests; there was 'considerable excitement among the inhabitants [of Fiume], who cannot believe that the performers are British Soldiers and not civilians'.

28   Graubard, *Military Demobilization*, p.310.
29   Gladden, *Piave*, p.218.
30   TNA: WO 95/4224, war diary, 2nd Gordon Highlanders, December 1918.
31   Sandilands, *23rd Division*, p.341.

For more than 1,200 of the men of the IEF, Italy would be their 'corner of a foreign field'. As with all wars the first months after hostilities were a time for collecting those bodies which lay unburied after the most recent fighting. But the work of the burial parties also included the consolidation of those who were in isolated graves into larger military cemeteries. Here is not the place to trace the history of the Commonwealth War Graves Commission (CWGC), the involvement of Sir Fabian Ware, or the arguments over whether or not to repatriate the bodies of the fallen. However, some brief comments will suffice. In May 1917, with the casualty lists yet to be swollen by the events at Passchendaele, the Imperial War Graves Commission (IWGC) was formed, with the Prince of Wales as President and Sir Fabian Ware as Vice-Chairman. In 1960, with 'Imperial' no longer appropriate, the IWGC became the CWGC. The memorialisation of the Great War is a subject in its own right, and very well covered by Jay Winter[32] and George Mosse.[33] In the design of the cemeteries Ware and his colleagues laid down a number of principles which are common to all of the CWGC sites around the world, and which make them instantly recognisable to those who visit these peaceful places of remembrance. Apart from some of the very early burial sites (Béthune Town Cemetery is one example), all the dead are treated equally, with soldiers and officers being inter-mixed and with similar headstones. By the use of flowers, especially in France and Flanders, the cemeteries were to portray the theme of an English country garden – this is more difficult in countries with a dry, arid, climate. Those sites with more than 40 graves were to have a Cross of Sacrifice, designed by Sir Reginald Blomfield, while those with 1,000 burials or more also had Sir Edwin Lutyen's Stone of Remembrance. The cemeteries in Italy are much smaller than those on the Western Front but most have the Cross, also, contrary to the comment that the Stone of Remembrance required 1,000 graves (or names on a memorial to the missing), the cemetery at Montecchio Precalcino has a stone, but only 438 burials. Because of the nature of the war, and the destructive potential of the weapons used, many of the dead have never been found and these men have their names engraved on a memorial to the missing; the author's great-uncle was killed at Loos and is remembered at Dud Corner. However, for those men who had a physical burial each has his own headstone; if the man could not be identified then he is 'Known unto God'. Where the man can be identified then the headstone reflects his religion (Muslims, Hindus, Jews and Christians having an appropriate religious symbol), his rank, name, number and regimental 'hat badge' are also engraved on the stone. In many cases families also paid to have a personal message engraved at the bottom of the headstone. Made from white Portland stone, the serried ranks of grave markers, many with flowers around them, are a lasting and poignant reminder of how many fell in that war. It is very sobering to visit sites like Tyne Cot in Flanders, and impossible to keep

32   J. Winter, *Sites of Memory, Sites of Mourning. The Great War in European cultural history* (Cambridge, 1995).

33   G.L. Mosse, *Fallen Soldiers. Reshaping the Memory of the World Wars* (Oxford, 1990).

a dry eye. Figure 9.1 demonstrates the difference in scale between the cemeteries on the Asiago plateau and those on the Western Front. These small Italian cemeteries use the local granite for the Cross of Sacrifice rather than the white Portland stone. On the front row is the headstone of Sergeant Davenport, who we met earlier in the book; the poppy was placed there by the author.

The British war cemeteries are in stark contrast with the Italian memorial to their dead at Redipuglia. Built in 1938 – many of those interred here were exhumed from their original burial place at Colle St Elia which faces today's edifice – the huge 'stairway' is the final resting place of 39,857 known and 60,330 unknown Italian soldiers. This author visited on a wet day in July when the stone looked particularly dark and grey. More than 100,000 names are carved on 4,500 panels spread across the 22 terraces of the monument. To the British visitor the site is very impersonal. Mosse points out that many of the Italian cemeteries were 'developed and reconstructed [...] during the Fascist regime', and Redipuglia bears all the hallmarks of that triumphalist style of architecture.

But there is another difference between this and the British burial sites (apart from the obvious one of size), and that is in the equality accorded those buried there. As visitors approach the memorial they come first to the enormous tomb of the Duke

Figure 9.1 Granezza CWGC cemetery on the Asiago plateau. The author placed a British Legion cross against the headstone of Sergeant Henry Davenport. (© J. Dillon)

Figure 9.2 Italian war memorial at Redipuglia, the Duke of Aosta's tomb in the front centre.
(© J. Dillon)

of Aosta (commander of the Italian Third Army, on Cavan's right flank at Vittorio Veneto), his grave is covered with a 75 ton monolith of black porphyry. Immediately behind this is a row of five tombs of generals who were killed in the war. In a British cemetery, all six (had they died in the conflict) would have had a headstone in the same style as the ordinary soldiers. The CWGC sites are for those who fell in the conflict; the Duke died in 1931, he was not killed in the war and so would not have been buried in a British war cemetery. He was buried here at his own request, and no doubt the physical positioning of his tomb was intended to represent him as being at the head of the soldiers from his Third Army, many of whom were no doubt also interred at Redipuglia.

But there was a job to be done before the stonemasons and gardeners could leave to us those quiet plots that are so instantly recognisable as British war cemeteries. The heavy casualty toll on the Western Front had taught the authorities that the process of grave registration had to be formalised, and this was then replicated in the IEF. In April 1918 five officers and 67 men were allocated to the role, and their job would have been to locate the graves of those who had been buried, many of them adjacent to Advanced Dressing Stations, and to record the details of the interred soldier. Some of the men would have been buried by their friends, with their names, regimental numbers, date killed and battalion noted on a wooden cross. Figure 9.4 shows

Figure 9.3 The tombs of the five generals, with that of the Duke of Aosta in front of them.
(© J. Dillon)

the wooden grave marker put up for Sergeant Davenport[34] alongside that of Private
Crosby. They were buried shortly after they died, in ground that is now Granezza
cemetery. After the war, when the IWGC took over the site, Davenport and Crosby
remained side by side, but now with their white headstones (figure 9.1). These men
are just two of the 142 buried here, one of five British war cemeteries on the Asiago
plateau. Sadly, as deep snow makes these sites difficult to reach between November
and May, they receive few visitors. Many of those who died in the Vittorio Veneto
campaign are buried in Tezze cemetery, somewhat easier to reach. Not all medical
centres became burial sites for those who had died of their wounds; those from No.
9, 24 and 39 CCS were brought together and reinterred at Montecchio Precalcino,
17 Km. north of the city of Vicenza. Burying the dead would have been particularly
problematic on the rocky terrain of the Asiago plateau, and considerably more difficult than for burial parties working in the low-lying fields of Flanders. The work of
reinterring the bodies in the IWGC cemeteries could not have been pleasant, but was
necessary, particularly for the peace of mind of the families at home. In December
1918 one medical officer and three men from 23 Division were detailed 'to be attached

34   The author is grateful to the Davenport family for sending me a copy off the photo of the
      grave-marker.

Figure 9.4 Wooden grave marker put up
by Sergeant Davenport's unit; this has
been replaced by the CWGC headstone.
(© Michelle Flanaghan, Sergeant
Davonport's great-granddaughter)

to the party re-interring bodies in isolated graves [on the Asiago]'.[35] At the same time
other groups were doing the same for those killed in the final offensive:

> From the beginning of the month parties from all three divisions [7, 23 and 48]
> have been engaged in collecting bodies from isolated graves and burying grounds
> into specified cemeteries. This work has been carried out on the Altipiano,
> Montello and Grave di Papadopoli fronts.[36]

The author visited the cemeteries at Boscon and Granezza on a warm summer's day
in 2010; they may have died a long way from home, and are rarely visited, but they lie
now in a beautiful, well-tended, spot among the tall pines on that high plateau.

Throughout the war Italian politicians had succeeded in frustrating their British
and French allies either by putting forward (then postponing) offensives, repeatedly
claiming Austrian numerical superiority, threatening dire consequences for the alliance should Italy fall out of the war, or by putting forward territorial claims that their
allies did not feel were justified by Italian military effectiveness. With the German

35   TNA: WO 95/4231, war diary of 23 Division ADMS, 1 December 1918.
36   TNA: WO 95/4212 war diary 14 Corps, December 1918.

and Austrian armistices in place, and the Versailles peace negotiations under way, the pattern continued; the Italians demanded that the disputed city of Fiume should be gifted to them. The claim was voiced most strongly by the Italian nationalist, aeronaut, womaniser and war-poet, Gabriele D'Annunzio. Fiume, or Rijeka in modern-day Croatia, is a harbour town in a large bay at the northern end of the Adriatic – it is difficult to see it as geographically part of Italy. The claims of the nationalists were based on the language spoken by the population, or that segment that they defined as the city's inhabitants. Although the city had a large proportion of Italian speakers it was governed by a Magyar mayor and the language of the city bureaucracy was Hungarian. In 1914 Fiume was 61% 'Italian', but if the suburb of Sussak was included then the figure dropped to slightly less than 50%[37] – it all depended on how the extent of the city was defined. Among Italian speakers, and especially among the younger citizens, there was a growing wish for Italy to annex the city; Fiumans basing their claim that it was Italian on the grounds of 'ethnicity'. For mainland Italian politicians annexation was attractive as it would give them an Adriatic port, albeit one on the Dalmatian coast, to offset their own lack of good natural harbours on their eastern coastline.[38] With the end of the war, Italian politicians put forward their claims to the spoils of victory at the Paris Peace Conference; after all, the country had entered the war specifically for territorial gain. Sir Edward Grey had commented in 1915 that the view of the Italian Ambassador was that for Italy to join the war against Germany 'there must be a great substantial advantage put before the Italian nation'. While the process and deliberations of the Versailles agreement (well covered in Margaret MacMillan's *Peacemakers*) are beyond the scope of this book, the Italian demands are relevant to the rump of the IEF that had to stay in the theatre until 1920.

At the conference the Italian delegates insisted on adherence to the terms of the Treaty of London, plus the annexation of Fiume. Once more the Italians were trying their allies, who (despite the many Italians who died on the Isonzo) were convinced that their involvement in the war did not justify the claims being made. Demands for territory in Asia Minor could 'hardly be justified by the effort hitherto made by Italy in the war as compared with the sacrifices already made by Great Britain, France and Russia'. But their justification for the annexation of Fiume flew in the face of the principles of the American President, Woodrow Wilson. He wanted a break up of European empires and a consequent independence (based on nationality) for those states ruled by them; Fiume was regarded by Wilson as Italian territorial expansion, and unlikely to receive his approval. For the Italian negotiators their demand for the 'Treaty of London plus Fiume' became the petard on which they had hoisted themselves. They had whipped up such a level of enthusiasm for it within the ultra-nationalists at home that they could not step down. With their economy in dire straits immediately after

37   TNA: WO 106/857, *The Problem of Fiume (translation).*
38   M. MacMillan, *Peacemakers. The Paris Conference of 1919 and Its Attempt to End War* (London, 2001), p.294.

the war they now faced American threats[39] to the stability of the Lira and to grain shipments (on which they were reliant to feed the population), because of Fiume. The justification for their bargaining position would have echoes in later proclamations by German and Italian Fascists; it was 'not a question of greedy territorial claims. It is also a question of the duty of Italy, of the rights of the Italians at Fiume and of universal justice'.[40] But D'Annunzio could do better than that when it came to why Fiume must be Italian: 'Oh, victory, you shall not be mutilated'.[41]

With growing nationalist unrest over Fiume, it fell to the lot of a battalion of British soldiers to see their time in Italy extended as they became part of an Inter-Allied garrison force intended to keep order in the city. This was precisely what Lord Cavan had warned against before he left Italy in November 1918, when he feared that there might be an outbreak of revolution in the country. Recognising that British troops would be there for some months he believed that their role should be limited.

> [It] should be such as to safeguard our cantonments [a term more appropriate to his time in the Boer War] and stores, our Lines of Communication and our Base, but <u>not</u> on any account to assist in keeping order outside our own area […] they should take no part in disturbances'.[42] [Underlining in the original]

Cavan's concern had been for socialist unrest on the mainland, not nationalist annexation claims in Dalmatia. However, he did warn Sir Henry Wilson that it was his impression, gained during a visit to Rome, 'that Italy meant to stay in DALMATIA [*sic*] if she could', and that following Versailles 'there will certainly be some difficult days no matter what the decision may be'. Even as he was writing, preparations were in hand to move the 8th Battalion of the York and Lancaster regiment to Fiume. They left for garrison duty – one can only imagine with what enthusiasm – on 23 November, arriving two days later.[43]

The situation for the British troops, warned against by Cavan, would have been bad enough had they only had the Italians to contend with. As part of an Inter-Allied garrison force they did not only have to hold the ring between the Italians and the Croatians. When the new state of Yugoslavia grew out of the demise of the Austro-Hungarian Empire, France gave its support to the 'historic' Croatian claims to the city, a stance which created problems between the Allies. The largest military force within the city was Italian, they had 9,000 troops, the French were close to 2,000-strong while the British had only a little over 600. As the British commander expressed it, there was less of an inter-allied character to the garrison 'because we are quite

---

39   Ledeen, *D'Annunzio*, p.16.
40   TNA: WO 106/857, *The problem of Fiume*, p.1.
41   Ledeen, *D'Annunzio*, p.14.
42   TNA: WO 79/68, *Private Papers Earl of Cavan*, letter from Cavan to CIGS, 14 November 1918.
43   TNA: WO 95/4240, war diary 8 York and Lancs, 23-25 November 1918.

swamped by the Italians'.[44] The battalion of British troops now found themselves in an invidious position. They were the smallest contingent in Fiume, they did not want to get involved between the various bickering parties, and yet they felt that the Italians and French looked to them 'more or less as their go-betweens'.[45] Unlike the armies of occupation in Germany and Austria, the British and French were not trying to control the actions of a previous enemy; the Italians had been their ally. The proposal was made to the Italians, in a committee formed of Admirals from Britain, France, the United States and Italy,[46] that they should reduce their force to 2,000 and so come into line with the other allied detachments. This was opposed by Admiral Vittorio Mola who protested that the other representatives had not taken into account 'the Italian character of the town [Mola had ignored the suburb of Sussak] and the feelings of the great majority of the population'; they had ignored the 'feeling of "Italianity" (Italianità) of its population' and the meeting was 'misled by partisan statements of the parties opposed to the Italian point of view'.[47] Mola resigned from the committee and the Italians did not reduce their force level in the city.

For the British soldier in Fiume – who had little interest in nationalistic claims based on language – garrison duty was a chore, interspersed with sports and lectures. The war was over, all they wanted to do was go home, see their families again and get into the civilian job market. Although there were some small disturbances, particularly in January 1919, the battalion war diary does not mention any until May of that year, with an increasing incidence after that. In his November letter to Wilson, Cavan had stated that the troops should not get involved in local disturbances, and the battalion's war diary shows that they tried to adhere to that by remaining in barracks – which begs the question of exactly why they were still there. On 1 May 'all British troops in Fiume were confined to billets during the whole of the day, in view of possible disturbances'. By July the situation had worsened, as the following diary entries record:

2 July; Much friction between the Italians and French soldiers during the evening. The Battalion was ordered to 'Stand-To' but nothing to justify its turning out occurred.

5 July; During the evening there were several disturbances in the town, French soldiers again being attacked and mobbed by the civilian population.

6 July; Again, there was much trouble in the town at night, both French and Italian soldiers being killed.

Both nationalities had been allies during the war. The British Ambassador wrote to the Foreign Office to say that nine French soldiers had been killed, while the British

44   TNA: WO 106/859, report from Brig-Gen Gordon to CIGS.
45   TNA: WO 106/858, letter to CIGS.
46   TNA: WO 32/5129, *Proposal for Inter-Allied organisation of Fiume.*
47   TNA: WO 32/5129, letter from Mola to Naval Committee, 12 January 1919.

Military Attaché opined that 'both Italians and French at Fiume have lost their heads'.[48] The British, confining themselves to camp, were considered by the Chief of the Italian General Staff, General Pietro Badoglio, to have been 'irreprochable [*sic*] and that not even the slightest incident of irritability of any kind has occurred' concerning them – did he know they had remained in their billets? According to Delmé-Radcliffe, Badoglio considered the chief blame 'for [the] disturbances rests on French troops and General Savy [their commander] who appears to be quite unable to exact obedience from his men'. Meanwhile the British blamed the local Italian commander who made 'no determined effort to keep order in the town'. It was all blame and counter-blame, while the British stuck to their billets. However, in September 1919 an incident occurred which required the battalion to take a more demonstrative stance. On the evening of 4 September a crowd approached the British billets, chanting and throwing stones, causing the troops to 'Stand-To', and in the words of the war diary 'the sound of the men loading their rifles and preparing Lewis Guns for action disheartened them [the demonstrators] and after about five minutes they cleared off'. But the time for the British to leave was fast approaching, the Italians did not want them in the city, and their effectiveness as peacekeepers was questionable.

On 12 September bands of Arditi troops took possession of the town, headed by the mouthpiece for the annexation of Fiume, D'Annunzio. In June Francesco Nitti had become Prime Minister, and he regarded D'Annunzio's activities as a threat to his government in Rome, so much so that he tried to have the poet's march on Fiume stopped. To that end, Diaz had promised Nitti that the army would prevent the entry of the volunteers into the city. However, between them they had failed to recognise how much support D'Annunzio had. General Vittorio Pittagula, the Italian commander in Fiume, led his men out to oppose Colonel Raffaele Repetto and his approaching Arditi. Confronting the volunteers, Pittagula called on D'Annunzio to turn back. In a scene straight out of a cheap Italian opera, D'Annunzio lifted his coat to show a gold medal over his heart and called on Pittagula to 'order the troops to shoot me'.[49] They did not and so the poet and his followers entered the city. For the remaining British troops the coup was the signal for them to leave. The battalion war diary for 14 September states that 'it was decided to evacuate Fiume […] An officer was sent to inform the Rebel Leaders [*sic*] of the projected move of the British troops from Fiume'.[50]

In November 1917 the British troops, sent to fight alongside their Italian ally after the defeat of Caporetto, were greeted with flowers, cheering and enthusiasm. The nature of their leaving must have been disappointing to those who had had to stay on in the country for almost a year after the armistice was signed. The British requested

48   TNA: WO 32/5004, *Establishment of Allied Commission to investigate incidents involving French troops and Italians at Fiume.*
49   Ledeen, *D'Annunzio*, p.67.
50   TNA: WO 95/4240, war diary 8 York and Lancs, 14 September 1919.

that they be allowed to start leaving at 10.00 on 14 September 'in order that the population might have an opportunity of expressing their sympathy with the British'.[51] The Italian authorities did not consider this to be advisable and the battalion had to leave in the early hours of the morning, with no bands playing. The appearance of a hurried, unplanned, evacuation is reinforced by the entry in the war diary: 'Everything possible was done by the Royal Navy to accommodate and feed the Battalion whilst on H.M. Ships'. The frustration of the men was not eased by their having to remain on board in Fiume harbour, until they set sail for Malta at 16.00 on 18 September – the involvement of the IEF in Italy was finally over.

The battalion arrived in Malta on 20 September where they were accommodated in the barracks at Tigné Fort, at the entrance to Valletta harbour. As a fitting close to the story of the IEF the 8th Battalion of the York and Lancaster Regiment was drawn up for inspection on 23 September. The inspecting officer was Field Marshal Sir Herbert Plumer, Governor and Commander in Chief of the forces on Malta, and previously commander of the IEF, of which the battalion had been one of the first to arrive in Italy. Fittingly, Plumer was also Colonel in Chief of the York and Lancaster Regiment. Although some small headquarters and staff units remained in Italy until April 1920, the withdrawal of the battalion from Fiume effectively ended the British army's involvement in that country until the 1943 landings of the Second World War.

51   TNA: WO 95/4240.

10

Conclusions

When the war ended, the majority of the soldiers did not rush to see their experiences published and sold from the shelves of the high-street bookshops. These men returned to their families, the majority of whom had never travelled more than a few miles from their home towns and villages, how could they possibly understand the squalor of trench life, the pettiness of army discipline, the horror of mass industrial killing, or the intense friendships and camaraderie that these conditions engendered. The majority believed that their experience was beyond the comprehension of their families and friends, and so they did not talk about it; they resumed their lives as best they could. Some, however, did turn to writing, both during and after the war and as a consequence the conflict, particularly since the 1960s, has been 'learnt' through the accounts of men like Robert Graves and Edmund Blunden, together with their contemporaries, the war-poets. This small number of authors, largely unrepresentative of the vast majority of the men who fought, has caused the war to be regarded as senseless and futile; those who fought were duped by blundering generals into throwing away their lives to no end. But these accounts, as well as the output of many British military historians over the last four or five decades, concentrating as they have done on the iconic battles in France and Flanders, have resulted in the Western Front becoming the paradigm for the British soldiers' experience of the war. Although this was the theatre in which the German army had to be fought and defeated, it was not the only front on which the Allies faced the Central Powers. To fully understand the First World War the other areas of conflict have to be explored, those who fought and died there deserve no less. It has been the aim of this book to draw back the curtain a little on the British soldiers' experience of the Italian Front, one which has received little attention from British military historians.

The first and most obvious contrast between the French and Italian theatres was the terrain. France and Flanders were low-lying, with fields of rich earth and heavy clay. This area of farmland very quickly became water-logged due to the high water table and the destruction of the field drainage systems under heavy artillery bombardment. Some of the most iconic photographs of the war are those which show stretcher-bearers, knee-deep in the liquid mud of Passchendaele, carrying their wounded comrades to medical aid posts. It was just such conditions that the men of the IEF were glad to see the back of as they took their cattle-truck journey to Italy. The positions taken over by the British for the majority of their time in that country, the Asiago plateau, could not have been more different from those they had left behind in France: a tree-covered, limestone plateau, at a height of 3,000 feet; covered in snow and ice in winter but warm in summer. In these conditions, and with careful management, trench foot – so closely associated with the mud of Flanders – occurred in the IEF at only 10% of the rate on the Western Front. However, the Italian limestone presented its own problems. Defence lines could not be dug out of soft earth as in France, they had to be blasted. The limestone also affected the nature of the soldiers' injuries, many of which were due to the high velocity rock splinters which resulted from artillery shells hitting the hard ground – very different from the effects of a bombardment on soft Flanders mud. Consequently, 'accidental' wounding in Italy was three times greater than in the BEF.

During 1916 and 1917 the Italian theatre had witnessed huge losses as Cadorna threw his men into attritional assaults against the Austro-Hungarian army, especially across the River Isonzo. In 1918, following Caporetto and the retreat to the Piave, the number of casualties dropped appreciably as the British, French and Italians settled into a relatively quiet war, watching the Austrians, but making little effort to take the war to them. The extent of the contrast between the Italian and Western Fronts can be gauged by the soldiers' references to their 'quiet' and even 'cushy' war. In their letters home the men reassured their families of how much safer they were after their move and just why they felt this to be so is demonstrated by an example from 7th Division. This unit was in reserve in June 1918 when the Austrians launched their attack, but they were in the van during Cavan's crossing of the Piave in October of that year. In their time in France they had been involved in the battles at First Ypres, Neuve Chapelle, Festubert, Givenchy, Loos, the Somme, the Ancre, Arras, Bullecourt and Passchendaele.[1] But it was not only the number of battles that made a difference between France and Italy, it was also their duration: many – like the Somme, Arras and Passchendaele – went on for weeks, if not months; the operation to take Vittorio Veneto and end the war against Austria lasted only 10 days. The British also regarded the Germans as tougher opponents than the Austrians. During an interview with Peter Liddle, in 1974, one old soldier recalled his time in Italy as 'an absolute picnic. We all loved it there',[2] while one officer found it 'deliciously amusing' to read newspaper accounts of 'intense artillery activity' along the Italian Front, while he saw so little for himself.[3] Mitchell's analysis of the British war casualties demonstrated that shell shock victims, usually associated with artillery bombardment, were on a scale of one in the IEF for every five in France – a reflection of the lower intensity of

1   Crosse, *Defeat of Austria*, p.114.
2   A. Acland, Interview with P. Liddle, August 1974, Liddle Archive, GS 0003.
3   Cotton, Private Papers, letter, 4 December 1917.

the shelling in Italy. Another crude comparison of the level of conflict is the number of dead and wounded. From October 1914 to the end of the war the 7th Division (normally 10-12,000 men) suffered 68,000 casualties, but only 729 during the battle of Vittorio Veneto. Statistics used in Chapter Four indicate that a man had 12 times the risk of being killed on the Western Front, and 21 times as much chance of being a casualty, as he did in Italy. While they were unaware of the actual numbers, this feeling of greater safety – and the belief that they might now survive – was constantly emphasised by the men in their letters home. On the other hand the reduced level of activity was a constant frustration for Cavan who, while commanding the IEF, had to defer to Diaz on the question of when to launch assaults against the Austrians. The lack of aggressive action by the Italian C-in-C also caused the British high command to begin the recall of two of their divisions, intending to replace them with tired units from France, on the grounds that so little was happening in Italy. The move was stopped when plans were finally drawn up for the October assault across the Piave.

But quiet fronts presented their own problems; NCOs and Officers had the challenge of maintaining the troops' preparation for battle, while at the same time the men saw little likelihood of that happening. The majority of the soldiers were not regulars and resented the continued restrictions and discipline which they believed were more appropriate to an active than an inactive theatre; they had either volunteered for the duration, or been conscripted, but they did not consider the army, and its rules, as their career future. It would not be unreasonable to infer that the high incidence of drunkenness and insubordination, in the early months of their deployment, was a reaction to the reduced intensity of the conflict from that which they had previously been used to, and the feeling that the war was drawing to a close. Maintaining morale, fitness and a feeling of 'purpose' was more difficult when the men saw less relationship between these activities and the war around them, and their improved chances of surviving it.

The British army of 1918 was more of a 'top down' organisation than its modern-day counterpart, requiring strict adherence to all orders and regulations; any deviation or infraction was likely to result in a 'charge' and consequent disciplinary action. Although the *Manual of Military Law* was the standard reference throughout the service, this book has demonstrated that sentences, for the same offence, varied widely between Italy and France. Reference has been made to the problems associated with the collation of the data relating to disciplinary charges; the paperwork for trials at different organisational levels, other than for those courts martial which resulted in the application of the death sentence, is no longer available. For those cases which did not result in the 'extreme penalty' the only records are those in the courts martial registers at Kew. Previous writers have analysed the disciplinary record of the IEF, but have restricted their research to trials for desertion, and especially to those where the man was executed. Apart from one soldier who was put to death for murder in 1919, all other death sentences in the IEF were commuted to some form of imprisonment. Discipline, while strictly enforced in Italy, tended to be tailored to meet the exigencies of local circumstances – such as insufficient facilities for incarcerating offenders.

Cases involving desertion were more likely to result in the man being found 'guilty of absence', which did not carry a capital sentence, than was the case in France. Similarly, and possibly because of a lack of confinement facilities, terms of imprisonment were more frequently commuted to Field Punishment. The trial records also demonstrate that Field Punishment was used more harshly in Italy than in France, with particular emphasis on FP1; commanders did not want their superiors, or the men, to think that the disciplinary regime was lax. This book has gone further than others in its use of all the courts martial data for the IEF, and in comparing this with similar records for the whole of the British army.

Soldiers and their officers knew that at some point they might be called on to fight and kill the enemy, but that required – among other attributes such as good leadership – that the morale of the units should be maintained as high as possible. The point has been made that the 'mood' and the 'spirit' of military units are not necessarily one and the same thing; the first could and did vary with the weather, the food, the prevalence of disease, and many other factors. This fickle temperament was detectable in the 'grousing' to which British soldiers were (and still are) so prone. The censor considered it a safety valve for vexations and grumbles, so venting an issue which might have otherwise resulted in insubordination, or worse: according to Captain Hardie it was 'good for a dog to have fleas, keeps him from brooding over being a dog'.[4] But while the mood varied, morale within the IEF did not decline to any significant degree. It was tested by the unavailability of home leave, and here the soldiers in Italy were worse off than their comrades in France, who were considerably closer to 'Blighty'. Journeys by train took five days each way from Italy, which meant that fewer men could be released; this strained morale more than any other issue. However, the real test of a military unit is its performance in action, and here the IEF did well on the two occasions that mattered: the Austrian attack on the 15 June and the Allied offensive in late October 1918. In spite of the effect of influenza on the availability of troops to repel the June attack, within 24 hours all ground taken by the Austrians had been reclaimed. Cavan's reaction to the temporary break-in on the front of 48th Division was the removal of Fanshawe from command. While Cavan gave differing explanations for his action, misplaced British pride may be one that he did not record. British commanders had frequently told the Italians that the Austrians were lesser opponents than the Germans, and that the Italian defensive positions at Caporetto had been poor – too many men had been too far forward. Against that background Cavan, in his first major action while holding independent command, had seen his line penetrated by the weaker enemy. Additionally, he had received Italian help on his left to recover the situation; not the scenario he would have wished for. The troops of the IEF, to their credit, performed as they were trained to do, and as they had rehearsed. Had there been any problems over the state of morale, the Austrians would not have been held by the scattered units of the 48th Division.

4   Hardie, report, October 1917.

The bigger test for Cavan's men was their part in the October offensive across the River Piave. By September 1918 General Diaz and the Italian politicians were conscious that, with the impending collapse of the Germans in France, their army could not afford to be static on the line of the Piave when the war ended, and with the Austrians still holding the ground they had taken after Caporetto. The Italians had to attack if they were to have any chance of holding the Allies to the terms of the Treaty of London during the post-armistice peace process. The role played by the IEF in the victory of Vittorio Veneto is covered in Chapter Nine, as is the resentment at the way in which the British contribution was perceived to have been down-played by the Italians. Cavan's occupation of the Grave di Papadopoli during the October attack made it possible for him to secure the left bank of the Piave when the full attack went ahead. Had he not done this in the early stages of the operation then the right flank of the Italian Eighth Army would have been exposed when it struck north to Vittorio Veneto. As a result of the slower crossing of the river by the Italians, Cavan's XIV Corps became the spearhead of the attack, rather than the Italians on his left flank, as had been Diaz's plan. An American historian, James Burgwyn, must have been comparing the numbers of boots on the ground, rather than outcomes, when he wrote that '*without substantial Allied* or American support, Diaz had broken through and rolled up the Hapsburg armies';[5] [my emphasis]. With the British and French involvement so easily dismissed (while mention is made of an almost inconsequential American participation), it is no wonder that their participation on the Italian Front is overlooked in so many histories of the war.

And what of the timing and preparation for the final offensive: readers can draw their own conclusions regarding the 'spatchcock' planning of the October attack. This author finds it difficult to reconcile the Italian claims that they had been making ready for this well ahead of time. Cavan, whose role was to protect the Italian Eighth Army's right flank was not told of his promotion from Corps to Army command until 6 October; Diaz did little to stop nine battalions leaving Italy in mid-September at the very point when it is claimed that he was planning the offensive; the 7th and 23rd Divisions began their move back to the Western Front (because they were not being used in Italy), to be replaced by 'tired' divisions from France, and this was only halted on 7 October. Both the recall of the nine battalions, and the replacement of two fit divisions with tired ones, would have reduced Diaz's strength and it is difficult to believe that they would have been contemplated if he had told Foch that he was planning a major offensive – one which the Allied *Generalisimo* had been demanding for some time. As the 23rd Division history records; 'a sudden complete change of plan had been made by the *Comando Supremo*'.[6]

5   H. J. Burgwyn, T*he legend of the mutilated victory: Italy, the Great War, and the Paris Peace Conference, 1915-1919* (London, 1993), p.190.
6   Sandilands, *The 23rd Division*, p.293.

The divisions that made up the IEF were battle-hardened, they brought with them the experience, skills and techniques which had been hard-learnt during their time in France and Flanders; some of these were transferable to their new theatre of operations, but some were not. This issue of 'transferability' was the source of some friction between British and French commanders, and their Italian hosts. The British were not above projecting the chauvinistic and patronising attitude that the Italians had a lot to learn about 'real war', and the Brits were just the people to teach them. The attritional battles on the Western Front had demonstrated the need for defence in depth – multiple trench lines, with only a small percentage of the troops in the forward trenches – and the sophisticated use of artillery. The British gunners had well-developed techniques for 'indirect' counter-battery fire which did not require the pre-registration of the guns, thereby enabling the 'deep battle'[7] which had become such a feature of the war in France; unfortunately the Italians had not yet developed these skills. By 1917 both sides in Flanders had learnt that a successful advance could only go ahead under the cover of a 'creeping barrage'. With this tactic the infantry advanced to the attack behind an artillery bombardment which (theoretically) moved forward at the same speed as the men, so affording them protection from the defenders. Again, this had not been perfected by the Italians but Cavan's Tenth Army, in the crossing of the Piave, used it to great effect and it was described as having been 'exceedingly accurate'.[8] This artillery success was in large part due to the photo-reconnaissance sorties flown by the RAF prior to the attack, where the whole front was covered in 5,000 photos.[9] This technique of army/air cooperation, brought to Italy from France, allowed enemy gun batteries to be pinpointed, and accurately shelled, without prior registration by the artillery.

But not all of the skills brought with them from Flanders were directly relevant to the Italian theatre, and for some new ones that related to mountain warfare, they would need to rely on their new ally. Differences in terrain demanded that compromises had to be made in the construction and layout of the defensive trench systems; areas of cover had to be blasted from rock rather than dug from the earth, while the steepness of the ground on the Asiago required support trenches to be sited closer to those in the front-line than was the case in France. Also, telephone lines, so essential for command and control, could be laid in triplicate on the Western Front, and buried up to six feet down as protection against shellfire. The limestone of the Asiago plateau precluded this and the IEF had to string them above ground, among the trees, where they were vulnerable to be being cut during a bombardment. Although the British were critical of the Italians for what they saw as a failure to adopt the new techniques of modern warfare, there were areas where the IEF could in turn learn from their ally. Road building was one good example. The Italians built a new 23 Km road for the

---

7   P. Griffith, *Battle Tactics of the Western Front* (London, 1994), p.158.
8   Crosse, Defeat of Austria, p.69.
9   Jones, *War in the Air*, p.290.

British in less than eight weeks, this piece of engineering (which included the switch-back road on the southern slope of the Asiago plateau) reinforced their reputation with the British as excellent engineers. Motor transport: British lorries were completely unsuitable for the mountain roads and were no match for the Italian short-wheelbase Fiat trucks. River crossings: Cavan acknowledged that his Tenth Army would not have made their rapid crossing of the River Piave without the essential help of the *pontieri*.

In all theatres of the war commanders and their subordinates had to 'learn the living and the operational aspects [of war] simultaneously';[10] they did not only have to prepare their troops to fight, but also had to look after their well-being. Medical facilities in Italy were provided on the basis of the experience learnt from the Western Front, but the casualty rates there were not replicated in the IEF, resulting in a much higher ratio of hospital places to ration strength than in the BEF. Consequently, when they were hit by the influenza epidemic, the troops in Italy had no shortage of beds. Much attention was paid in the British army to the role of sanitation officers and their teams in the prevention of disease and its subsequent possibility of spreading among the soldiers. Italy, with its freezing winters on the Asiago and hot, humid, summers on the plains, presented new challenges to those charged with policing the 'cleanliness' of the IEF and its vulnerability to the different enteric diseases that could spread so easily in those conditions. Using Macpherson's history and the statistics of Mitchell, this book has demonstrated that there were many ways in which the Western and Italian Fronts differed in terms of the illnesses the troops contracted, and how the IEF tried to assist the Italians in improving their own sanitation standards.

There has been much reference in preceding chapters to the views expressed by senior British commanders, and the troops under them, towards their Italian allies, soldiers as well as civilians. Frequently those commenting resorted to the racial stereo-types of the time, but it should also be pointed out that they did not restrict themselves to the one ally. The correspondence of Haig and Robertson contains many examples of their unflattering views of the French. Junior regimental officers, and the troops they commanded, had a limited view of the war: Carrington, a company officer, 'had not the slightest hint'[11] of the collapse of Nivelle's offensive or the mutinies in the French army. The soldiers had much less contact with French and Italian civilians than we might expect, yet it was based on these infrequent opportunities that they made their sweeping generalisations in their letters home. Skirth claimed that in one six month period in France he 'never set eyes on a single civilian',[12] while Carrington (also in France) 'moved eighty times' in 1916,[13] which would have made any meaningful

---

10   M. Crawshore, 'The impact of technology on the BEF and its commander' in B. Bond and
      N. Cave (eds.), *Haig: A Reappraisal 80 Years On* (Barnsley, 1999), p.158.
11   Carrington, *Soldier from the wars returning*, p.147.
12   Skirth, *Reluctant Tommy*, p.50.
13   Carrington, *Soldier from the wars returning*, p.148.

contact with the French rather problematic. The letters and memoirs referred to in this book also indicate that relationships between British soldiers and French and Italian civilians were limited, often going not far beyond the family they may have been billeted with. In their writings from France those who later moved with the IEF rarely mention French soldiers or civilians; they were preoccupied with 'the war'. In contrast these same men, in the 'quieter' environs of Italy, focused more on how they imagined the Italians to be. Comments on the local people and the countryside replaced 'the war' in their letters and memoirs. However, the limited opportunity to mix with the local civilians meant that a soldier's view was biased; if one landlord over-charged for an item, then all Italians became cheats and robbers – general conclusions were drawn from particular personal experiences.

While the soldiers were largely working men, untraveled, and with a very limited view of the world outside their hometowns, the senior commanders might have been expected to show a more rounded appreciation of their foreign allies; instead, some of their comments demonstrate an arrogant jingoism. Haig referred to the Italians as 'a wretched people, useless as fighters',[14] and he resented having to send them some of his divisions. His dismissive statement reflected a fundamental difference between the military histories of Britain and Italy; while the former had one stretching back centuries, Italy had only been a unified country for two generations. The Roman Empire and its legions were long gone, modern Italy's military past was not a glorious one: in the Austro-Prussian war of 1866 Italy's face was 'rubbed in the dirt'[15] as its army and navy were humiliated at Custoza and Lissa; their army was defeated in 1896 by the Ethiopians at Adowa; the 1911 expedition to Libya was only a 'fragile national conquest'.[16] With this recent history, British and French generals did not consider Italy to be a military power of any weight. With more French troops on the ground than British, and with the war being fought on their territory, French generals took the *generalisimo* role in the alliance, one that was resented by Haig and Robertson; Haig referred to Nivelle as a 'junior foreign commander'[17] [italics in original], while Robertson was 'trying to see that the fine British army is not placed at the mercy of irresponsible people – & [*sic*] some of them foreigners at that'.[18] There was an 'otherness' in the way these men regarded their allies; Robertson again:

14   W. Philpott, 'Haig and Britain's European Allies', in B. Bond and N. Cave (eds.), *Haig: A Reappraisal 80 Years On* (Barnsley, 1999), p.138.
15   Duggan, *The force of destiny*, p.253.
16   Bosworth, *Mussolini*, p.205.
17   Sheffield and Bourne, *Douglas Haig*, p.274.
18   Woodward, *Robertson*, p.286.

The great thing to remember in dealing with them is that they are Frenchmen and not Englishmen, and do not and never will look at things in the way we look at them. I suppose that they they that we are queer people.[19]

The British just could not get past their predilection for regarding the Italians and the French as 'Johnny foreigner', and this assumed superiority came through in their comments on their allies' martial abilities. Following the German gas attack at Ypres in 1915 Haig confided to his diary that:

These French leaders are a queer mixture of fair ability (not more than fair) and ignorance of the practical side of war [an accusation also levelled at the Italians]. They are not built for it by nature. They are too excitable and they never seem to think of what the enemy may do.[20]

Only a few months later Haig (and the BEF) would be involved in the debacle at Loos.

The view that 'allies are a tiresome lot' would no doubt have some resonance with those given overall command in World War Two, the Second Gulf War and the last 13 years of Afghanistan; the skill lies in making the coalition work, even when the Allies are considered to be of limited military worth, or just difficult to work with. When Plumer went to Italy to command the IEF he was told by Robertson that:

We could see Italy and even Russia drop out, and still continue the war with France and America. But if France drops out we not only cannot continue the war on land but our armies in France will be in a very difficult position.[21]

Sir Edward Grey and Lloyd George, separately, may have seen the political advantage of having Italy as an active member of the Entente, but the Chief of the Imperial General Staff saw little military benefit.

It is preposterous that they [the Italians] should have all the millions of able-bodied men that they have and that we should be called upon to send 150,000 to 200,000 of our good soldiers to look after their wretched country.[22]

In the first 12 months of the war the opinion of the British Foreign Secretary was that Italy should join the Entente as a belligerent. Had Italy not declared neutrality

19   R. Blake (ed.), *The Private Papers of Douglas Haig 1914-1919* (London, 1952), Robertson to Haig, 5 January 1916, p.122.
20   Blake, *Douglas Haig*, p.91.
21   Woodward, *Robertson*, p.258.
22   Woodward, *Robertson*, p.258.

on the outbreak of hostilities then the British and French armies (in the first two years of the war) would have been even more sorely pressed than they were. The Allied success at the Marne was in part due to Italy refusing to join the Triple Alliance and so allowing the release of French divisions that would have been needed to cover the French-Italian border. Similarly, had Italy not joined the Entente in May 1915 then those Austro-Hungarian divisions which launched the *Strafexpedition* of May 1916, and absorbed Cadorna's eleven assaults on the Isonzo, would have been free to join their German ally in France and Flanders. Either way the outlook would have been bleaker for Britain and France. Unfortunately the Italians were given little credit by the British at the time, or by later historians, for the indirect assistance they had given to the Western Front. Robertson in particular could not see this ally as other than a distraction from British efforts in Flanders. When the war ended and peace negotiations opened in Versailles, Italian politicians found yet more ways to frustrate their allies, but with hostilities ended there was less reason for the British to accede to what they regarded as an increasing Italian appetite for territorial advantage. Italian negotiators, spurred on by the romantic oratory and writings of D'Annunzio, demanded 'The Treaty of London plus Fiume'. Strident as the claims were, and backed up by the melodramatic walkout of the Italian representatives at Versailles, the British judged these claims against Italy's perceived commitment to the war. From London's perspective the Italian commitment, especially in blood and treasure, was weighed and found wanting. In 1917 Lloyd George had told the War Cabinet that Italian aspirations in Asia Minor could 'hardly be regarded as justified' when their military effort was compared with 'the sacrifices already made by Great Britain, France and Russia'.[23] When it came to the division of spoils the British were to remember the prevarications of Cadorna, the loan of guns for promised assaults that were then postponed, and the shroud-waving pronouncements of doom should Britain not deliver that assistance which the Italians were convinced they needed against inflated estimates of Austrian strength. Overlooking the size of Italian casualty figures – which were proportional to those of Britain – Lord Derby (British Ambassador in Paris in 1919) gave voice to an opinion held by others at the time, and since; the armistice was 'the signal for Italy to begin to fight'.[24] Now that the war was over the generous terms of the Treaty of London were something of an embarrassment to British and French politicians and Italy would again, as before the war, be treated as the Least of the Great Powers. The negotiations at Versailles were dominated by the wish of the American president, Woodrow Wilson, so see the break-up of old European empires and their replacement by national self-determination. The Italian demands for territorial expansion under the terms of the Treaty of London, together with D'Annunzio's tenuous claim on the city of Fiume, flew in the face of Wilson's Fourteen Points. If Italy persisted in its stance then America threatened to withdraw economic aid to the country until

23   TNA: CAB 23/2, War Cabinet 126, 25 April 1917.
24   MacMillan, *Peacemakers*, p.292.

it fell into line. It was against this background of international 'bickering' and fervent nationalism, that the last battalion of the IEF found itself in the unenviable position of trying to hold the ring in Fiume, while also being effectively confined to barracks.

Not unnaturally, with the fighting finished and the armistice signed, the soldiers of the IEF had expected a rapid return home to their families and the chance to resume their civilian lives, but many were disappointed. Until Germany signed a peace treaty the government felt obliged to maintain an army of sufficient strength to take up hostilities again if necessary – demobilisation would be slow, and initially it was also unfair. However, there is no evidence that their distance from England was itself a disadvantage to the men in Italy, although that was one of their fears. Keeping the men occupied between the end of hostilities and their eventual return home was a challenge for those left in charge of the IEF; discipline could not be allowed to completely collapse, but neither could it be kept at the previous levels when there was no conflict to give it a rationale. To occupy their time strenuous efforts were made to lay on sports, concerts and lectures on all subjects, and to be fair the officers and NCOs appear to have done a good job of filling the men's time until their return home. The period following the armistice, a time of frustration with the process of demobilisation and garrison duty in Fiume, is not one that receives much attention from historians, but it formed an important part of the experience of the IEF in Italy.

Rather than focus on the limited military action in which the Italian Expeditionary Force was involved, this book has focused on the whole experience of the British soldiers who fought and died in a theatre separate from Flanders. It has demonstrated that while the Western Front became the paradigm for the First World War, and as such has dominated British military histories of that conflict, conditions there did not hold true for all fronts. It was a *World* War, and as such the other theatres have to be studied to hold that perspective. For many of those who wear their poppy every November the Great War is encapsulated by the battles, losses and experience of the events in France and Flanders. To a great extent the visual symbols of that war will be the great memorials to the missing at Ypres and Thiepval, together with the serried ranks of white headstones that punctuate that 'Fatal Avenue'[25] through northern France and Belgium In these centenary years, 2014-18, it is likely that this geographic and Anglo-centric interpretation of the war will be even more pronounced. It is because of this that those who lie in the much smaller (often rarely-visited) cemeteries of the Asiago plateau and the Venetian plain, deserve their place in the histories of that war and the coming commemorations. They also 'gave their tomorrows'.

25   R. Holmes, *Fatal Avenue. A Traveller's History of Northern France and Flanders, 1346-1945* (London, 1992), p.1.

Bibliography

PRIMARY SOURCES

Archival material

House of Lords
Lloyd George papers.
LG/F/14/4/78, Parliamentary Archives.
LG/F/44/3/19, Parliamentary Archives.
LG/F/44/3/27, Parliamentary Archives.
LG/F/44/3/28, Parliamentary Archives.
LG F/44/3/30, Parliamentary Archives.

The National Archives
TNA CAB 21/89 Development of military plans of the Allies during 1917; Support to Italy.
TNA CAB 23/2, Cabinet minutes and papers; nos. 83-153.
TNA CAB 23/4, Cabinet minutes and papers; nos. 227-308.
TNA CAB 23/5, Cabinet Minutes and Papers; 309-378.
TNA CAB 23/6, Cabinet Minutes and Papers; 379-437.
TNA CAB 23/7, Cabinet Minutes and Papers; 438-479.
TNA CAB 23/44a, Committee of Prime Ministers of the Dominions: I.W.C. meetings 19A – 36A.
TNA CAB 24/26, Cabinet Minutes and Papers; 2001-2100.
TNA CAB 24/40, Cabinet Minutes and Papers; 3401-3500.
TNA CAB 45/83, Official Report of the Convention in the event of Co-operation of British Troops in Italy.
TNA CAB 45/84, Original letters, comments and personal accounts.
TNA FO 371/1660, Italy, 1913.
TNA FO 371/2007, General Corrspondence; Italy.
TNA FO 371/2375, Italy, 1915.
TNA FO 371/2507, The War: General Correspondence.

TNA FO 371/2508, The War, 1915.

TNA FO 371/2687, Italy, 1916.

TNA FO 371/3229, Italy, 1918.

TNA FO 371/3230, Italy: 1918.

TNA FO 371/3232, Italy, 1918.

TNA FO 800/377, Miscellaneous correspondence.

TNA WO 32/4512, Report of the Committee on Punishments on Active Service.

TNA WO 32/5004, Establishment of Allied Commission to investigate incidents involving French troops and Italians at Fiume.

TNA WO 32/5129, Proposal for Inter-Allied organisation of Fiume.

TNA WO 32/5460, Discipline: Field Punishment: Question of abolition or retention of Field Punishment No.1.

TNA WO 32/5461, Enquiry into Field Punishment No.1.

TNA WO 32/5597, Medical: Diseases; Prevention of Venereal Disease.

TNA WO 79/67 Private Papers Earl of Cavan.

TNA WO 79/68 Private Papers Earl of Cavan.

TNA WO 79/70, Earl of Cavan; Campaign in Italy, 1917-1918, draft account.

TNA WO 90/8, Court martial register; officers.

TNA WO 93/50, Extracts from the Statistics of the military effort of the British Empire during the Great War 1914-1920.

TNA WO 95/495, War Diary, 6th Battalion British West Indies Regiment.

TNA WO 95/4197, Adjutant and Quarter-Master General.

TNA WO 95/4198, Director Medical Services.

TNA WO 95/4207, 9 Casualty Clearing Station.

TNA WO 95/4212, War Diary 14 Corps.

TNA WO 95/4224, War Diary 7 Division.

TNA WO 95/4231, Assistant Director Medical Sevices.

TNA WO 95/4240, War Diary 23 Division.

TNA WO 95/4245, 48 Division: Adjutant and Quarter-Master General.

TNA WO 95/4254, War Diary, Lines of Communication, Arquata Base.

TNA WO 95/4255, Taranto Base: Commandant.

TNA WO 95/4259, Detention hospital (VOGHERA).

TNA WO 95/4261, 43 Ambulance Train.

TNA WO 95/4262, British West Indies Regiment.

TNA WO 106/308, General War Policy and Situation Reports.

TNA WO 106/761, Brig. Gen. Delmé-Radcliffe British Mission Italy: Reports.

TNA WO 106/762, Brig Gen Delmé-Radcliffe British Mission Italy: Reports.

TNA WO 106/765, Allied co-operation in operations on Italian Front.

TNA WO 106/770, Telegrams; March-October.

TNA WO 106/773, Impressions of the Italian Army during the autumn retreat 1917; Lt. Col. Buzzard, Jan 1918.

TNA WO 106/796 Situation in Italy; November 1917.

TNA WO 106/805 Italy.

TNA WO 106/810, Report by General Plumer on the condition of the Italian Army; 20 January 1918.

TNA WO 106/837, Royal Italian Army, Battle of Vittorio Veneto: Report by Comando Supremo.

TNA WO 106/852, Full story of campaign in Italy, 1918, as wired to CIGS by Earl Cavan.

TNA WO 106/857, The Problem of Fiume (translation).

TNA WO 106/858, Copy of letter to CIGS from GHQ Italy.

TNA WO 106/859, Brig-Gen Gordon Commanding British troops Fiume: Copy of report to CIGS.

TNA WO 106/1512, General Sir George Macdonogh, Director of Military Intelligence; miscellaneous papers.

TNA WO 106/1516, General Sir George Macdonogh, Director of Military Intelligence: Miscellaneous Papers.

TNA WO 158/23, C-in-C & CIGS correspondence and signals.

TNA WO 158/24, Communication between C-in-C BEF and CIGS.

TNA WO 213/18-30, Field General Courts Martial.

TNA WO 394/5, Statistical Abstract of information regarding Armies at Home and Abroad.

TNA WO 394/6, Statistical Abstract of information regarding Armies at Home and Abroad.

TNA WO 394/7, Statistical Abstract of information regarding Armies at Home and Abroad.

TNA WO 394/11, Statistical Abstract of information regarding the Armies at Home and Abroad.

TNA WO 394/12, Statistical Abstract of information regarding the Armies at Home and Abroad.

TNA WO 394/13, Statistical Abstract of information regarding the Armies at Home and Abroad.

The Imperial War Museum

Cotton, V.E. Private papers, Doc. 93/25/1, IWM.

Dible, J.H. Private papers Doc. 10927, IWM.

Eberle, V.E. Private papers, Doc. 7033, IWM.

Gameson, Lawrence. Private papers Doc. 612, IWM.

Hardie, M. Private papers Doc. 4041, IWM.

Morshead, Owen. Private papers Doc. 05/50/1, IWM.

Skirth, Ronald. Private papers, Doc. 9023, IWM.

Warner, H. Private papers Doc. 11465, IWM.

Wilson, Henry. Diary of Sir Henry Wilson, CIGS, Microfiche DS/MISC/80 reel 7, IWM

Trench journals
The Fifth Glo'ster Gazette. The Trenches, 1915-1919.
Gunfire. The Trenches, 1918.
The Old Firm Unlimited. The Trenches, 1918.

The Liddle Collection, Brotherton Library, University of Leeds
Acland, Arthur. Private papers GS 0003, Liddle Collection
Bradley, W.J. Private papers GS 0183, Liddle Collection.
Cresswell, W.F. Private papers GS 0389, Liddle Collection.
Dannatt, Cecil. Private papers GS 0419, Liddle Collection.
Faviall, J.V. Private papers GS 0543, Liddle Collection.
Hancock, Frank. Private papers GS 0701, Liddle Collection.
Todd, James. Private papers GS 1607, Liddle Collection.

The National Army Museum
Cadorna, Luigi. "The End of a Legend." *Army Quarterly* Vol. 7, (1924): 235-244.
Gathorne-Hardy, John F. "A summary of the Campaign in Italy, and an account of the Battle of Vittorio Veneto." *Army Quarterly* Vol.3, (1921): 23-25.

Private collections
Walton, Private Papers of Private George. Held by his granddaughter, Clare Pilkington.

SECONDARY SOURCES

Books
Albertini, Luigi. *The Origins of the War of 1914. Volume 3*. Translated by I Massey. Oxford, 1965.
Aldington, Richard. *Death Of A Hero*. London, 1929.
Arthur, Max. *When This Bloody War is Over. Soldiers' Songs of the First World War*. London, 2001.
Ashworth, Tony. *Trench Warfare 1914-1918. The Live and Let Live System*. London, 1980.
Atkinson, Christopher T. *The Seventh Division 1914-1918*. London, 1927.
Barker, Ralph. *The Royal Flying Corps in World War 1*. London, 1995.
Barrett, Duncan, (ed.). *The Reluctant Tommy. Ronald Skirth*. (London, 2010).
Bickersteth, John, (ed.). *The Bickersteth Diaries*. London, 1995.
Bishop, Alan and Mark Bostridge, (eds.). *Letters from a Lost Generation. First World War Letters of Vera Brittain and Four Friends*. London, 1999.
Blake, Robert, (ed.). *The Private Papers of Douglas Haig 1914-1919*. London, 1952.
Bond, Brian. *The Unquiet Western Front*. Cambridge, 2002.
Bosworth, Richard. *Italy, the least of the Great Powers: Italian foreign policy before the First World War*. Cambridge, 1979.

Bosworth, Richard. *Mussolini*. London, 2010.

Bosworth, Richard. *Mussolini's Italy. Life under the Dictatorship 1915-1945*. London, 2006.

Bourke, Joanna. *An Intimate History of Killing*. New York, 1999.

Bourne, John. 'The British Working Man in Arms'. In *Facing Armageddon.*, edited by Hugh Cecil and Peter Liddle, 336-352. London, 1996.

Brown, Malcolm. *The Imperial War Book of The Somme*. London, 1997.

Burgwyn, H James. *The legend of the mutilated victory: Italy, the Great War, and the Paris Peace Conference, 1915-1919*. London, 1993.

Burleigh, Michael. 'Religion and the Great War'. In *A Part of History. Aspects of the British experience of the First World War*, edited by Michael Howard, 74-81. London, 2008.

Carrington, Charles. *Soldier From The Wars Returning. [2006 Pen & Sword edition]*. Barnsley, 1965.

Cassar, George H. *The Forgotten Front. The British Campaign in Italy 1917-1918*. London, 1998.

Cecil, Hugh and Peter Liddle, (eds.). *Facing Armageddon. The First World War Experienced*. London, 1996.

Clark, Alan. *The Donkeys*. London, 1961.

Clark, Christopher. *The Sleepwalkers. How Europe Went to War in 1914*. London, 2012.

Corner, Paul and Giovanna Procacci. 'The Italian experience of 'total' mobilization 1915-1920'. In *State, society, and mobilization in Europe during the First World War*, edited by J Horne, pp. 223-240. Cambridge, 1997.

Corns, Cathryn and John Hughes-Wilson. *Blindfold and Alone. British Military Executions in The Great War*. London, 2001.

Corrigan, Gordon. *Mud, Blood and Poppycock. Britain and the First World War*. London, 2003.

Crawshore, Michael. 'The impact of Technology on the BEF and its Commander'. In *Haig: A Reappraisal 80 Years On*, edited by Brian Bond and Nigel Cave, pp.155-75. Barnsley, 1999.

Crosse, Ernest C. *The Defeat of Austria As Seen By The 7th Division*. London, 1919.

Dalton, Hugh. *With British Guns in Italy: A Tribute to Italian Achievement*. Teddington, 2007.

Duggan, Christopher. *The force of destiny: a history of Italy since 1796*. London, 2008.

Dunn, J.C. *The War the Infantry Knew 1914-1919*. London, 1987.

Edmonds, James E and H.R Davies. *Military Operations Italy, 1915-1919*. London, 1949.

Englander, David. 'Discipline and morale in the British Army, 1917-1918'. In *State, society and mobilization in Europe during the First World War*, edited by J Horne, 125-143. Cambridge, 1997.

Falls, Cyril. *Caporetto 1917*. London, 1966.

Ferguson, Niall. *The Pity of War 1914-1918*. London, 1998.

Ford, Ford Madox. *Parade's End*. London, 1982.

France, John. *Perilous Glory: The Rise of Western Military Power*. London, 2011.

Fuller, John G. *Troop Morale and Popular Culture in the British and Dominion Armies 1914-1918*. Oxford, 1990.

Fussell, Paul. *The Great War and Modern Memory*. Oxford, 1975.

Gladden, Norman. *Across the Piave*. London, 1971.

Gladden, Norman. *Ypres 1917. A Personal Account*. Guildford, 1967.

Gooch, John. 'Italy Before 1915: The Quandary Of The Vulnerable'. In *Knowing One's Enemies. Intelligence Assessment Before The Two World Wars*, edited by Ernest R May, 205-233. Princeton, 1986.

Gooch, John. 'Italy during the First World War'. In *Military Effectiveness, Volume 1, The First World War*, edited by Allan R Millett and Williamson Murray, 157-189. London, 1988.

Gooch, John. 'Morale and Discipline in the Italian Army, 1915-18'. In *Facing Armageddon. The First World War Experienced*, edited by Hugh Cecil and Peter Liddle, 434-447. London, 1996.

Gooch, John. 'Soldiers, Strategy and War Aims in Britain 1914-18'. In *War Aims and Strategic Policy in the Great War*, edited by Barry Hunt and Adrian Preston, pp.21-40. London, 1977.

Gooch, John. *The Italian Army and the First World War*. Cambridge, 2014.

Gottlieb, Wolfram W. *Studies in Secret Diplomacy during the First World War*. London, 1957.

Graves, Robert. *Goodbye to All That*. London, 1929.

Greenwell, Graham H. *An Infant in Arms. War Letters of a Company Officer 1914-1918*. London, 1935.

Griffith, Paddy. *Battle Tactics of the Western Front*. London, 1994.

Gudmundsson, Bruce I. *Stormtroop Tactics. Innovation in the German Army, 1914-1918*. Westport, 1989.

Hankey, Maurice. *The Supreme Command, 1914-1918 Volume Two*. London, 1961.

Hastings, Max. *Catastrophe. Europe Goes To War 1914*. London, 2013.

Hemingway, Ernest. *A Farewell to Arms*. London, 1929.

Hennessey, Patrick. *The Junior Officers' Reading Club: Killing Time and Fighting Wars*. London, 2009.

Henniker, Alan M. *Transportation on the Western Front 1914-1918*. London, 1937.

Herbert, Alan P. *The Secret Battle. A Tragedy of the First World War*. Barnsley, 2009.

Holmes, Richard. *Dusty Warriors. Modern Soldiers at War*. London, 2006.

Holmes, Richard. *Fatal Avenue. A Traveller's History of Northern France and Flanders, 1346-1945*. London, 1992.

Holmes, Richard. *Soldiers. Army Lives and Loyalties from Redcoats to Dusty Warriors*. London, 2011.

Holmes, Richard. *Tommy. The British Soldier on the Western Front 1914-1918*. London, 2004.

Howard, Michael, (ed.). *A Part of History. Aspects of the British Experience of the First World War*. London, 2008.

Hussey, Arthur H. and D.S Inman. *The Fifth Division in the Great War*. London, 1921.

Jeffery, Keith, (ed.). *The Military Correspondence of Field Marshal Sir Henry Wilson 1918-1922*. London, 1985.

Joll, James and G. Martel. *The Origins of the First World War*. Harlow, 2007.

Jones, Henry A. *The War in the Air*. London, 1937.

Lambert, Arthur. *Over The Top. A "P.B.I." in the H.A.C.* London, 1930.

Lamin, Bill. *Letters from the Trenches. A Soldier of the Great War*. London, 2009.

Ledeen, Michael. *D'Annunzio. The First Duce*. New Brunswick, 2009. Reprint, 3rd.

Lewis-Stempel, John. *Six Weeks: The Short and Gallant Life of the British Officer in the First World War*. London, 2011.

Lloyd George, David. *War memoirs; 3*. London, 1934.

Lloyd George, David. *War memoirs; 4*. London, 1934.

Lussu, Emilio. *Sardinian Brigade*. Translated by M Rawson. London, 2000.

Mackay, Francis. *Asiago 15/16 June 1918. Battle in the woods and clouds*. Battleground Europe. Barnsley: Leo Cooper, 2001.

MacMillan, Margaret. *Peacemakers. The Paris Conference of 1919 and Its Attempt to End War*. London, 2001.

MacMillan, Margaret. *The War That Ended Peace. How Europe Abandoned Peace for the First World War*. London, 2013.

Macpherson, William G. *History of the Great War based on official documents: Medical Services, Vol.3*. London, 1923.

Mitchell, T J and G M Smith. *History of the Great War based on official documents: Medical Services. Casualties and Medical Statistics of the Great War*. London, 1931.

Moran, Lord. *The Anatomy of Courage*. London: Robinson, 1945.

Moore-Bic, Christopher. *Playing the Game: The British Junior Infantry Officer on the Western Front 1914-18*. Solihull, 2011.

Mosse, George L. *Fallen Soldiers. Reshaping the Memory of the World Wars*. Oxford, 1990.

Murray, Nicholas. *The Red Sweet Wine of Youth*. London, 2011.

Owen, David. *The Hidden Perspective. The Military Conversations 1906-1914*. London, 2014.

Philpott, William. 'Haig and Britain's European Allies'. In *Haig: A Reappraisal 80 Years On*, edited by Brian Bond and Nigel Cave, pp.128-44. Barnsley, 1999.

Plowman, Max. *A Subaltern on the Somme*. New York, 1928.

Powell, Geoffrey. *Plumer. The Soldiers' General*. Barnsley, 2004.

Richards, Frank. *Old Soldiers Never Die*. . Eastbourne, 1933.

Robbins, Keith. *The First World War*. Oxford, 2002.

Roberts, Andrew. *A History of the English-Speaking Peoples Since 1900*. London, 2006.

Rodd, James R. *Social and Diplomatic Memories 1902-1919*. London, 1925.

Roper, Michael. *The Secret Battle. Emotional Survival in the Great War*. Manchester, 2009.

Sandilands, Harold R. *The 23rd Division 1914-1919*. London, 1925.

Senior, Michael. *Haking, a Dutiful Soldier*. Barnsley, 2012.

Seth, Ronald. *Caporetto. The Scapegoat Battle*. London, 1965.

Sheffield, Gary. *Forgotten Victory. The First World War: Myths And Realities*. London, 2001.

Sheffield, Gary. *The Chief. Douglas Haig and the British Army*. London, 2011.

Sheffield, Gary and Dan Todman. *Command and Control on the Western Front*. Staplehurst, 2004.

Sheffield, Gary and John Bourne. *Douglas Haig. War Diaries and Letters 1914-1918*. London, 2005.

Sherriff, Robert C. *Journey's End*. London, 1929.

Sicurezza, Renato. 'Italy and the War in the Adriatic'. In *Facing Armageddon*, edited by Hugh Cecil and Peter Liddle, 180-92. London, 1996.

Silkin, Jon. *The Penguin Book of First World War Poetry*. London, 1996.

Skirth, Ronald. *The Reluctant Tommy*, Edited by Duncan Barrett. London, 2010.

Snape, Michael F. *God and the British Soldier. Religion and the British Army in the First and Second World Wars*. London, 2005.

Snyder, Louis. *Historic Documents of World War 1*. New York, 1958.

Spears, Edward. *Liaison 1914*. London, 1968.

Spencer, W. *Army Service Records of the First World War*. Trowbridge, 2001.

Starling, John and Ivor Lee. *No Labour, No Battle. Military Labour during the First World War*. Stroud, 2009.

Strachan, Hew. *The First World War*. London, 2006.

Strachan, Hew. *The First World War. Volume 1: To Arms*. Oxford, 2001.

Strachan, Hew. *The Oxford Illustrated History of the First World War. New edition*. Oxford, 2014: Kindle.

Taylor, Alan J. P. *The First World War*. Harmondsworth, 1963.

Terraine, John. *Douglas Haig. The Educated Soldier*. London, 1963.

Thompson, Mark. *The White War. Life and Death on the Italian Front 1915-1919*. Croydon: Faber and Faber, 2009.

Todman, Dan. *The Great War. Myth and Memory*. London, 2005.

Tomassini, Luigi. 'The Home Front in Italy'. In *Facing Armageddon. The First World War Experienced*, edited by Hugh Cecil and Peter Liddle, 577-595. London, 1996.

Trevelyan, George M. *Scenes from Italy's War*. London, 1919.

Tuchman, Barbara. *August 1914*. London, 1994.

Van Emden, Richard. *The Last Fighting Tommy*. London, 2007.

War Office. *Manual of Military Law*. London, 1914.

Watson, Alexander. *Ring of Steel. Germany and Austria-Hungary at War, 1914-1918*. London, 2014.

Weber, Thomas. *Hitler's First War. Adolf Hitler, the Men of the List Regiment, and the First World War*. Oxford, 2010.

Whittam, John. 'War Aims and Strategy: the Italian Government and High Command 1914-1919'. In *War Aims and Strategic Policy in The Great War 1914-1918*, edited by Barry Hunt and Adrian Preston, 85-104. London, 1977.

Wilks, John and Eileen. *Rommel and Caporetto*. Barnsley, 2001.

Wilks, John and Eileen. *The British Army in Italy 1917-1918.* Barnsley, 1998.

Wilson, Trevor. *The Myriad Faces of War.* Cambridge, 1986.

Winter, Dennis. *Haig's Command. A Reassessment.* London, 1991.

Winter, Jay. *Sites of Memory, Sites of Mourning. The Great War in European cultural history.* Cambridge, 1995.

Woodward, David R, ed. *The Military Correspondence of Field-Marshal Sir William Robertson.* London: Army Records Society, 1989.

Journal articles

Agutter, Karen. 'Captive Allies: Italian Immigrants in World War One Australia'. *Australian Studies,* Vol.1 (2009), pp.1-20.

Bellany, Ian. 'Men at War: The Sources of Morale'. *RUSI Journal* , Vol.148 (2003), pp.58-62.

Black, Jeremy. 'The Resonance of Waterloo'. *RUSI Journal* , Vol.156 (2011), pp.96-100.

Carrington, Charles. 'The Defence of the Cesuna Re-entrant in the Italian Alps by the 48th (South Midland) Division, 15th June 1918. A Study of Minor Tactics in the Defensive'. *Army Quarterly,* Vol.XIV (1927), pp.306-18.

Cavan, Lord. 'Some Tactical and Strategic Considerations of the Italian Campaign in 1917-1918'. *The Army Quarterly,* Vol. 1 (1920), pp.11-18.

Collins, Tony. 'English Rugby Union and the First World War'. *The Historical Journal* , Vol. 45, no. 4 (2002), pp.797-817.

Crozier, William Percival. 'Demobilization in England'. *Atlantic Monthly,* Vol.123 (1919), pp.275-83.

De Filippi, Filippo. 'The Geography of the Italian Front'. *The Geographical Journal,* Vol. 51, no. 2 (1917), pp.65-75.

Duffett, Rachel. 'Beyond the Ration: Sharing and Scrounging on the Western Front'. *Twentieth Century British History,* Vol. 22 (2011), pp. 453-473.

Graubard, Stephen R. 'Military Demobilization in Great Britain Following the First World War'. *The Journal of Modern History,* Vol.19, no. 4 (1947). pp.297-311.

Harrison, Mark. 'The British Army and the Problem of Venereal Disease in France and Egypt during the First World War'. *Medical History,* Vol.39, no. 2 (1995), pp. 133-158.

Kronenbitter, Günther. 'The Austro-Hungarian Experience of Coalition Warfare, 1914-18'. *RUSI Journal,* Vol. 159 (2014), pp.76-82.

Oram, Gerard. 'Pious Perjury: Discipline and Morale in the British Force in Italy, 1917-1918'. *War in History,* Vol. 9, no. 4 (2002), pp. 412-430.

Petter, Martin. "Temporary Gentlemen' in the Aftermath of the Great War: Rank, Status and the Ex-Officer Problem'. *The Historical Journal,* Vol.37, no. 1 (1994), pp.127-152.

Prior, Robin and Trevor Wilson. 'Debate. Paul Fussell at War'. *War in History,* Vol. 1, no. 1 (1994), pp.63-80.

Sforza, Carlo. 'Cadorna and Diaz'. *Foreign Affairs* , Vol. 8, no. 2 (1930), pp.282-293.

Sheffield, Gary. 'War of Words'. *BBC History Magazine,* (August, 2014), pp.76-7.

Ure, James. 'The Warwickshire (Mountain) Brigade'. *The Journal of the Western Front Association,* No. 53 (1998), pp. 25-29.

Wade, Ashton. 'Youthful memories of war (2)'. *The Journal of the Western Front Association,* No. 27 (1989), pp.28-31.

Whittam, John. 'War and Italian Society 1914-16'. *War and Society,* Vol.1 (1975), pp.144-161.

PhD thesis

Oram, Gerard. '"What alternative punishment is there?" Military Executions during World War One'. Open University, 2000.

Sheffield, Gary. 'Officer-Man Relations, Morale and Discipline in the British Army, 1902-22'. King's College, London, 1994.

Newspaper articles

Hellen, Nicholas and Richard Brooks. 'Don't mention that we won the First World War'. *The Sunday Times,* 13 January 2013, pp.1-2.

Jones, N. 'Living and dying in the trenches'. First World War Supplement, *Sunday Telegraph,* 1 June 2014, p.5.

Radio Broadcast

Clark, Christopher. 'Month of Madness'. Radio series, *BBC 4,* 26 June 2014.

Web based sources

Geoff Barr, 'Military Discipline. Policing the 1st Australian Imperial Force 1914-1920'. http://books.google.co.uk/books.

Norton-Taylor, R. 'Executed WW1 soldiers to be given pardon'. The Guardian, 16 August 2006, www.theguardian.com, last accessed 24 June 2014.

The Times Digital Archive http://infotrac.galegroup.com

Index

INDEX OF PEOPLE

INDEX OF PLACES

INDEX OF MILITARY UNITS & FORMATIONS

INDEX OF GENERAL & MISCELLANEOUS TERMS